W9-DGT-215

School Restructuring, Chicago Style

To
Randy and Sarah
for their patience with their preoccupied father

and to
Mary
for her understanding, help, and love in shaping this effort

School Restructuring, Chicago Style

G. Alfred Hess, Jr.

For information address:

Corwin Press, Inc.
A Sage Publications Company
2455 Teller Road
Newbury Park, California 91320

SAGE Publications Ltd.
6 Bonhill Street
London EC2A 4PU
United Kingdom

SAGE Publications India Pvt. Ltd.
M-32 Market
Greater Kailash I
New Delhi 110 048 India

Printed in the United States of America

Library of Congress Cataloging-in-Publication Data

Main entry under title:

Hess, G. Alfred, Jr., 1938–
School restructuring, Chicago style / G. Alfred Hess, Jr.
p. cm.
Includes bibliographical references and index.
ISBN 0-8039-6001-8 — ISBN 0-8039-6002-6 (pbk.)
1. Educational change—Illinois—Chicago. 2. Public schools—Illinois—Chicago—Administration. 3. School management and organization—Illinois—Chicago. 4. Education and state—Illinois—Chicago. I. Title.
LA269.C4H48 1991
371.2'09773'11—dc20 90-27612
CIP

FIRST PRINTING, 1991

Corwin Press Production Editor: Judith L. Hunter

Contents

Foreword

Chicago is embarked on a novel and far-reaching educational reform. This reform stands apart from virtually all others of the last decade, an unprecedented period of educational reform across the nation. First, it originated from a grass roots political movement, formed around a nucleus of business, philanthropic, and community organizations, in response to increasing evidence of chronic failure of schools to educate children. Most other reforms have originated from the action of policymakers, legislatures and governors, at the state level; and, at the local level, coalitions of superintendents, unions leaders, and board members.

Second, the Chicago reform is, more than any other, based mainly on the theory that schools can be improved by strengthening democratic control at the school-community level. Most other reforms have been based either on theories of regulatory control—increased standards for teachers and students—or professional control—investments in the improvement of teachers' competence and increased decision making authority at the school site. While the Chicago reform has elements of both regulatory and professional control, it is mainly based on a theory of democratic control.

Third, the Chicago reform is probably more ambitious—some would say radical—than any other current reform in its departure from the established structure of school organization. The creation of 542 Local School Councils with significant decision making authority for schools is, by itself, an enormous departure from established patterns of school organization. The departure is even greater when democratic control is coupled with the other elements of the reform—commitments to reduce central administration, reallocation of resources to the school level, changes in school principals' roles and responsibilities, and the like.

To a large degree, the Chicago reform was a product of particular local circumstances—serious fiscal problems, a long and acrimonious teachers' strike, and, most of all, a deeply-rooted tradition of community-based political mobilization. But the problems of Chicago's schools are, in most key respects, the problems of large urban school systems across the country: alarming physical deterioration, declining teacher morale, dramatic shifts in the social, cultural, racial, and ethnic backgrounds of students, and increasing public dissatisfaction with such measures of performance as drop-out rates, achievement scores, and readiness of graduates for work. Those with a concern for the future of urban public school systems are watching Chicago closely.

G. Alfred Hess, Jr., has performed a valuable service to the large number of people with a scholarly and practical interest in the Chicago reform by describing and analyzing the early stages of its formation and implementation, and by locating the Chicago reform in the context of other reforms of the past decade. Those of us who do research on contemporary education policy making know all too well that the historical record of most reforms is incomplete, fragile, and temporary. It matters a great deal that Fred Hess has taken the care to put his own experience and the considerable collection of research and analysis that accompanied the reform into a coherent, well-argued form.

Hess brings two important qualifications to this task. He is a scholar with experience analyzing and interpreting the inscrutable jumble of information produced by urban school bureaucracy. He was also an active participant in the reform. He makes no bones about his support for the reform and his interest in seeing it succeed. His perspective, while analytic, then, is hardly detached. This combination, while it may trouble traditional social scientists, adds greatly to this book. He has both the analytic temperament and the sympathy required to make an understanding and understandable account of the Chicago reform.

This book will be of considerable value to students of education policy and reform, both as an account of the Chicago reform and as an example of how to use existing analyses to assemble an historical and analytic record. As Hess himself says, it will be a long time before there is enough experience with the reform to draw conclusions about its effects. But this book sets a standard for future accounts. It describes the basic logic and structure of the reform proposal. It documents the evidence of failure leading to the reform. And it provides a context for interpreting what the reform is about, relative to other school reform measures. In all these respects, it is a useful book for students and practitioners of school reform.

Richard F. Elmore
Graduate School of Education
Harvard University

Preface

This book is a case study of the third-largest urban school system in the United States and the reform movement that was mobilized to address its problems. The effort to restructure the Chicago Public Schools is unique in the 1980s reform movement in that reform is imposed from outside the system by mandating legislation. Not since decentralization to community subdistricts was imposed on New York City and Detroit in the early 1970s has a state legislature tried to address the educational problems in its major urban center. Most present efforts to improve urban school systems have been led by enlightened superintendents within the system, like Richard Wallace in Pittsburgh, Tom Payzant in San Diego, and Joseph Fernandez, formerly of Dade County (Miami) and now New York.

But Chicago has not been blessed with innovative and capable superintendents over the last 20 years. Instead, it has wavered between caretaker insiders and flamboyant, but ineffective, outsiders. In that vacuum of leadership, it became obvious that a reformation of the public schools in Chicago would happen only if it was imposed from the outside. This book describes the situation that gave rise to the Chicago school reform movement, the political, civic, and business forces that came together to impose reform, the restructuring mandated by the reform legislation, and the initial implementation of that reform.

BACKGROUND

This book grew out of my experiences as one of the participants in that reform movement; as such, it is a participant-observer's account of events. I first began to look at the problems of public education in Chicago 10 years ago as a postdoctoral fellow in Northwestern University's Program in Ethnography and Public Policy. For that fellowship, I did a more classic participant-observer study of popular participation in the development of a desegregation plan for the Chicago Public Schools (Hess, 1984). Under the terms of a consent decree between the school system and the federal government, the desegregation planning process was required to involve parents and community activists. While a process was developed to receive continuing reaction and input from more than a hundred such persons, the final plan was only marginally affected by that process.

In 1982 I began my association with the Chicago Panel on Public School Policy and Finance by being the primary investigator on the panel's first research into the policies and practices of the Chicago Public Schools (Hallett & Hess, 1982). As the system's fiscal crisis eased, we turned our attention from finance and management to educational outcomes; what emerged were five studies of different dimensions of the dropout problem in Chicago. In each study, we not only described and analyzed the issues involved in the dropout problem, but the Panel also offered a series of recommendations about how to address this problem.

The school reform movement emerged from an education summit convened by Mayor Harold Washington in 1986. The summit began with 40 designated participants but included more than a hundred who contributed to six task forces. It dramatically expanded and gained momentum with the 19-day school strike in September and October of 1987. In its second year, the summit directly involved more than a hundred persons, with several hundred more attending hearings and participating in organizing efforts.

Although I was just one of this throng of people involved in creating the reform movement, I brought to my participation my training as an anthropologist. Early on it became clear to me that someone needed to keep a careful record of what was happening in this extraordinary effort. For the first year of the mayor's summit, I was its official chronicler, preparing minutes of the meetings of the entire summit, of its steering committee, and of the planning staff, led by the mayor's chief policy advisor, Hal Baron. After resigning from the summit staff in June 1987, I continued active participation in the summit, and continued to compile extensive field notes, files of all of its reports, meeting minutes, news files, and analyses of the various proposals for reform that surfaced both inside and outside the summit. At the same time, the Panel was actively involved with the leaders of the state legislature in designing reform legislation introduced both in 1987 and 1988. The 1988 bill was incorporated with two other pieces of legislation into the Chicago School Reform Act of 1988.

Thus, this book is the product of a decade of experience with the Chicago Public Schools. That experience began as fairly traditional, detached research on the problems and difficulties of the school system. It eventually evolved into a passionate effort to help turn around a school system that was horrifying in its failure to provide an adequate education to the city's 400,000 public school students. Now, at the end of the decade, it has been a privilege to be able to return to my notes and my papers and to try to portray the significance of this amazing exercise in citizen participation in restructuring a major urban school system.

This book is not the final word on school reform in Chicago. Certainly others will tell the story from their own perspectives. A participant-observer's account is always constrained by his or her inability to see everything that is going on. And it is too early even to begin to assess whether or not the Chicago experiment will be successful. The Chicago Panel, returning to its more characteristic research orientation, has begun a five-year project monitoring the implementation and effects of the restructuring of the Chicago Public Schools. The initial comprehensive assessment can only be undertaken at the end of that period. This book is designed to explain what the restructuring of schools, Chicago style, is and why it came to be. It places the Chicago experiment in the context of its own unique history and in the national context of the school reform movement of the 1980s.

AUDIENCE AND COVERAGE

This book is intended for students of the management of public schools, for policymakers who are contemplating how to improve their own public school systems, and for practitioners in urban school systems, in state departments of education, and in county-wide school districts. It is a case study, not a typical text on educational administration. I have tried to keep it straightforward and readable.

Describing the Chicago Scene

After a brief introduction that focuses on the policy problem of improving urban schools, the first chapter describes why school reform is necessary in Chicago. It reviews the specific research that documented the failure of the system to educate the children in Chicago and the organizational misdirection that focused the system's resources away from the teaching and learning process and into a bloated and growing bureaucracy. Chapter 2 focuses more intensely on a single high school in that system and shows the difficulties encountered in trying to improve its performance through a prime example of the much-ballyhooed, but largely ineffective, "private-public partnerships." Chapter 3 completes this initial section by describing the citizen initiative in "mobilizing a movement for school reform." The chapter provides both a chronology of the reform effort and an analysis of the major elements of the successful reform mobilization. In that chapter I have attempted to show what is necessary if a movement for reform from outside the system itself is to be successful.

Restructuring a School System

The second part of the book describes what is involved in restructuring a major urban school system. Chapter 4 reviews the national movement for reform in the 1980s, with specific attention to those aspects with direct impact on the Chicago restructuring experiment. In particular, attention is given to the research on effective schools, to the efforts to enhance the professionalization of teachers, to the emergence of school-based management as a dominant theme in school restructuring, and to the focus on decentralization in the private sector that helped mobilize business support for school reform in Chicago.

Chapter 5 describes the major elements in the Chicago restructuring plan: its goals, the reallocation of resources to the school level, and the central focus on establishing school-based management through local school councils with control over program, budget, and the principal. Chapters 6 and 7 examine the shift in roles of the major actors involved in school-based management: the principals, the teachers, parents, and community residents. Implications are drawn for schools of education in preparing educational professionals for their changed roles under school restructuring.

Implementation and Implications

The final two chapters address the significance of the restructuring experiment in Chicago. Chapter 8 describes the initial year of implementation of the school reform act: the election of the local school councils, their first hectic year, the selection of new principals, and the interactions of the school reform effort with the changing pattern of municipal politics in this most political of American cities. The final chapter sets the Chicago experiment back in its national context. In that chapter I seek to show why other reform efforts would not have been sufficient to turn around the Chicago Public Schools, while acknowledging that the adequacy of the current restructuring effort is not assured either and can only be assessed empirically after five years of implementation, if then. I do provide a series of interim "marks of success" that would indicate whether reform is moving in the right direction in Chicago.

ACKNOWLEDGMENTS

This book describes the efforts of hundreds of people who were working to improve the Chicago Public Schools, most of whom could not be named. Without their contribution, there would be no book to write.

Most directly, this volume has been made possible by the officers and members of the Chicago Panel on Public School Policy and Finance, who authorized, supported, and guided the work referenced throughout. Tee Gallay served as president of the Panel during the reform mobilization years, represented the Panel on the Mayor's Education Summit during its second year, and helped shape many of the events described here; the current president is the Reverend Harold W. Smith. I am grateful for the support of both of these colleagues and for their dedication to the children of Chicago. The member organizations of the Panel are listed in Appendix B. I am particularly indebted to members of the staff of the Panel who assisted me in the research reported here and in the preparation of this text: John Q. Easton, Virginia Lazarus, Hilary Addington, Sandra Storey, and former staff members Diana Lauber and Christina Warden.

I am grateful to Mitch Allen of Sage Publications and Gracia Alkema of Corwin Press who encouraged me to write this book, and to Daniel Brown of the University of British Columbia who reviewed the manuscript for the publisher and who made innumerable valuable suggestions about how to approach this subject and how to enhance its usefulness. I am also indebted to many colleagues in Chicago and across the country who have read earlier versions of chapters in this book, have corrected errors or pointed out significant omissions, and generally have helped broaden my understanding of the events in which I was caught up. The continuing limitations of the study are my own responsibility.

G. Alfred Hess, Jr.
Chicago, Illinois
October 1990

About the Author

G. Alfred Hess, Jr., is Executive Director of the Chicago Panel on Public School Policy and Finance, a multiracial, multiethnic coalition of 20 nonprofit agencies dedicated to improving public education in Chicago. He coauthored the Panel's first study and many of those that followed, and has been Executive Director since 1983.

He was trained as an educational anthropologist, receiving a Ph.D. from Northwestern University in 1980. That year he received the university's first postdoctoral fellowship in ethnography and public policy; he used the fellowship to do a participant-observation study of popular participation of parents and community activists in desegregation planning for the Chicago Public Schools, which introduced him to the problems of public education in Chicago and launched the decade-long research that culminates in this book.

Hess was invited by Mayor Harold Washington to help conceptualize and staff the Mayor's Education Summit in the fall of 1986. His primary responsibility was to assist the summit in developing a set of strategic objectives for reforming the school system. At the request of the Speaker of the House, Hess developed draft legislation to launch a pilot program in school autonomy in 1987. While the proposal died in the Illinois senate that year, an expanded version was one of the three bills merged to create the Chicago School Reform Act in 1988. This book utilizes Hess's participant-observation training to describe the movement toward reform in Chicago, the restructuring experiment established by the reform act, and the initial year of implementation of school reform in Chicago.

Prior to attending Northwestern University, Hess received a B.A. from the College of Wooster in 1959 and a bachelor of sacred theology degree from Boston University in 1962, having spent a year of his graduate study at Cambridge University as a visiting international fellow. He was ordained a Methodist minister in 1962 and served churches in New England before joining the staff of the Institute of Cultural Affairs in 1966. He conducted adult education programs for the institute, first in inner-city locations in Chicago, Oklahoma City, and Memphis and then as Director of International Training, leading intensive residential programs in Venezuela, England, India, Hong Kong, the Philippines, Australia, and Korea.

Introduction: The Need for Reform

On December 2, 1988, the Illinois State Legislature voted nearly unanimously to adopt the Chicago School Reform Act (P.A. 85-1418). The act fundamentally changed the structure of public education by creating Local School Councils consisting of two teachers, six parents, two community representatives, the principal, and, in high schools, a nonvoting student. Based on educational research on effective schools and school restructuring and on business and management practices of decentralization of authority and participatory decision-making, the councils are the vehicle through which the goals of Chicago school reform are to be achieved.

Educational researchers and school practitioners have called Chicago school reform the most radical experiment in the history of public education. Some worry that the reform movement has gone too far. However, there are some who believe only market forces can save this nation's schools; for the market advocates, the Chicago reforms do not go far enough. The success or failure of the Chicago experiment will have a major impact on how urban American children are educated.

This book describes the failings of the Chicago Public Schools and the reforms that were designed to overcome them. It depicts the evolution of Chicago's particular type of school reform, and the mobilization of support for school reform from citizen activists, parents, business executives, and state legislators that was necessary to set the reform in place. Finally, the book describes the initial year of implementation and addresses how the Chicago reform effort relates to other reform experiments currently under way or revolutionary schemes that have recently been proposed.

THE CHICAGO PUBLIC SCHOOLS: IN NEED OF REFORM

The Chicago School Reform Act builds upon the unique history of the Chicago Public School system. In 1985, Chicago schools enrolled some 435,000 students, down from a high of 585,000 in 1968 (Chicago Board of Education, 1985). The school system was recovering from a fiscal crisis in 1979-1980, when it had failed to meet its payroll and required a state financial bailout. This bailout included subjecting many of its financial decisions to the review and approval of an oversight board, the Chicago School Finance Authority. Under the terms of the bailout, the system was forced to cut more than 8,000 positions from its budget (Hallett & Hess, 1982).

The school system was also operating under a desegregation consent decree and had virtually eliminated all predominantly white schools. However, in a school system that had only about 15% white enrollment, that left the vast majority of minority students continuing to attend completely segregated schools and not benefiting significantly from desegregation (Hess & Warden, 1987).

The system had involved parents in advisory roles for a number of years. Local advisory councils had been established at virtually all schools, starting in 1970 (Cibulka, 1975). Chapter I parent advisory councils were maintained at Chicago schools even after the federal government allowed their discontinuance. Bilingual advisory councils were functioning in most schools serving large numbers of limited-English-proficient students. (Chicago provided special instruction to students from more than 80 different language backgrounds.) Further, the local school advisory councils or PTAs had been involved in the selection of school principals since 1970 (Cibulka, 1975), interviewing candidates and recommending their three preferences, which were almost always followed in the general superintendent's recommended appointments.

The system, however, was not being very successful in educating the children enrolled in its schools. Only one out of three graduating seniors was capable of reading at the national norm. Two out of five (43%) entering freshmen dropped out before graduation, with dropout rates in inner-city schools reaching 67%. Of the 8,000 positions cut during the financial crisis, teachers and other student contact staff were cut the most. Thus, a picture was created of a school system failing its students and more interested in protecting bureaucratic jobs than in improving its schools. The school reform movement was launched to address these problems.

THE INEFFECTIVENESS OF PREVIOUS STATE REFORM EFFORTS

In 1985, Illinois, like other states before it, enacted statewide school reform legislation in response to the report *A Nation At Risk* (National Commission, 1983). The 1985 reform act (P.A. 84-126) was long on accountability and short on serious efforts to improve the state's schools (Nelson, Hess, & Yong, 1985). It did not seriously address the shortcomings of the Chicago schools, though the reports of high dropout rates and low graduate reading scores appeared as the bill was being debated. In a special section devoted to Chicago, the act did create Local School Improvement Councils at every school, which were encouraged to engage in school improvement planning and were given the right to review discretionary spending by the principal.

The accountability provisions may have been more important, in the long run, for they helped highlight how poorly Chicago schools were performing. In 1987, the state report card showed that 33 of 64 Chicago high schools scored in the lowest 1% of all high schools in the country on the American College Test (ACT). In fact, on this college entrance test, Chicago schools dominated that lowest percentile, which consisted of only 56 schools nationwide. Only seven Chicago high schools scored higher than the 10th percentile. At the elementary grades, 60%-70% of all students were reading below the national norms on the Iowa Test of Basic Skills.

It is not surprising that state school reform had little effect on Chicago. Most state reforms have had little effect on urban school systems, and Chicago is not very different from other large urban school districts. Dropout rates in Boston, for instance, when calculated the same way we did in Chicago, are 53% (Camayd-Freixas, 1986), and that does not include the 35% who never make it into high school (Massachusetts Advocacy Center, 1986). Using similar statistics, the Dade County public schools, which include both the city of Miami and its suburbs, report a 28% dropout rate (Stephenson, 1985). New York reports a 33% rate, though knowledgeable critics point out that the figure would be much higher if New York counted the students transferred into the night school and then allowed to drop out (*New York Times,* August 24, 1988).

Meanwhile, suburban schools graduate upwards of 95% of their students. In fact, in Illinois, according to the state report card, some suburban districts graduate up to 105% of their students! (The state report card is based on a comparison of the size of the graduating class with the ninth-grade class four years previously; this method is called an attrition study. Schools with large numbers of transfers in, primarily those in the fast-growing suburbs, graduate more students than they originally had in the ninth grade, creating graduation rates in excess of 100%. By contrast, the urban dropout rates reported above are based on a longitudinal tracking of individuals, called cohort studies, rather than the less sophisticated aggregate enrollment comparisons.)

In short, urban schools are not like suburban schools, a fact recognized by most people. Rural schools are often different from both urban and suburban ones. But state policymakers too frequently ignore these differences, except to complain about their costs to the state. Urban districts are frequently described as "black holes," and the color reference is usually not unintentional. Rural districts are too small and inefficient. Both cost the state too much and perform too poorly. On the other hand, suburban districts cost the state little and perform well. Even without much state aid, they spend much more on each pupil than the rest of the state.

If we all know these differences exist, why do states continue to search for the "one best solution"? Why do we try to enact the one set of policies that will fix all of these schools? In fact, the problems faced by urban schools are quite different from those faced by suburban schools, and the solutions must be different, as well.

The Council of Great City Schools (1987:2) reports that a quarter of all youths live in central cities. Students who attend urban schools are predominantly from disadvantaged homes and these students dominate inner-city schools. In Chicago, for example, more than half of the entering freshmen at Austin High School come from low-income homes, and 82% of those freshmen are reading at least two grades below normal. These students are not a few problem kids on the margin of the school population; these disadvantaged kids dominate the school enrollment. Yet from a policy perspective, Austin is treated like any other high school in the state!

In addition, urban school districts are organized differently than are other school districts in the state. Outside of Chicago, the average school district in Illinois has 1,385 students in about four schools of 300 to 350 students each. In 1988, Chicago enrolled 410,000 students in 542 regular attendance centers and 55 other specialty sites. There were 36 high schools and 10 elementary schools with more students enrolled than in the average Illinois district! In the suburbs, most districts have 10 or fewer administrators. In Chicago, there were 4,380 persons who worked in the administrative units in the central or subdistrict offices. There were another 38,000 employees working in the system's schools. Unlike most other districts in the state, urban school systems are large, rigid bureaucracies. They are controlled by central office staff who are far removed from the system's large schools, which are not successfully educating kids or saving money.

The Chicago restructuring of an urban school system is an attempt to create a solution geared to the urban school problem. It would not be very appropriate for problems in suburban or rural schools, except in those states utilizing large county districts with their own bureaucracies. There may be aspects of the Chicago restructuring effort that would be appropriate in other settings, but the effort as a whole is aimed at the urban problem. States with large urban centers may find elements of the Chicago experiment that would address their own urban problems.

The first two chapters of this book examine the problems faced by a large urban school system, and the frustrations and difficulties encountered in attempting to deal with those problems in individual schools. Only when the problem is clear is it appropriate to describe the reform effort seeking to provide a radical solution.

Profile of a Failing School System

In early November 1987, just a month after the end of the longest teacher strike in the city's history, Secretary of Education William Bennett came to Chicago to declare its public schools the "worst in America" (*Chicago Sun Times,* November 7, 1987). Bennett was commenting on recently published data from the state's school report card, which showed that half of Chicago's high schools ranked in the lowest 1% of all high schools in the country on the basis of results of the American College Test.

School officials disputed Bennett, who has never been known for understatement. They pointed out that Chicago's median ACT score ranked the city 16th out of the 21 largest systems using the ACT exam. They cited higher dropout rates in Boston (53%) than in Chicago (43%). They pointed to lower per-pupil revenues in Chicago and attendance rates better than those in New York City or Los Angeles. There were many available statistics that showed Chicago was not the worst, but none that showed Chicago's schools were successful. Despite Bennett's obvious overstatement, there was no defense against the charge that Chicago had a failing school system.

THE FAILURE TO EDUCATE

By the fall of 1987, the failure of the Chicago Public Schools had been well documented. For more than a decade, the Chicago Board of Education had published test score data for every grade in every school in the system. However, those data were released in very low-profile ways and were often ignored by the daily press. In the late 1970s, a local investigative newsletter, *The Chicago Reporter* (Gelder & Rawles, 1980), first called attention to the dropout problem. A few years later, Father Charles Kyle focused on two predominantly Hispanic high schools to examine the dropout problem for his doctoral dissertation at Northwestern University (Kyle, 1984). Sponsored by a local social service agency, Aspira, and other neighborhood groups through the Network for Youth Services, the study was released to the press and used as an organizing focus in the northwestside Hispanic community.

But the real focus on the failure adequately to educate Chicago children was a series of reports by several of the city's independent nonprofit agencies that were focused on public education. Perhaps as a legacy of the early organizing efforts of Saul Alinsky (1946), Chicago is blessed with a number of citywide policy-oriented nonprofit agencies, often referred to as "watchdogs." These agencies, from time to time, publish reports focusing on various aspects of the school system. Starting in 1984, three of these agencies issued a series of reports that focused on the educational failures of the school system.

Early Reports of Problems

The first of these reports, which appeared in May 1984, was not originally intended to focus on educational failure, but on educational opportunity. The Citizens Schools Committee (CSC), originally formed during the depression of the 1930s when the school system was paying its teachers in script rather than cash, had been closely monitoring the development of the system's desegregation plan following a 1980 consent decree signed with the U.S. Department of Justice. (For a fuller history of the development of the consent decree, see Hess, 1984.) CSC was concerned that too few parents were aware of the options they had in choosing what schools their children could attend under the provisions of the desegregation plan developed by the board of education. CSC's School Standards Committee, under my chairmanship and with the assistance of a small grant from the Spencer Foundation, set out to describe these various options. A *Consumer's Guide to Chicago Public High Schools* (Citizens Schools Committee, 1984) was published in May 1984. The guide contained a two-page

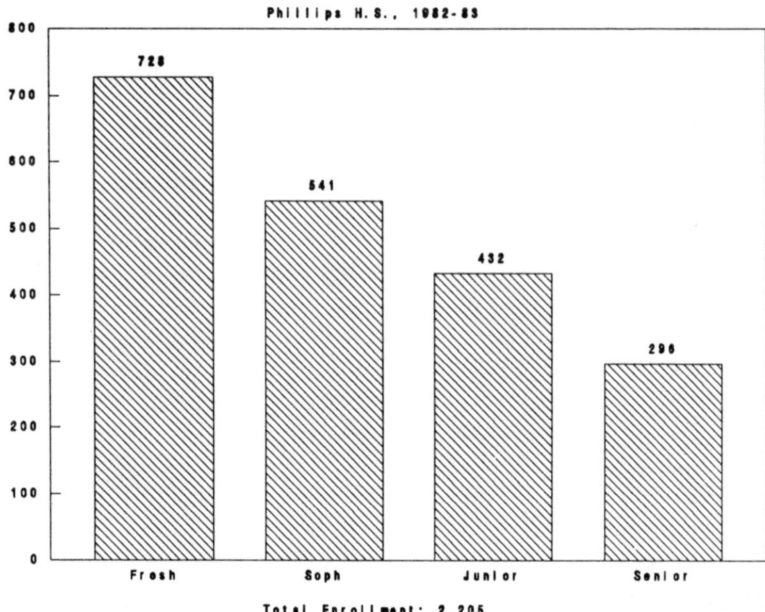

Figure 1.1. Class Enrollment

description of each of 65 general high schools, including graphs of enrollment by race and grade and reading scores compared to the citywide average and the national norm. In school after school, we discovered that senior class enrollments were typically half the size of enrollments in the freshman or sophomore classes. In predominantly minority schools, we found similar down-step patterns in reading scores, with the national norm at 50%, the Chicago average at 30%, and the school average near 15%. Figures 1.1 and 1.2 from Phillips High School were typical of these inner-city high schools.

Thus, the *Consumer's Guide* began to give a particular picture of the departure of students prior to graduation and of the low performance of students in many Chicago high schools. However, because the primary purpose of the report was to be a resource for parents making choices in student enrollment, its portrayal of the low level of educational success in many Chicago high schools was not widely noticed.

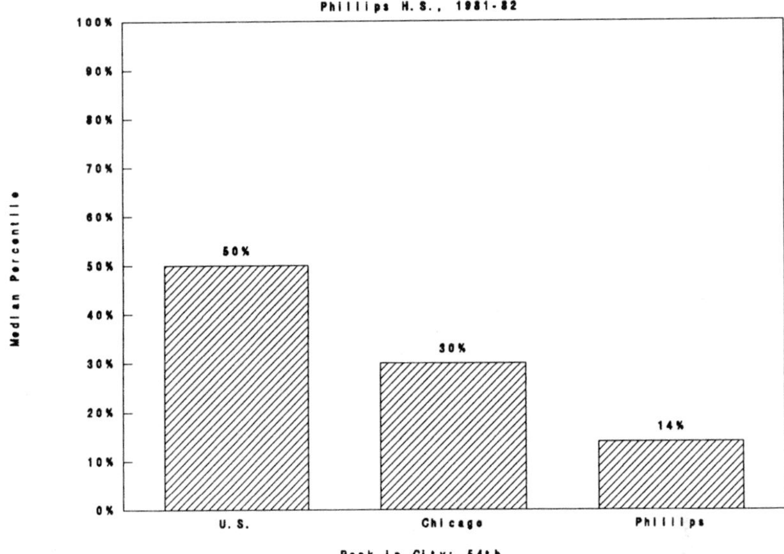

Figure 1.2. 11th-Grade Reading Scores

Much more attention was given to a report released in January 1985 by Designs for Change titled *The Bottom Line: Chicago's Failing Schools and How to Save Them* (Designs for Change, 1985). Using very similar data, Designs for Change analyzed the data citywide and by groupings of schools on the basis of the proportion of schools with minority students. Using an attrition approach, Designs for Change divided the number of seniors enrolled in the Class of 1984 by the number of freshmen enrolled four years earlier and called the result the completion rate, implying in their press releases that the inverse was the dropout rate. They further analyzed the reading scores of the senior class to show the proportion reading at or above the national norm. They combined these two figures and reported that less than half of all students (47%) completed high school and of those only a third were well prepared, (i.e., reading at or above the national norm). They went on to show that completion and preparation rates were higher in selective academic and vocational high schools and in integrated high schools, but significantly lower in nonselective high schools. The report then briefly reviewed the effective schools literature (see

Chapter 4) and suggested an approach to using the findings of that research effort to help parents evaluate the school their children attend and to devise methods of improvement.

The Bottom Line received considerable attention from the daily press in Chicago. The soon-to-be-departing general superintendent, Ruth Love, however, dismissed the claims of the report as based on faulty enrollment estimates, for individual students had not been tracked. Instead, she insisted that the proper way to calculate the dropout rate is the annualized method, which the state requires to be reported each year (the number of students who drop out between September and June of each year divided by the total enrollment of all four grades at the beginning of the year), which hovered about 8%. Thus, there was a dispute as to whether or not there was a real dropout problem.

Dropouts from the Chicago Public Schools

The dispute lasted only a few months. On April 24, 1985, the Chicago Panel on Public School Finances, as it was then known, released its study *Dropouts from the Chicago Public Schools* (Hess & Lauber, 1985). The Panel is a nonprofit agency, which is a coalition of other nonprofit groups concerned about improving public education in Chicago. At the time it had 16 members, including both Citizens Schools Committee and Designs for Change. This study contained a much more precise analysis of the dropout rate, for it tracked individual students from their entry into ninth grade to their departure from the Chicago Public Schools. The study, whose data were already being analyzed when Designs for Change released its report based on rough attrition estimates, accounted for each of the 33,000 entering ninth-grade students and tracked each student for up to six and a half years, at which time all but 0.5% of all students had left the Chicago Public Schools. The study, which I and my colleague Diana Lauber conducted cooperatively with the board of education's Department of Research and Evaluation, examined for legitimacy the individual record of each claimed transfer, ultimately reclassifying 1,500 of these claimed transfers as dropouts (e.g., about 500 students were reported to have transferred to the Roseland Christian Academy, which did not exist during the period these students were in high school).

The Chicago Panel study had several significant advantages over *The Bottom Line.* Utilizing a longitudinal cohort student tracking approach, the study could produce far more precise figures than could the enrollment attrition approach, which *The Bottom Line* clearly acknowledged. The Panel's study, together with a similar study by Robert Stephenson of the Dade County public schools, established the longitudinal cohort approach as the preferred method for analyzing dropout rates in urban school systems (cf. Hammack, 1986). Second, since the study was conducted cooperatively with a department of the board of education, using the system's own student record data, its results could not easily be attacked by other staff of the board. Finally, between the release of *The Bottom Line* and the Panel's study, a new general superintendent, Manford Byrd, Jr., was installed who was not reluctant to acknowledge the problems in the system that he was inheriting as he took office. Thus, the Panel's dropout study marked the end of the debate about whether or not there was an educational problem in the Chicago Public Schools.

The study, which reported 43% of the entering freshmen in the Class of 1982 never graduated, was the first of five interrelated studies of the dropout problem in the Chicago Public Schools. The basic dropout statistics were reanalyzed and the basic conclusions confirmed by a group of scholars, which included Father Kyle, at DePaul University (Kyle, Lane, Sween, & Triana, 1986; also Kyle, 1984). These studies, together with data from the new state-mandated school report cards, began to spell out convincingly the failure of the Chicago Public Schools to educate the city's children adequately.

Dropouts from the Chicago Public Schools was primarily a descriptive study that showed both systemwide and school-level data on school completion and related factors for the classes of 1982, 1983, and 1984. (Some scholars criticized the study for being "underanalyzed," [e.g., Hammack, 1986.] A later reprinting of the study included a more sophisticated statistical analysis, which supported the basic findings reported here.) We focused on the Class of 1982, for we could follow its students for an additional 28 months after the class graduated. This allowed us to assess the outcomes of those students taking more than four years to graduate or finally leave the system (only 0.5% of the class was still enrolled in September 1984, presumably special education

Table 1.1
Dropout Rates by Eighth-Grade Reading Score

Level	*Stanine*	*Grade Equivalent*	*Dropout Rate*
Below	1	0.5-4.6	67.8%
Normal	2 & 3	4.7-6.7	49.9%
Normal	4	6.8-8.0	39.3%
	5	8.1-9.2	28.0%
Normal & Above	6-9	9.3-13.9	18.8%

students, who may remain enrolled until they reach age 21). Results for the classes of 1983 and 1984 were similar to those for the focus cohort, though the rate for 1984 declined somewhat due to a new promotion policy implemented in the spring of 1980. Matching our prediction, a follow-up study by the board of education showed a higher dropout rate for the Class of 1985 (44.9%) followed by a return, for the Class of 1986, to 41.4%, closer to the level of the first two classes.

Some 33,142 students entered a Chicago high school as part of the Class of 1982. As of September 30, 1984, 140 were still actively enrolled, and 3,060 had transferred out to another diploma-granting secondary school system. Since the ultimate academic outcomes of the transfers could not be determined, we eliminated both the still active and validly transferring students, leaving a base for analysis of 29,942 students. Of this number, 12,804 (42.8%) dropped out; 17,138 graduated. The study pointed out that this was nearly half again the national rate of 27% reported by the U.S. Department of Education.

Statistical analysis revealed that two factors were highly correlated with the dropout rate of any particular high school: the percentage of students entering ninth grade reading below normal rates (defined as stanine 3 or lower on the Iowa Test of Basic Skills for the eighth grade; *Pearson's* $r = 0.85$) and the percentage of students entering at least a year over age ($r = 0.80$). Dropout rates declined for students in higher reading categories, as Table 1.1 shows.

Similarly, dropout rates increased as the age of students at entry into ninth grade increased:

Entry Age	*Dropout Rate*
13/less	26.0%
14	37.0%
15	59.9%
16/more	68.8%

Dropout rates were higher for males (49.2%) than for females (36.2%), meaning that one of two males dropped out, while only one in three females did so. Rates also varied by race, with Hispanics highest at 46.9%, then blacks at 45.1%, whites at 34.5%, and Asians with the lowest rate at 19.4%. A later reanalysis of the data indicated that the percent of students in poverty was also positively correlated to the school dropout rate ($r = 0.54$).

One of the Panel's primary concerns in this study was to show the differences in student success and failure at different schools in the system. While the systemwide dropout rate for the Class of 1982 was 43%, individual school rates varied from a low of 11% to a high of 63%. We divided the 63 high schools into thirds for comparative purposes. Nearly half of all graduates in the Class of 1982 (47%) attended one of the top 21 schools. Only a quarter of the students attending these schools dropped out. At 18 of these 21 schools, two-thirds or more of the students graduated. A primary factor in these low dropout rates is that these schools received the best-prepared elementary students. Only 13% of the students attending these high schools entered overage, compared with 26% systemwide. Only 28% of the students entering these high schools entered reading below the normal level, compared to 47% systemwide. These schools were more heavily white (34%) than the system as a whole (21% across the high schools of the system), with fewer blacks (57% vs. 63%) and Hispanics (6% vs. 14% systemwide). Of the 21 schools, 13 were located in the more affluent lakefront or fringe of the city areas; among the 8 in the inner city, 6 maintained selection criteria for their entering students.

By contrast, among the 21 schools with the highest dropout rates, all lost more than half of their students. Together, the dropouts from these schools made up half (49%) of all dropouts in the system, with a cumulative dropout rate of 56%. Twenty of these

21 schools were located in the inner city, and together they attracted students who were not nearly as well prepared for high school. More than a third of the entering students in these schools were overage (one school had half its entering students arrive overage). Seventy percent of the entering students were reading below normal rates. At two schools, more than four in five students were below normal in reading (Austin, 82%; Manley, 80%). A disproportionate number of the students attending these schools were black (76%) and Hispanic (18%); few were white (6%).

It was the conclusion of the study that received a great deal of attention:

> **The Chicago Public School system operates a two-tiered high school system, which concentrates dropout-prone students into inner-city black and Hispanic high schools.**
>
> It appears that, for the freshmen entering high school in September 1978, the system was functioning under an operative policy of **educational triage,** in which some schools were designed to save the best students, some were designed to be holding pens for the worst-prepared students, and a small midrange just plodded along. (Hess & Lauber, 1985, p. 10)

The study's primary recommendations broke with the conventional wisdom that dropout reduction efforts should focus on special efforts in high schools: peer tutoring, alternative schools within schools, and additional counseling. Instead, the Panel called for "a major assault on the dropout problem [which] should be focused on the elementary schools" (Hess & Lauber, 1985, p. 11). Specifically, the study called for an effort to bring the achievement levels of elementary students up to the normal range, particularly in reading levels. Finally, the study called for a special focus to be given to schools that were performing less successfully than others with similar kinds of students. The study noted (Hess & Lauber, 1985, p. 12) that

> It is unrealistic to expect Crane High School, which received 60% of its entering students reading below normal levels and 38% who were overage, to have as high a Graduation Rate as Lane Tech, with none of its students reading at below normal rates, and only 3% overage. But 18 other schools received a higher proportion of their students reading below normal and yet had lower Dropout Rates than did Crane.

A Comparative Study of High Schools

We then set out to examine a number of high schools to try to understand why these differences in school effects existed. Our methodology was to undertake a matched pairs ethnographic study. A regression analysis isolated pairs of schools with similar entering freshman classes but with significantly different dropout rates. Four pairs of schools were chosen, two with high percentages of entering students reading below normal and two with few such entering students. The schools were also matched on the race and poverty levels of their students.

The study was designed to replicate, in Chicago, the kind of studies conducted as part of the effective schools research (see Chapter 4). In fact, it did produce similar findings:

1. The principal at the school with the lower dropout rate in each pair was judged to exert stronger overall leadership.
2. Students in the lower dropout school were more orderly and disciplined in the halls, lunchroom, and other common areas of the school.
3. Student attendance at the lower dropout school was significantly better in three out of the four pairs of schools.
4. The school with the lower dropout rate also had a lower failure rate in the years 1984-1986.
5. Teachers in the school with the lower dropout rate devoted more time to active classroom instruction of the entire class.
6. More interactive teaching took place in the lower dropout school.
7. The physical facilities were in better condition at the school with the lower dropout rate in those cases where there was a difference. (Hess, Wells, Prindle, Kaplan, & Liffman, 1986, pp. v-vi)

For those familiar with the effective schools research, these findings are not unusual. But they do point to some things that high schools can do to improve the performance of their students: hire a principal with strong leadership skills, emphasize order and discipline, focus on student attendance, concentrate on improving student pass rates, use active instructional techniques that emphasize interaction with students, and assure that the building looks cared for. These are all items that can be controlled at the local level, if local-level people have the decision-making capacity. In some cases, an active school administration can see to it that these conditions prevail. Frequently, however, the principal's assignment is not within the control of persons at the school level. In Chicago at that time, advisory councils did have some input on selection of a principal when a vacancy occurred, but little influence on firing a principal who was not exercising effective leadership.

The unexpected findings, however, were ones that were common to all schools and appeared to contribute to high dropout rates at all Chicago high schools. The first of these was that "Chicago public high schools shortchange students on instructional time" (Hess et al., 1986, P. iii). The study noted that, while Illinois state law requires that students receive "five clock hours" of instruction each day, a combination of short periods (40 minutes) and excessive use of study halls (at least one and frequently two study halls per day) meant that most students received less than 240 minutes of instruction per day, and frequently as little as 200 minutes per day. In some of the schools, study halls were scheduled for first and last period, so that students did not need to come to school during those periods. In one school, students were scheduled to a nonexistent room for those early and late study halls, which led us to title the study, *"Where's Room 185?"* This was the question our researcher asked as he tried to find students he wanted to interview during their study hall; only after three days of searching was he informed by some students that the room did not exist and that students knew that that room on their schedules meant they were not to be in school at that hour.

The use of 40-minute periods, a practice prescribed in the board of education's contract with the Chicago Teachers Union, meant that Chicago students would receive 200 minutes of instruction each week in major subject areas such as English, math, science, history, and foreign languages. A quick survey of suburban school districts revealed that class periods in their schools averaged 48 minutes in length. Thus, the average suburban student was receiving one whole period of additional instruction each week in each major subject on his or her schedule. Annually they received 20% more instruction in English, 20% more in math, 20% more in history, etc.

Time on task has been clearly identified as one of the most important factors in differential achievement of students (Walberg, 1984). It should not be surprising, with this advantage in instructional time, that suburban students would do better on examinations testing knowledge of these subjects, such as college entrance tests like the American College Test. While it is clear that inner-city students bring other disadvantages to the classroom, as we have been discussing, length of the period is an issue that is within the control of those persons, administrators and union, who are making policy decisions for the school system. But even here, it seemed, policymakers frequently sought to blame the victims (Ryan, 1976), claiming the reason Chicago utilizes 40-minute periods is that inner-city students' attention spans are shorter than those of students in the suburbs. Therefore, expectations for inner-city students should be lower.

A second finding of the study was that a "culture of cutting" existed in all eight schools studied.

> A clear pattern of cutting early morning and later afternoon classes was observed in all eight studied schools. Thus, many students further reduced the already shortened instructional school day. . . . In most of the studied schools, there were no effective plans to counter the popular practice of cutting. (Hess, Wells, Prindle, Kaplan, & Liffman, 1986, p. iii)

A third finding related to the anonymity of high school life. The study noted that the average student received less than 10 minutes of individual attention each day. Similarly, counselors carried such heavy case loads, over 450 students per counselor, that they had little time to devote to any particular student. Thus, students had to be self-sufficient to survive in a Chicago public high school.

"Where's Room 185?" showed that there were things that could be done at the local school level, if school personnel were committed to improving their school. The mechanisms for allowing local school personnel to assume this responsibility, however, were not clearly present at most Chicago schools. But even the most enterprising of school administrators was not likely to overcome a steady diet of poorly prepared entering students.

The Elementary School Effect

The Panel next set out to examine the relationship of elementary school preparation to dropping out. The first part of that examination, *Bending the Twig: The Elementary Years and Dropout Rates in the Chicago Public Schools* (Hess & Greer, 1987), was released during the summer of 1987. The second part of the study was not released until the summer of 1989, after the school reform legislation was enacted. It was called *Against the Odds: The Early Identification of Dropouts* (Hess, Lyons, & Corsino, 1989).

In *Bending the Twig,* we extended our analysis of high school dropout rates back into the elementary schools from which those students came. By tracking the entering freshmen back to their sending elementary schools, my colleague, Jim Greer, and I were able to ascribe an elementary school dropout rate, i.e., a rate at which elementary school graduates from each school eventually dropped out of high school. (We were not tracking the proportion of students dropping out during their elementary schools years.) By comparing eighth-grade reading scores and students entering ninth grade, we were able to determine that about 1.5% of eighth graders did not appear in a Chicago high school or validly transfer. This was a surprisingly small number, much smaller than activists in some Hispanic neighborhoods were claiming.

This study examined 381 elementary schools that graduated at least 10 students who entered ninth grade as part of the Class of 1982. For the most part, these students were in Chicago elementary schools from 1970 through 1978. A comparison with elementary school statistics for 1986 showed some small improvement in reading scores and a small decrease in the number of students in poverty, leading us to predict a small decrease in the dropout rate for the Class of 1990.

Ascribed dropout rates varied widely across the system. Some elementary schools had a perfect record; every leaving eighth grader eventually graduated from high school. Others, primarily those organized exclusively for special education problem students, had none graduate. Eighty percent of the elementary schools had ascribed dropout rates above the national average of 27%.

With the larger number of schools in the elementary school analysis (n = 381), the factors associated with dropping out were more strongly identified than in our study of high schools (n = 63). Just as in the high school study, below normal reading was the most important factor (*Pearson's* r = 0.57), followed by percent overage (r = 0.47) and percent low income (r = 0.38).

When we examined the sending patterns of elementary schools to high schools, the educational triage picture identified in the high school study became even clearer. Different elementary schools had very different sending patterns, depending upon the part of the city in which they were located and the type of students enrolled. Some elementary schools sent all of their graduating eighth graders to the same high school; others sent their graduates to as many as 32 different high schools across the city. Predominantly white elementary schools tended to send all of their graduates to the neighborhood, predominantly white high school. Inner-city minority elementary schools sent their graduates to different schools across the city. Typically, their highest-achieving students enrolled in one of the selective technical or vocational or magnet high schools or used public transportation to attend a predominantly white school along the lakefront or near the fringes of the city. By tracking individual students from their elementary schools to high school, and by assessing the resulting reading scores in the neighborhood high school, the actual pattern of triage, perceived in the high school study by the results, was evident. Magnet high schools like Whitney Young and selective vocational high schools like Westinghouse, both located in the West Side ghetto, could and did attract the best performing students from West Side and other citywide elementary schools. Meanwhile, neighborhood schools, like Austin High School, would receive only students from the bottom half of these already poorly performing West Side elementary schools, with the result that 80% of their entering ninth graders were reading below normal rates.

When we looked more carefully at these differential sending patterns, we began to realize that parents had different academic opportunities for their children in different parts of the city. For white parents wishing to avoid sending their children to predominantly minority schools, there were few choices. The vast majority of their children went from the neighborhood elementary school to the neighborhood high school. Thus, white parents focused their attention on making sure that their neighborhood schools were the best they could possibly be. Active parent groups and parent leaders in subdistrict and citywide groups were predominantly from these areas of the city, despite the fact that only a quarter of the students in the system were white. For black parents, the best opportunities, usually, were to opt out of the local high school and seek to enroll their children in one of the selective entrance high schools or to provide transportation to a distant predominantly white high school. The target school was almost inevitably some distance from the home of the black student, discouraging active parent involvement in the attended high school. At the same time, the parents most availing themselves of the transportation option were also those most likely to be involved in the schools their children were attending. Thus, the neighborhood high school was left with the most poorly prepared students whose parents tended to be those least likely to be involved.

Thus, we concluded, the opportunity structure was quite different for white and black parents. White parents, given their prejudices and preferences,

> had an interest in *collectively* assuring the high quality of these community elementary and high schools. In contrast, [parents of] inner city minority students, because of the existence of selective high schools with an enhanced curriculum, had a strong interest in *individually* utilizing the educational opportunities of the Chicago Public Schools. (Hess & Greer, 1987, p. iv)

Finally, we noted that size and grade organization of elementary schools, which were within the control of the Chicago Board of Education, were significantly related to the dropout rate of individual schools. When we analyzed these schools separately, we discovered that dropout rates were higher in larger schools and in middle schools, as was the percentage of students leaving those schools reading below normal and overage. We also found that the larger middle schools were more commonly found in all-minority inner-city neighborhoods. Those familiar with the history of Chicago recognize the location and construction of those schools as part of the system's desegregation avoidance tactics of the 1960s. Thus, again, through conscious policy decisions of the board of education, inner-city students were isolated and housed in larger, anonymous middle schools, which were not adequately preparing most of their graduates for entrance into high school.

Since the passage of the Chicago School Reform Act, the Chicago Panel has released two further dropout studies. The first, released in December 1988 just as the governor was signing the reform act, was a study of the experiences of 87 young girls who became pregnant while students in a Chicago public high school. Called *Invisibly Pregnant* (Hess, Green, Stapleton, & Reyes, 1988), the study describes the lack of attention paid to these girls as pregnant teenaged students. The most recent study, *Against the Odds: The Early Identification of Dropouts* (Hess, Lyons, & Corsino, 1989), examined a sample of 473 individual student records from the Class of 1982. The students were tracked back to their entry into a Chicago Public School. Their records were analyzed year by year to determine how early potential dropouts could be identified. Utilizing primary attendance and academic grade data for three years for boys and girls separately, eventual graduates and dropouts could be distinguished with nearly 90% accuracy as early as the end of the fourth grade. Both of these studies provided practical insights into changes at the school level that might make schools more successful in assuring the educational success of their students.

The State Report Card

During the same time period that the three Chicago nonprofit agencies were publishing their research reports showing the shortcomings of the educational system in Chicago, the state of Illinois embarked upon its own legislatively mandated accountability effort. On July 2, 1985, Illinois finally joined other states in enacting a statewide school reform bill, Public Act 84-126. The Panel's analysis of this legislation was that it was "long on accountability, but short on programs which will significantly alter the way schooling is done in Illinois" (Nelson, Hess, & Yong, 1985, p. iii). In our assessment, the accountability reforms were the ones most likely to have long-range possibilities. One of the elements of accountability was the establishment of annually released school report cards to be issued, through the state, by each district for each school in the district. These report cards were first issued in October 1986. Each year they were extensively reported in both the daily Chicago newspapers, including results for each Chicago elementary and high school.

On October 27, 1987, the *Chicago Tribune* published the state report card data for 64 Chicago high schools. Statewide, the average ACT score (score on the American College Test, the college entrance test used most frequently in the Midwest) was 18.9 out of a perfect 35. The Chicago average was 13.9, lower than in any other metropolitan school district. A 13.9 average score would be lower than the average ACT score in 95% of all high schools in the country. As previously noted, 33 of the 64 schools scored in the lowest 1% of all schools in the country. Since there were only 56 schools in the bottom percentile nationwide, Chicago schools comprised 59% of the lowest-ranked high schools taking the ACT. The average scores at three other Chicago high schools would have included them in that group, but they had too few students even taking the test to be counted in the official rankings. Only five Chicago high schools ranked above the 10th percentile; however, two of these, Lane and Young, were at the 60th percentile, 10 ranks above the national average. Average scores ranged from a low of 8.2 at Flower Vocational to highs of 19.7 at Lane Tech and Young Magnet.

In the same report, graduation rates were listed. The state utilized an enrollment attrition approach to graduation rates, which, as noted previously, is not a very reliable methodology. The rate is determined by dividing the number of graduates by the number of enrolled ninth graders four years earlier. As mentioned earlier, in rapidly growing school districts, graduation rates exceeded 100%! The longitudinal cohort method now adopted by many urban school districts provides far more reliable data. Still, as inexact as the state measure is, it gives some grounds for comparison with other school districts around the state. The state average graduation rate for the Class of 1987 was 82.6%. The Chicago rate was 63.0%.

These dismal educational results were also reflected in other school report card data. When the panel, through its semiautonomous division METROSTAT, compiled and analyzed elementary reading scores on the new Illinois Goal Assessment Program (I-GAP) tests (METROSTAT, 1989), more than 70% of the suburban elementary schools scored above the state norms at the third, sixth, and eighth grades (the only grades tested). In Chicago, fewer than 20% of the schools scored above the norm in each grade. While Chicago school officials could and did point to the much higher proportion of low-income students in Chicago, other elementary school districts with even higher proportions of low-income students had higher average scores in both third and sixth grades. Chicago's students scored more highly in eighth grade. This is shown in Table 1.2.

Thus, by several different educational measures, the Chicago Public Schools were seen to be failing in their charge to educate our young people to be effective and well-rounded citizens of the city. Dropout rates were high. Reading achievement was low. The problems to be overcome were great, but the system was not focused on solving those problems. It provided avenues for its most ambitious users to escape the worst of its schools, but that only depressed achievement and expectations in the schools on the lowest rungs.

Table 1.2
I-Gap Reading Scores for 1987-1988 School Year

District	*Low Income*	*Third Grade*	*Sixth Grade*	*Eighth Grade*
Harvey #152	74.2%	215	221	210
Chicago Hts #170	76.5%	214	205	209
Chicago #299	68.4%	192	198	217
State Norm	28.9%	250	250	250

Combining the dropout studies of the Chicago Panel and Designs for Change, it was noted repeatedly that fewer than three out of five entering freshmen ever graduated from a Chicago public high school, and only one of them could read at the national average level. That means only one in five entering ninth graders would graduate reading at the national norms. No account of excuse-making could justify such a low performance rating. The need for radical reform was obvious.

ORGANIZATIONAL MISDIRECTION

The failure to educate the children of Chicago adequately would have been sufficient grounds, by itself, to fuel a movement to reform the public schools. However, the outcome failure was inextricably related to the managerial failures of the school administration. These failures dominated the newspaper and television accounts of the school system throughout the 1980s. They started with the financial collapse of the system in 1979. When the board of education's efforts to borrow money acknowledged that the funds sought would be used to pay off previous debts in order to keep the system afloat, the banks and bonding agencies refused to extend credit. Without fresh cash, the board failed to meet its December payroll, employees went on strike, and the schools were shut down.

A financial bailout plan was assembled at a New Year's weekend summit in the governor's mansion in Springfield. A financial oversight agency, the Chicago School Finance Authority (CSFA), was created and given part of the board's taxing authority. The CSFA

Table 1.3
Staff Cuts During Fiscal Crisis

Type Employees	*FY 1979*	*FY 1982*	*Decrease*	*Percent*
Student Contact	30,063	24,624	5,439	18%
Admin/Technical	3,628	3,125	503	14%
Support	15,161	12,606	2,555	17%
Total	48,852	40,355	8,497	17%

was authorized to use this tax authority to sell nearly $600 million of bonds to be used to help balance the board's budget for the 1979-1980 through 1981-1982 school years. Thereafter, the board's budget was required to be balanced before schools could open, and a three-year financial plan was required to show a reasonable likelihood of balancing the two succeeding years' budgets. In addition, the CSFA was given the right to approve the appointment of an independent chief financial officer who would have ultimate control of the board's fiscal affairs.

The Growth of the Bureaucracy

In 1982, shortly after its founding, the Chicago Panel on Public School Finances initiated a study of staffing changes resulting from the resolution of the fiscal crisis (Hallett & Hess, 1982). We compared the budgets and expenditures of four years just preceding and during the fiscal crisis (see Table 1.3). We categorized employees by job function and then grouped them by task. Between FY 1979 (the 1978-1979 school year) and FY 1981, 11,562 positions were cut, but more than 3,000 of those cuts were restored in FY 1982. In FY 1982, there were 8,497 fewer staff than in 1979. Student contact personnel (teachers, educational support staff like counselors, psychologists, speech therapists, etc., and classroom aides) took the largest cuts, both proportionally and in gross numbers. Support staff, including clerks, lunchroom attendants, custodians, and tradesmen, took the next largest cuts. Administrative and technical staff were most protected.

After noting that these budget cuts had most directly affected the number of staff with direct contact with students, we noted, "The Panel believes that when staff must be cut, as has been true, student contact positions should be the last cut. The instructional staff should take precedence over those who do not work directly with students" (Hallett & Hess, 1982, p. 16).

Each year thereafter, the panel analyzed the proposed budgets of the board of education and noted changes in the staffing patterns between categories of employees and the locations in which they worked. These analyses were presented at the annual hearings on the board's proposed budgets. One of the primary criticisms of the Chicago Public Schools during these annual hearings was the continual growth of the central bureaucracy, while local schools were starved for adequate numbers of teachers, texts, supplies, and other resources. The most telling analysis came in 1987, in testimony on the general superintendent's proposed budget following the 19-day school strike (Hess, 1987b). In that testimony, I showed the growth of the administrative bureaucracy in each year since 1981, while total student enrollment was dropping. This growth proceeded from the low point reached during the depth of the fiscal crisis, FY 1981. Our testimony examined the number of staff, supported by operating funds, working in administrative units (the central office and subdistrict administrative offices) and compared that number with those working in schools and with the total enrollment. From 1981 onward, there was a steady growth in the number of administrators and in the percentage of staff who worked in administrative offices (see Figure 1.3 and Table 1.4). By comparison, staff in the schools were severely cut in 1982, returned to 1981 levels only in 1985, and by 1988 was projected to be only 2% higher than in 1981. During that same period, staff in the administrative units had grown by 29%! When calculated against the declining enrollment base, the "bureaucrats" per 1,000 students increased by 37%. Something was desperately wrong with the focus of the system. The system's priorities were clearly not on providing as many resources as possible better to meet the needs of low-achieving Chicago students.

Diverting Compensatory Aid

In addition, the panel had identified an illegal diversion of state compensatory aid from serving disadvantaged students into supporting the central bureaucracy (Chicago Panel, 1988b). Illinois, unlike most other states, has a poverty impaction aspect in its

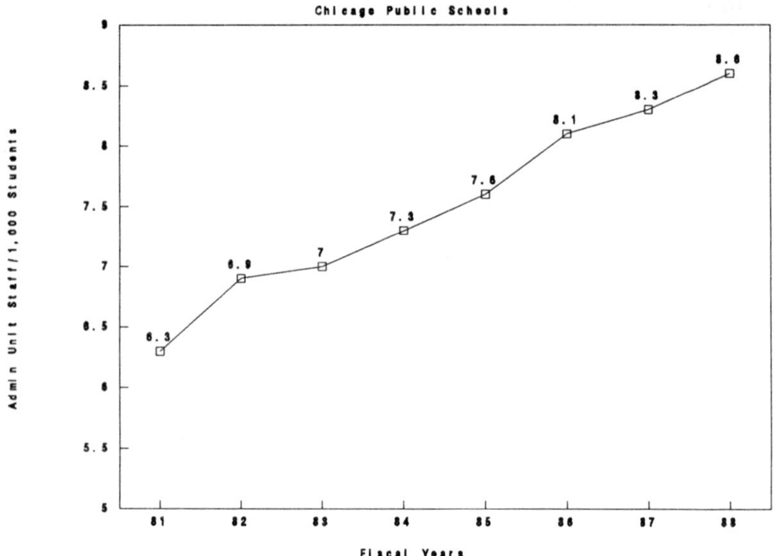

Figure 1.3. Bureaucrats Per 1,000 Students

school aid formula, which is based upon the proportion of economically disadvantaged students in enrollment. Districts with a proportion higher than the state level (about 18% in 1987-1988) received additional weighting for those students in the school aid formula. In 1987-1988, the Chicago Public Schools received $238 million in compensatory aid as part of total state aid of $832 million. Under 1978 legislation, Chicago was to distribute 60% of this state compensatory aid (called State Chapter I aid) to attendance centers on the basis of free lunch counts, while 40% was to be distributed to attendance centers on the basis of total enrollment. In fact, the Chicago Board of Education diverted nearly a third ($42 million) of the funds targeted for disadvantaged students to support central administrative costs under the pseudonym of "Program Support." In addition, contrary to the intent of the law, but unfortunately not directly proscribed in this state law as it is in federal law, the board used these state compensatory funds to provide basic services, such as kindergarten, guidance counseling, and librarians, in schools with heavy concentrations of disadvantaged students, while providing the exact same levels of

Table 1.4
Bureaucratic Growth

LOCATION	*1981*	*1982*	*1983*	*1984*	*1985*	*1986*	*1987*	*1988*
Enrollment	458,497	442,889	435,843	434,042	431,226	430,908	431,298	430,000
School Staff	29,339	27,822	28,855	29,185	29,418	29,462	29,919	29,964
Admin Units	2,884	3,036	3,043	3,156	3,295	3,470	3,598	3,708
Total Staff	32,223	30,858	31,898	32,341	32,713	32,932	33,518	33,672
% Admin	9.0%	9.8%	9.5%	9.8%	10.1%	10.5%	10.7%	11.0%
Admin/1,000	6.3	6.9	7.0	7.3	7.6	8.1	8.3	8.6

these services at other schools with regular education fund resources.

Once again, the priorities of the board of education were clearly not in favor of providing assistance to the students who needed the most help. Not only was it diverting resources away from schools to support what Secretary of Education Bennett called "a bloated bureaucracy" (*Chicago Sun Times*, November 7, 1987), the resources at the school level were being focused on the least needy students. This pattern was the same pattern seen in the system of educational triage identified in the Panel's dropout studies.

Racial Steering in Special Education

The same pattern had earlier been identified in a study of special education practices conducted by Designs for Change. *Caught in the Web* (Moore & Radford-Hill, 1982) was based, in part, on a survey of major city school systems, and their use of various special education programs (Office of Civil Rights, 1982). The report showed that Chicago classified more students, over 12,000 annually, as needing special education services for the "educable mentally handicapped" (EMH) than any other large city school district in the country. Moore and Radford-Hill charged that at least 7,000 of these students were misclassified. They further demonstrated that Chicago classified black students as EMH at far higher rates than any of the comparable major city systems (percentages in

Table 1.5
Students Classified as EMH

City	*Enrolled*	*In EMH*	*Black*	*White*	*Hispanic*
New York	943,952	6,629 0.70%	3,276 0.91%	1,009 0.41%	2,286 0.80%
Los Angeles	538,038	2,765 0.51%	1,339 1.07%	503 0.39%	858 0.51%
Chicago	458,523	13,077 2.85%	10,658 3.83%	1,493 1.74%	701 0.83%
Philadelphia	224,152	4,559 2.03%	3,351 2.39%	887 1.38%	312 1.95%
Detroit	213,077	3,659 1.72%	3,200 1.75%	430 1.66%	22 0.61%
Houston	194,060	1,707 0.88%	1,058 1.21%	280 0.57%	357 0.66%

Source: Adapted from Table A-1 in Moore & Radford-Hill, 1982, p. 58.

Table 1.5 indicate the proportion of all students or all students of a particular race classified as EMH).

Staff from Designs for Change attacked the reclassification project already being undertaken by the Chicago Board of Education, claiming that its evaluation criteria were seriously flawed. But staff from the board of education, disdaining to recognize the validity of outside research, had for a number of years regularly dismissed the charges by Designs for Change. Finally, the U.S. Office of Civil Rights (OCR), utilizing data supplied by Designs for Change and by the Chicago Panel, brought suit to deny further federal funds (the system was then receiving about $200 million from the federal government for a variety of programs). In 1989, an administrative law judge affirmed the OCR suit and ordered an end to all federal aid to the Chicago Public Schools until a remedy had been designed. One of the first acts of the new interim board of education installed under the Chicago School Reform Act was to enter into a consent decree with the Office of Civil Rights to remedy this long-standing injustice to disadvantaged students in the school system. Without the decade-long pressure exerted by

Designs for Change, it is unlikely that change in special education practices would have occurred.

Mismanagement at the Board of Education

Two other related reports deserve a prominent place in portraying the problems of the Chicago Public Schools. Immediately following the fiscal crisis, the business community, through Chicago United, a nonprofit association of major businesses and civil rights groups, created a Special Task Force on Education. It enlisted the services of over 82 loaned executives of major businesses, universities, and civic groups for 14 weeks of intensive effort. Following hard on the fiscal collapse of the system and guided by business interests, the *Report of the Special Task Force on Education: Chicago School System* (Chicago United, 1981) focused on changing the management and administration of the system more than on improving school-level instruction. However, the report recognized that the problems were more than simply managerial. "Broadly stated, the proposals presented have a common goal: Improve the quality of public education by enhancing accountability and control" (Chicago United, 1981, p. iii). The connection between the 253 primarily managerial recommendations and the quality of instruction is spelled out in the report's first recommendation:

> 1. *Decentralize authority at the central office in favor of adding talent at the school and district level.* To improve the system's responsiveness to the individual needs of students and parents, decisions should be made as close to the classroom as possible. Teaching and management capabilities at the school level should be strengthened. (Chicago United, 1981, pp. vii-viii)

Over the next several years, loaned executives were continually made available to the board of education, and many of the managerial recommendations were implemented. However, when Chicago United commissioned a *Reassessment of the Report of the 1981 Special Task Force on Education* (King, 1987), their consultant reported that, although 59% of the original report's recommendations had been fully or partially implemented, "the most important recommendations of the 1981 Report were not implemented or were buried in classic obfuscation presented as 'more study,' 'reorganization,' 'long term plan,' and 'too costly,'" and, "the fundamental causes of the problems that beset the Chicago Public Schools in 1981 and before remain the same today" (King, 1987, p. 7).

The reassessment focused particularly on the original report's first recommendation, which advocated decentralization. Its finding was succinct: "These essential elements of management, so clearly and deeply of concern to the 1981 analysts have not been addressed at all by the Chicago Public School" (King, 1987, p. 8).

It was on the occasion of the release of this reassessment report that Secretary of Education Bennett made his "worst in America" comment, and described the school situation in Chicago as "educational meltdown" (*Chicago Sun Times,* November 7, 1987). Whether totally accurate or not, Bennett's comment capsulized the growing awareness of Chicagoans that their public schools were not working and that the leadership of the school system was not focusing its resources on dealing with the problem.

But it was also recognized that fixing the Chicago Public Schools was not an easy task. Some business leaders had been working actively to support improvement efforts in individual schools and were finding the going very rough. The next chapter describes one such effort.

2

South West High: A Failing School

In 1988, a large Chicago company, which I will call National Diversified Foods (NDF), asked the Chicago Panel to do an assessment of its Adopt-A-School program at a Chicago high school. The NDF president had been the graduation speaker at the school the previous June and had asked the principal of the school, which I will call South West High, if NDF's assistance had had any impact on student achievement. When the principal equivocated, the president decided to ask his own staff.

The initial NDF staff analysis was inconclusive, and staff members turned to the Chicago Panel for assistance. The Panel's semiautonomous division METROSTAT conducted the assessment using a multidisciplinary approach. (The assessment team consisted of G. Alfred Hess; Virginia Lazarus, the new director of METROSTAT; and two research assistants, Christina Warden and Denise O'Neil Green. This chapter is built on the assessment developed by the entire team.) We conducted a survey of the entire faculty about the Adopt-A-School (AAS) programs and their impact on South West High. We surveyed a sample of students, interviewed all administrators and department heads, interviewed the faculty sponsors of all AAS programs, and conducted focus group discussions with selected faculty members and with several groups of students—both those within AAS programs and noninvolved students. But we also examined student achievement. We looked at several gross measures, such as the median student achievement levels over five years and attendance rates over the same period. We also examined the individual records of selected students, both those within AAS programs and others. This examination showed the difficulties faced by those who would seek to improve an individual Chicago public school. It appeared to the assessment team that the officers of National Diversified Foods had dreamed of turning South West around so that its performance would rival that of the best suburban high schools, the kind of high schools that they themselves had attended. The reality at South West was much more grim.

A SNAPSHOT OF SOUTH WEST HIGH SCHOOL

On the basis of freshman sign-ups and membership in the previous year's freshman through junior classes, South West expected a Fall 1988 enrollment of 1,106 students. All of these students would be black. About 55% would be from low-income homes, thus qualifying for free or reduced-price lunch. An analysis of home addresses revealed that 87.5% lived in the post office zip code area that includes the South West neighborhood boundaries, with another 7.1% from the contiguous zip area to the south. A few students traveled from the southern edge of the city or from lakefront communities to attend South West. Few students transfer in or out of South West; the stability rate is 93.6%.

In September 1988, South West expected to begin with 236 freshmen, 311 sophomores, 290 juniors, 211 seniors, and 58 students in special education classrooms (see Figure 2.1). This projection envisioned a considerably smaller freshman class than in previous years, though it was recognized that walk-in enrollments at the beginning of the Fall semester might expand the entering class. The larger size for the sophomore class was normal, reflecting a promotion policy that automatically promoted all freshmen, but required sophomores to have acquired 8.5 credits to be promoted to junior status and 13.0 credits to achieve senior status.

For the past several years, South West had maintained a higher proportion of males than females in most grades. While the previous year's freshman class was more evenly divided, freshmen were again more heavily male in the fall of 1988. Males made up nearly two-thirds of all students in special education classrooms.

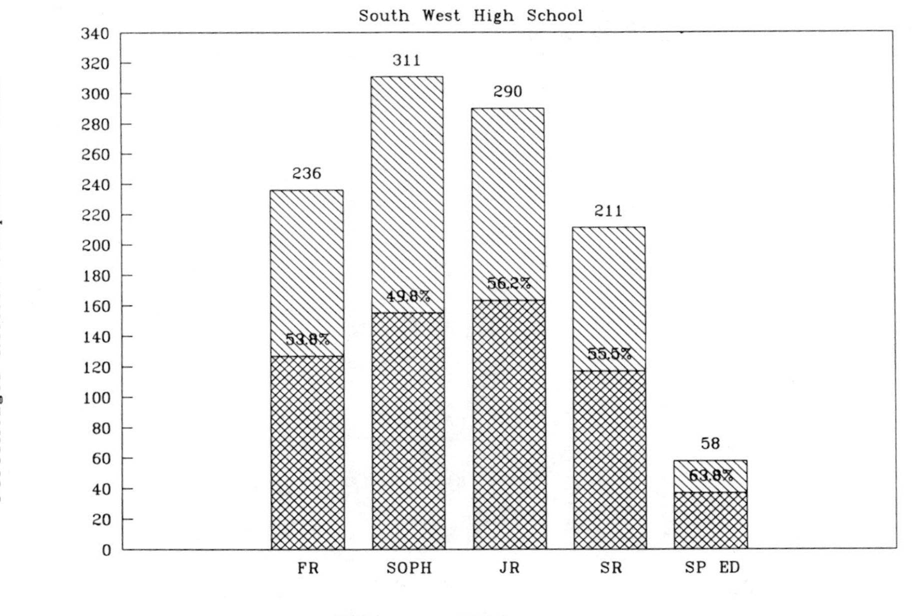

Figure 2.1. Class Enrollment, Fall 1988

Age data were not easily accessible for all classes, but an examination of the incoming freshman class revealed that 61.4% were overage at entrance. Without examining each student's school history, we felt it safe to assume that most of these students had been retained in grade level at least once during their elementary school careers.

Compared to national norms, students at South West High School were below normal in reading (and most other) skills. The most recently available data on the ACT college entrance test showed that South West students averaged a 9.2 score out of a possible 35. Only 40% of South West seniors took the test for college entrance. The national average score for that year, for the Class of 1987, was 18.7; the statewide Illinois average was 18.9. At 9.2, South West ranked in the first percentile of all high schools in the country using the ACT. It was one of more than 30 Chicago high schools that ranked in the nation's lowest percentile (see Introduction).

The normal distribution of scores on standardized tests follows a typical bell curve pattern, with 54% of tested students in the three middle (or average range) stanines. The curve for South West students is significantly skewed in the below-normal direction (Figure 2.2). When the three upper grades were examined individually, on the basis of the Test of Achievement and Proficiency (TAP) scores from fall 1987, there were few significant variations. The TAP is produced by the makers of the Iowa Test of Basic Skills, which is used in Chicago elementary schools.

We tracked end-of-year failure patterns over four years: 1984, 1986, 1987, and 1988. Data were missing for June, 1985. There was little consistent change in the failure patterns during these four years, except for a decline in the number of juniors with no failures. The compilation of the figures for these four years produced an average failure pattern that focused attention on the difficulties students have during their first two years at South West. Only 33% of freshmen passed all their subjects at the end of their first year. Sixteen percent failed one course. More than half (51%) failed two or more subjects, and more than half of these multiple failing students had failed four or more subjects! The picture shifted only slightly for sophomores, as might be expected since all freshmen are automatically promoted to the sophomore class. See Figure 2.3.

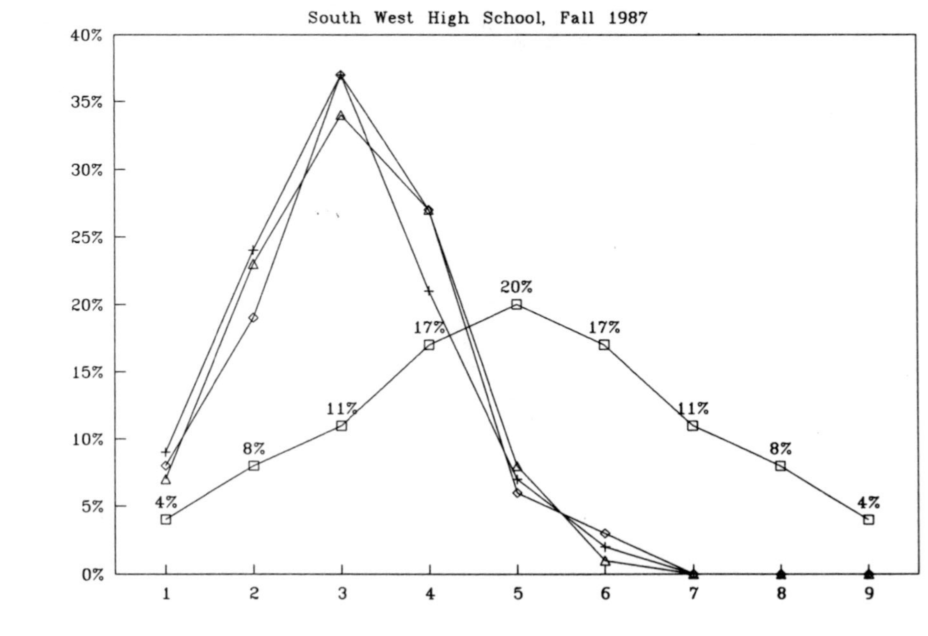

Figure 2.2. Reading Score Distribution by Stanines

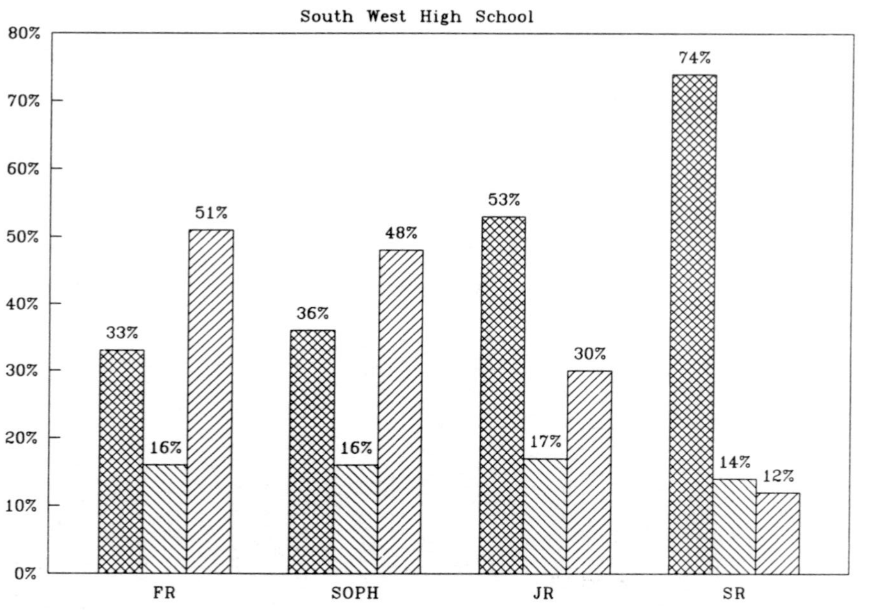

Figure 2.3. Failure Pattern, 1984-1988

The picture improved markedly for the junior class. At that grade, more than half (53%) passed all their subjects, 18% failed one subject, and 30% failed two or more. (Totals do not equal 100% due to rounding.) However, it must be acknowledged that most students dropped out before achieving junior ranking. Failure rates for the final semester of the senior year decreased significantly, but still involved a quarter (26%) of the class. In all probability, these students would not graduate with their class. Some would make up the credit in summer school so that they could graduate in the fall. Others would be required to spend an additional year at South West. The principal made it a point to encourage students who required an extra year to graduate to take that opportunity.

Course failures and course attendance are intimately connected. Very few of the students at South West who attended class regularly failed a course. The Panel staff examined in detail the course grade reports for each individual in the 1987-88 junior class. There were 244 juniors who received final grades that June; 112 passed all classes and their records were not examined further. The other 132 students had 424 Fs between them. For only 18 of those cases did the student miss fewer than 10 days of class. For 80.9% of the Fs, the student had missed more than 20 days. Many of these students were simply not in school for days on end. Others would be in school but consistently cut the class they failed. Failures were directly related to both low attendance and cutting.

Males failed more classes than did females. For all students in June 1988, 326 males failed at least one course, compared to 230 females. Similar numbers of males and females failed just one course (78 vs. 71, respectively), but more males (248) had multiple failures than did females (159).

Closely connected to the failure pattern is the distribution of students by grades. The composition of the student body, as demonstrated earlier, showed an enrollment peak among sophomores with a sharply smaller junior class and an even smaller senior class. When individual cohorts of students were tracked from entrance until completion at South West, the same pattern appeared (Figure 2.4). When the Class of 1987 first came to South West in 1983, there were 309 freshmen. The next year, with the addition of sophomores held back from preceding classes, there were 396. However, fewer than half of those students (165) achieved junior ranking. Most of those stayed to become seniors

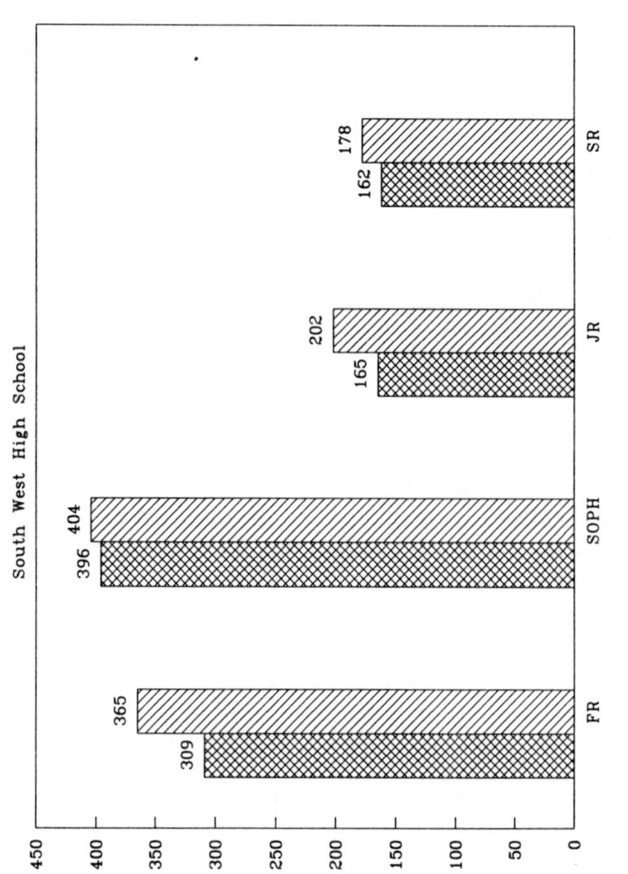

Figure 2.4. Change in Enrollment by Grade

(162). For the Class of 1988, the pattern was similar: 365 as freshmen, 404 as sophomores, 202 as juniors, and 178 seniors.

Dropout rates at South West stabilized at about 50% after reaching nearly 60% for the Class of 1983 (students who entered South West as freshmen the year before the principal had arrived at the school). When the dropout data were examined closely, it was possible to determine which students were most at risk. In the Class of 1985, nearly two-thirds (63.0%) of South West males dropped out before their class graduated; 39.9% of females dropped out. Among those who entered overage (15 or older on December 1 of their freshman year), 63.6% dropped out, while only 39.1% of those entering on time did so. More than half (56.7%) of those with entering reading scores in the first stanine dropped out, while 40.9% at the fifth stanine (those with scores +/– 10% from the national median) or higher did so. Thus, it is quite possible to identify students who are most at risk of dropping out: males who are overage and who have low reading scores. Still, the difficulties of improving South West High School are underlined by the fact that nearly 41% of students reading at average or higher levels when they entered the school eventually dropped out.

It seems clear from the foregoing analysis that many students entered South West at risk, did not successfully negotiate the transition into high school, piled up massive numbers of failures in their freshman and sophomore years, and then dropped out. These failures were directly related to absences from school and cut classes, indicators that could be tracked continuously to alert staff to students who are putting themselves at further risk of dropping out.

Of course, there were significant numbers of females and appropriately aged students who got caught in the same failure pattern. In addition, the principal pointed out that a "D syndrome" also existed at South West, in which students were satisfied with the lowest passing mark, even though they were capable of doing better work.

IMPROVED ATTITUDES AT SOUTH WEST HIGH SCHOOL

At the time we assessed the programs at South West High School, there had been three primary efforts at school improvement. The first was an effort by the principal and his staff, initiated several years before the arrival of National Diversified Foods, to improve attendance at the school. We examined the attendance pattern at South West. In 1981, the principal's first year at the school, the attendance rate was 78.4%. Just over three quarters of all students were in attendance on any given day. By 1983, through extensive teacher telephoning to homes, attendance had risen to 85.3%, where it hovered through 1985. During 1986 and 1987, attendance slipped, dropping to 83.1% during the latter year. In 1988, new board of education regulations, reflecting pressure from the State Board of Education in response to our study *Where's Room 185?*, deducted a half day's attendance for students who cut any class. Thus, attendance data for 1988 were not comparable to data for previous years. However, it was primarily faculty effort and the dedicated work of an administrator in charge of attendance, prior to NDF's involvement, that accounted for the increase in attendance rates during the early 1980s. Rates tailed off during the two years just prior to the assessment, reflecting the death of the attendance monitoring administrator and his replacement by an ineffective one, who was later transferred out of the school. According to the principal, this was a good example of the significant impact one excellent employee could have on the school. It was also an indication of the impact staff changes can have on the success of programs.

A second effort at improvement, launched by the principal, was to make South West a career academy, a high school with a specialty program focused on job preparation. In this regard, the principal saw South West primarily as a school providing terminal education, the final education in which most of its students would enroll. He embarked upon an effort to guide entering students into business or technical concentrations to prepare them more adequately for post-high school employment.

Student enrollments were changing in these various tracks. For seniors in the Class of 1989, 51.3% were enrolled in the academic track, with the rest of the students roughly divided between the other two tracks, business and technical. However, for the class that entered as freshmen in the fall of 1987, the Class of 1991, only a quarter (24.3%) were in the academic track, more than a third were in business (34.7%), and the largest group (41.0%) was in technical courses. Thus, more students were selecting business and technical tracks. The principal was successful in his effort to have South West viewed as a terminal education institution emphasizing job preparedness instead of preparation for college. The latest research, however, indicates this kind of a tracking pattern, emphasizing vocational and business education, is more likely to increase the dropout rate (Oakes, 1985; Braddock & McPartland, 1990).

Adopt-A-School Introduces New Programs

Another effort at improvement involved the Adopt-A-School programs supported by National Diversified Foods. At the time we made our assessment, these programs had been in the school for five years. Various programs had been added during NDF's tenure at South West so that at the time of the assessment, 10 major programs were functioning. These programs included the Academic Team, the International Academic Team, the School Store/Silk Screen Printing programs, Build-A-Better You (with both student and parent components), a peer tutorial program, the Adopt-A-Friend community service project, the Ambassador program, the NDF Scholarship Program, black history month, and teacher continuing education and small grants programs. The most important of these programs appeared to be the Academic Team, the School Store enterprises, Build-A-Better You, the peer tutoring, and the grants to teachers.

The *Academic Team* was a recognition and service program for qualifying South West students. Students were inducted onto the team when they met any of three criteria: 1) having a semester grade point average of B or above; 2) having perfect attendance while maintaining at least a C average; or 3) being the most improved student in their respective home rooms.

The *School Store and Silk Screen* enterprises were sponsored by an outstanding teacher in the business department. The student store was open daily, selling supplies, snacks, and clothing to South West students. The silk screening effort involved applying insignia and logos to T-shirts and other apparel for commercial sale. Both enterprises were student managed and staffed as entrepreneurial training for future employment.

The *Build-A-Better You* programs were focused on raising the self-esteem of both students and parents. With extensive use of local sports and media stars, the primary activities of these programs were schoolwide speakers and classroom workshops. During 1987-

1988, 20 speakers were brought to South West to encourage students to complete their education.

The *peer tutoring* program was run through the guidance department and matched student tutors with students recommended by their teachers as needing assistance. Tutors would work, during their study hall time, with students excused from the class subject in which they were having trouble.

Teachers received, on the basis of applications to the principal, *small grants* provided by NDF to pay for continuing courses at universities or for underwriting small class projects. NDF supplied the funds and the principal made the grants to requesting teachers he thought merited the support.

Creating a New Attitude

Our assessment at South West High School focused on these and the other Adopt-A-School (AAS) programs. NDF's efforts were concentrated on highly visible and motivational programs, providing students with many speakers and reward programs, and using well-known black role models. This approach was consistent with NDF's early theme, *South West High—A New Attitude.* The goals of the programs were to make it acceptable for students to want to get an education and to make it fun to be a student. There was little doubt, from the data we collected as part of the assessment, that these goals were met.

Since the focus of the goals was upon changing attitudes, our assessment utilized qualitative data collection methods. We surveyed and interviewed a significant proportion of the faculty and student body and a small representative sample of parents. Our assessment of the data collected from these various efforts was that attitudes had changed at South West, or at least that the current students and faculty felt that attitudes had changed.

Response to NDF's presence at South West was overwhelmingly positive. The vast majority of faculty (97%), students (93%), and parents (70%) surveyed reported that the AAS program had had a positive impact on the academic and social education of the students at South West. (Social education was defined as the learning and experiences related to student involvement, morale, rapport with faculty, etc.) However, faculty and students often mentioned that, although the individual programs were very valuable for those who qualified or were chosen to participate, far too many students were not reached by the current activities and honors. Both groups felt that more faculty, students, and parents should be involved.

The overall perception of South West High School itself was one of progress and improvement. The main contributors cited for this improvement were the school's administration, NDF's presence, and the improved efforts of teachers. The general reputation of the school had greatly improved. The AAS activities, as well as the implementation of stricter administrative policies and procedures, were seen as instrumental in this change.

Faculty and students emphasized the improvement in both teacher and student morale over the last few years. The teachers reported that the increased student involvement in AAS programs had improved the students' attitudes toward and behavior in school. For example, they believed that the academic team had provided the inspiration for achievement and had created an attitude that made staying in school socially acceptable to students. Students confirmed this in comments referring to the status and recognition they received for their participation on the team and for having an academic team jacket. Students reported that their sense of self-esteem and accomplishment had been enhanced by their involvement in the individual AAS programs such as the Build-A-Better You program, which was specifically designed for this purpose. This attitudinal effect was consistent with the initial goals of the AAS program.

The majority (84%) of the faculty surveyed reported that the AAS program had improved teacher morale and provided a new hope and enthusiasm for teaching. They commented that the AAS program encouraged them, with the financial support of the Mini Grants program, to implement innovative ideas in the classroom, allowing them to expand their curricula to include experiences and/or materials that enhanced student learning.

In addition tc the improved morale, the reputation of the school, as perceived by students, parents, and teachers, had vastly improved. South West was seen in the past as a dangerous school with gang violence and drug problems. While similar problems still existed, their presence had diminished at the time of the assessment. Students felt that the improvement was partially attributable to the Adopt-A-School programs because students were becoming less troublesome as they became more involved in the programs. Students reported that the school was not as bad as they had feared before attending, and parents agreed that it had improved significantly over the last five years. NDF's presence and new administrative policies were credited for this improvement. (However, a year later a student was killed in a gang-related incident in a South West High School classroom.)

Although the general response to NDF's programs at South West was positive, on specific items the various groups surveyed had differences of opinion. The majority of all parties identified vast improvements in the social climate at South West, but one sixth (17.6%) of the faculty felt that it had declined. Many still identified areas where further improvement was needed. Teachers mentioned apathy, ineffectiveness, and conflicts among both teachers and administrators, as well as insufficient communication, as major contributing factors to their perception of a decline. Students and teachers also commented on the continuing problems with discipline issues inside and outside the classrooms, teenage pregnancy, and gangs. Teachers, students, and parents all provided numerous suggestions for the further improvement of the social climate at South West.

In the academic climate at South West High, a majority of faculty, students, and parents also perceived an improvement. Our surveys showed that faculty (62%), students (63%), and parents (85%) all believed that the students' education at South West had improved. The perceived improvements in the academic climate were attributed to the AAS program, changes in administrative policies, and improved curriculum and teachers.

According to the faculty surveyed, teachers' efforts in the classroom were enhanced by the noticeable improvement in student attitudes toward course work as a result of the AAS programs. They reported that student concern for grades and attendance had increased and that the competitive drive to improve was helping in the quality of course work. It is clear that a perception of improvement had permeated both the faculty and student body. However, as I shall show, this perception of improvement was not substantiated by the data we collected on student achievement.

It must be noted that one quarter (26%) of the faculty surveyed felt that the academic climate had declined. Reasons given for the decline in academic achievement included perceptions that administrative policies were not consistently enforced, faculty members were apathetic, heterogeneous groupings among upperclassmen lowered the standards for average and above-average students, the curriculum did not prepare students for the job market, and the feeder schools did not adequately prepare students for high school. Teachers also listed socioeconomic issues such as problems with teenage pregnancy, gangs, lack of parental involvement, and the difficulties encountered when trying to contact parents.

Faculty members described three primary weaknesses of the AAS programs in relation to their impact on academic achievement: 1) the same students were targeted for the various activities and programs, and many students were excluded; 2) program activities disrupted classroom work too frequently and without enough previous notice; and, 3) AAS programs did not concentrate on improving basic skills.

Student concerns for academic achievement focused on the need for more effective teachers and more diverse curriculum choices. Students wanted to have more options for vocational courses and interesting electives.

ACADEMIC ACHIEVEMENT HAD NOT IMPROVED

Our staff from the Chicago Panel conducted a review of student achievement patterns at South West High School during the period when the NDF Corporation had sponsored its Adopt-A-School program there. This review assessed changes in student enrollment, student/teacher ratios, freshmen preparedness, and student achievement indicators.

Academic indicators showed that the enhancement of student motivation *did not* lead to academic improvement. An analysis of schoolwide achievement results indicated that no significant improvement in achievement occurred during the tenure of NDF's Adopt-A-School efforts. Although student/teacher ratios declined, as a result of reduced enrollment and staff additions for Options for Knowledge and special education programs, there was no consequential improvement in standardized test achievement scores, dropout rates, failure rates, or attendance rates.

Decline in Student Enrollment

The student enrollment at South West had changed significantly during the last decade. In 1978, there were 2,270 students at South West High School. In just five years, that number was cut in half; by 1983, the enrollment stood at 1,140. By 1986, the number had risen to 1,289, but had then fallen back to 1,214 (see Figure 2.5). The comfortable program capacity of the school, according to school administrators, is 1,350 students.

Reduction of Student/Teacher Ratio

The size of the faculty declined more slowly, dropping from 124 in 1978 to 72.2 in 1983, and then rose again to 83.1. This slower decline in the number of faculty had resulted in a reduction of the student/teacher ratio from 18.9 to 15.0 (see Figure 2.6). To some extent, this lower number was the result of new staff added to implement Options for Knowledge programs under the system's desegregation plan. This additional staff had given the principal added flexibility in designing programs for South West High School. An increase in special education staff also contributed to the decrease in the student/teacher ratio.

Improvement in Preparedness of Entering Freshmen

The preparedness of entering freshmen had improved at the same time that enrollment numbers had declined. The median reading score in grade equivalents (half the students had higher scores, half lower) for entering freshmen rose from 6.1 in 1981 to 7.4 in 1986 (the national norm for such students is 8.8). The median reading percentile for freshmen classes, which were tested after arriving at South West, between 1982 and 1986 improved from the 18th to the 21st percentile (1987 Test of Achievement and Proficiency [TAP] results were not available from the Chicago Public Schools). High school test scores on the TAP are expressed as the national percentile rank of the median student tested; thus, the national norm would be the 50th percentile. The improvement in median test scores for entering freshmen reflected primarily the systemwide improvement in elementary test scores between 1978 and 1983. Since 1983, systemwide test scores have remained flat.

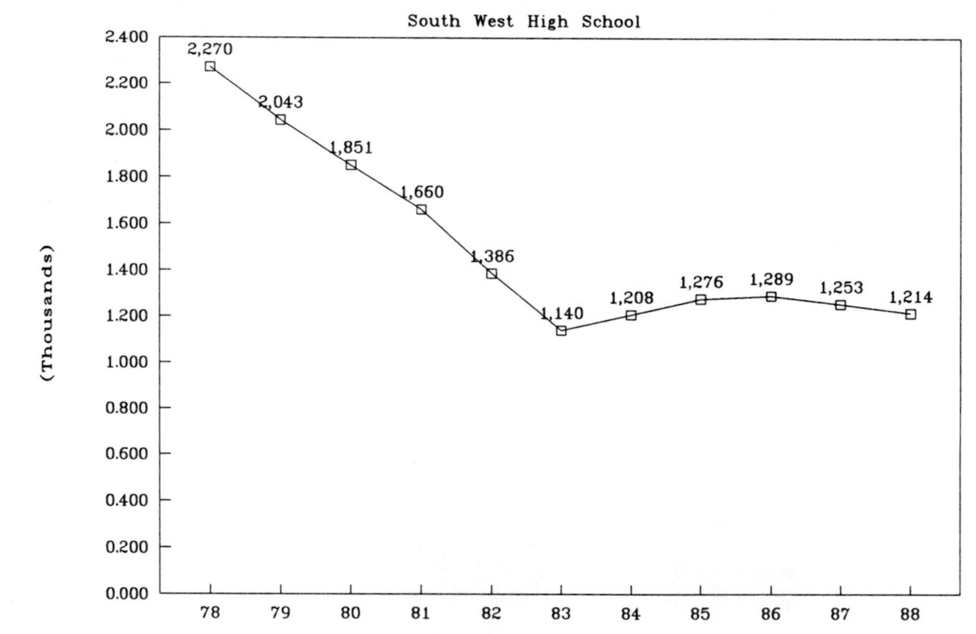

Figure 2.5. Decline in Student Enrollment

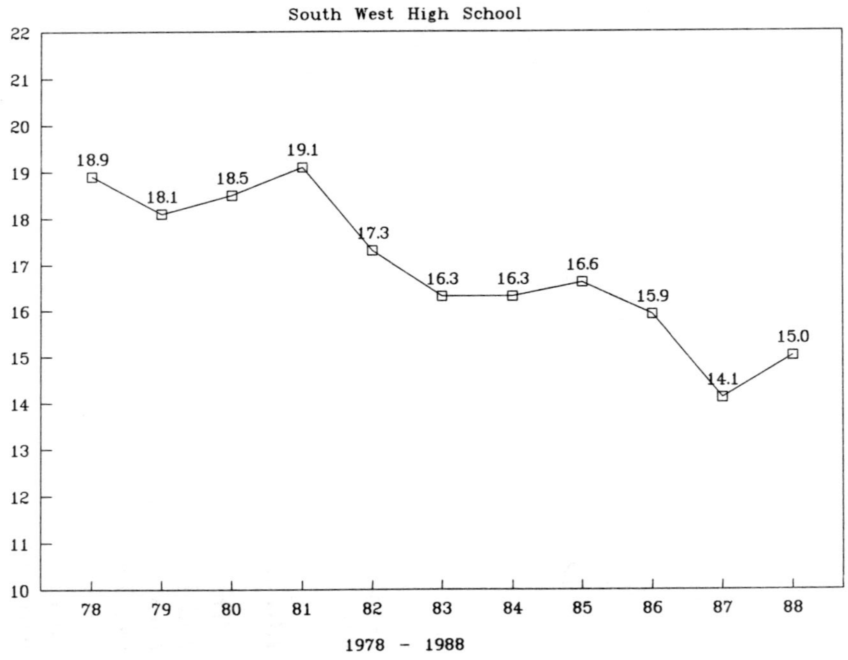

South West High School

22
21
20
19
18
17
16
15
14
13
12
11
10

18.9 18.1 18.5 19.1 17.3 16.3 16.3 16.6 15.9 14.1 15.0

78 79 80 81 82 83 84 85 86 87 88

1978 – 1988

Figure 2.6. Students Per Faculty Member

Table 2.1
Changes in Freshmen Enrollment and Reading Scores

	1980	1981	1982	1983	1984	1985	1986	1987
No. Freshmen	396	331	278	310	376	394	325	327
Median Percentile-Fresh	N/A	N/A	18%	19%	18%	21%	21%	N/A
Median Read-Grade 8	N/A	6.1	6.3	6.5	6.9	6.9	7.4	7.2
Avg Grade 8 Scores 4 Feeder Schools	6.7	6.8	N/A	8.2	7.8	8.0	8.0	N/A

As can be seen from the figures in Table 2.1, the median reading scores of entering South West freshmen were consistently below the median reading scores of its four primary feeder elementary schools. In the past, these four schools had supplied more than 70% of South West's entering class. Thus, it may be concluded that the higher-achieving students leaving these feeder schools were enrolling at more distant schools. The Chicago Panel's 1987 study, *Bending the Twig: The Elementary Years and Dropout Rates in the Chicago Public Schools* (Hess & Greer, 1987), demonstrated that such higher-achieving neighborhood-school eighth graders were, in fact, being drawn away from neighborhood high schools like South West to the system's selective magnet and vocational/technical high schools, such as Chicago Vocational, Simeon Vocational, Gage Park, and Lindblom Tech. (Contrary to the above-cited tracking literature, some Chicago vocational schools function primarily as selective college prep schools for the best-prepared students, while others are of the more conventional, dead-end variety.)

Rise in Senior Achievement Scores

The high school test scores for seniors on the Test of Achievement and Proficiency (TAP) also showed slight improvements in the early years of this decade, but had been flat since the fall of 1984 (see Table 2.2).

Since the fall of 1984, reading test scores for South West seniors have stayed the same, with 80% of all students taking the test nationally scoring higher than the median student at South West.

Table 2.2
Changes in Reading Scores of Seniors

	1982	*1983*	*1984*	*1985*	*1986*
Fall Tests of Seniors	18%	17%	20%	20%	20%

It was anticipated that the scores of seniors would rise during the several succeeding years, reflecting the better preparation of more recent entering freshmen classes.

Reduced Dropout Rates for Class of 1984, Flat Since Then

Closely related to the preparedness of entering freshmen is the dropout rate. The Chicago Panel's 1985 study, *Dropouts from the Chicago Public Schools* (Hess & Lauber, 1985), demonstrated that individual high school dropout rates are directly related to the proportion of entering freshmen reading below normal rates. In that study, the Panel and the Chicago Public Schools cooperatively calculated dropout rates for each high school for the graduating classes of 1982, 1983, and 1984. The study used a longitudinal approach calculating the proportion of entering freshmen who dropped out prior to graduation. The system produced two updates of that study for the classes of 1985 and 1986 (further promised updates for the classes of 1987 and beyond have been suppressed by the school system's administration).

The South West dropout rate peaked at 59.2% for the Class of 1983, which had started at South West two years before the arrival of the principal. Reflecting some decrease in the proportion of entering students reading below normal, the dropout rate for the Class of 1984 declined significantly, to 49.8%; the Class of 1985 maintained that position (50.0%), but the rate edged up to 51.2% for the Class of 1986. Annualized dropout data and anecdotal information from South West officials indicated that the unreported rate for the Class of 1987 would be close to those for 1984 to 1986. Thus, dropout rates improved after 1983, but had remained flat since then. Since dropout statistics for each class reflect experiences of students during their preceding four years, it is fair to say that the significant change in the dropout rate between 1983 and 1984 at South West High School was not the result of NDF's Adopt-A-School program.

Little Change Seen in Failure Rates

Our staff from the panel, with the assistance of South West High School staff, examined the schoolwide pattern of student failures. End-of-year failure rates at South West differed significantly by class, with the proportion of students with no failures doubling between the freshman and senior years. A four-year average showed 33% of freshmen with no failures compared with 74% of seniors with no failures (Figure 2.7). Part of this difference was the result of the departure of dropouts between the end of the freshman and senior years. However, over a four-year period, the proportion of students in each grade with no failures was generally mixed, except for a steady decline among juniors. Data for 1985 were not available for this assessment. This graph clearly shows that there had been no significant reduction of student failures during the period of NDF's Adopt-A-School program.

Summary: Little Significant Achievement Change During NDF's Tenure

In summary, an examination of student achievement, outcome, and attendance records revealed that, despite reduced student-teacher ratios and extensive morale building efforts, there had been no significant improvement in any of these areas during the tenure of NDF's Adopt-A-School efforts. This is not to say that the individual AAS programs had had no impact upon the school. Extensive evidence was uncovered that indicated NDF's efforts had significantly affected the attitudes of students and faculty who made up the South West school community. Since such an attitude change was the expressed intent of those programs, it is appropriate to say the programs achieved their explicit goals. However, it cannot be said that those AAS programs had any significant impact on the academic performance of the student body, as a whole.

COMPARING ACADEMIC TEAM TO NONPARTICIPANTS

We postulated, at the outset of the assessment, that individual AAS programs might have had an effect on some students that

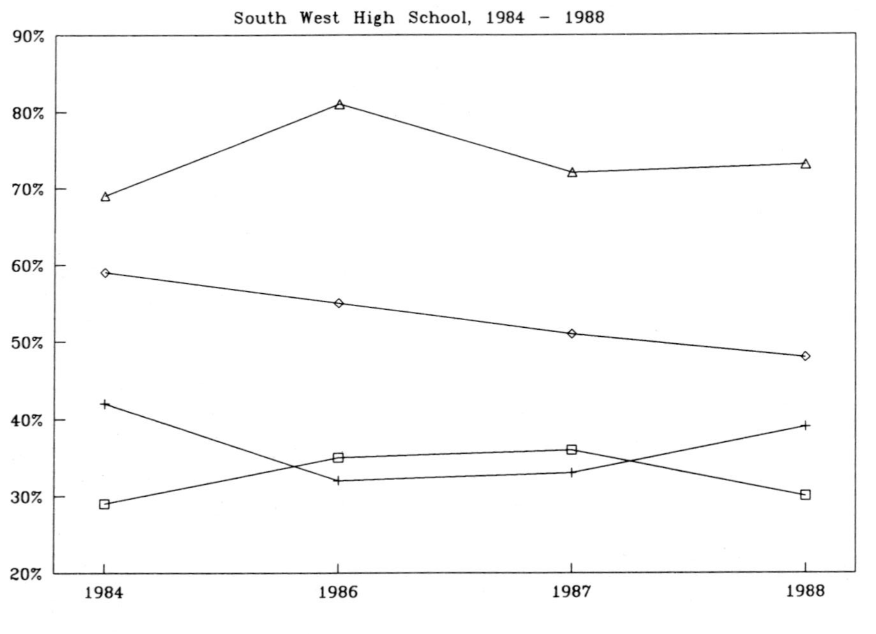

Figure 2.7. Students with No Failures

schoolwide statistics would not reflect. To test that possibility, we created two comparable groups of students, randomly selected in each case, to compare the experiences of students in the most academically oriented AAS program (the academic team) with those of students not participating in AAS programs.

A close assessment of the academic team led us to the conclusion that, as then implemented, the team had had no persisting effects on student achievement. Students who made the team in their first two years at South West manifested the same pattern of deterioration of academic performance in succeeding years as did nonparticipating students. On the whole, the academic team was made up of students at higher achievement levels, who had better attendance patterns. As might be expected, team members had fewer total course failures and lower failure rates. But having made the academic team, a majority of students were not then improving their subsequent academic performance. The success of the academic team was mitigated by the selection on the basis of nonacademic criteria of some students, who clearly fell short of the image purveyed by the name "academic team." The following data, based on our survey of individual records of a random sample of students who were on the academic team in 1985-1986 as freshmen and sophomores and a comparable group of other students, present comparisons between team members and nonmembers.

Team Member Reading Achievement Patterns Were Closer to the Normal Curve

Students who made the academic team had reading scores that were closer to the normal bell curve than did nonparticipating students (Figure 2.8). Note that, theoretically, the curve for academic team members would be expected to be to the right of the normal bell curve since their grades were supposed to be above average.

Similar Deterioration in Cumulative Grade Point Averages

The cumulative grade point average (GPA) of students first making the academic team as freshmen and sophomores changed in the same direction as for nonparticipants. However, it should be noted that the average cumulative GPA was higher for academic

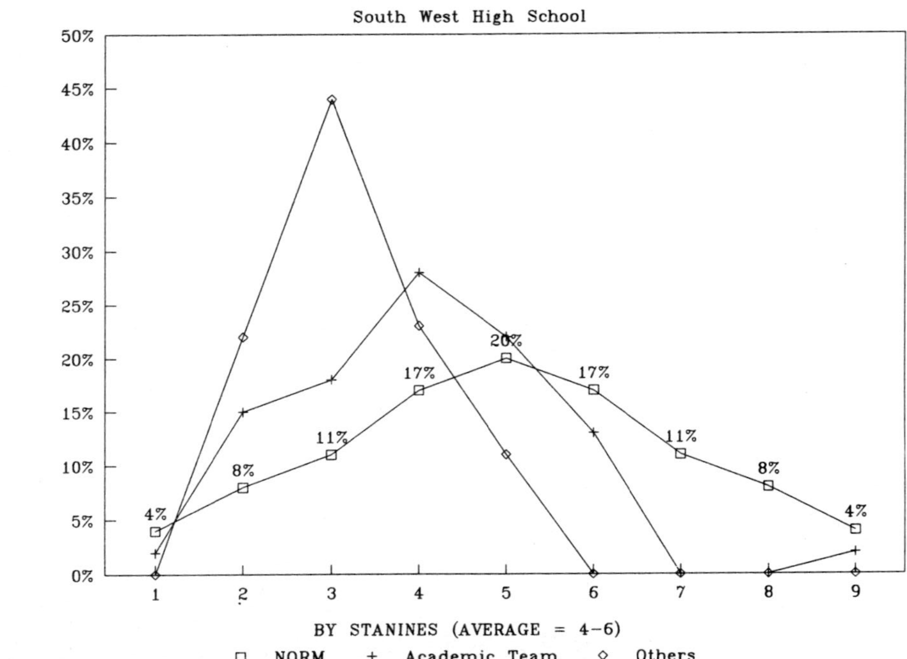

Figure 2.8. Reading Scores: Academic Team Versus Others

Table 2.3
Changes in Cumulative GPA, Fall 1985 to Spring 1988

	GPA		*Improved*	*Deteriorated*
	Fall '85	*Spring '88*	*GPA*	*GPA*
Academic Team	2.55	2.42	43.5%	56.5%
Other Students	1.26	1.42	45.8%	52.1%

NOTE: In the "other students" group, a few students had the same GPA in both marking periods.

Table 2.4
Cumulative Failure Rates, June 1988

	Seniors		*Juniors*	
	Courses	*Percent*	*Courses*	*Percent*
Academic Team	1.5	3.3%	3.0	9.0%
Other Students	9.6	18.5%	9.4	25.4%

team members at both the beginning and the end of the period. For the fall semester of 1985, the average GPA of academic team members was 2.55 (about a C+) compared to 1.26 (D) for other students. By the end of 1988, the team's GPA had dropped to 2.42, while the other students' GPA had improved to 1.42 (D+) (see Table 2.3). Thus, membership on the academic team, while indicating higher academic success, did not result in general improvement in grades. When the direction of change in GPA was calculated for each student, it was found that more students had lower GPAs in their senior year than in their freshman year. The deterioration was greater among academic team members than among nonparticipating students.

Lower Failure Rates for Team Members

Academic team members had lower failure rates than did nonmembers (see Table 2.4). Seniors in 1988 who had been on the team averaged 1.5 failures during their high school careers, with Fs in only 3.3% of their courses, compared to 9.6 failures (18.5% of courses) for nonparticipants. Academic team juniors did not do as well. In 1988, they averaged 3.0 failures (9.0% of courses taken) compared to 9.4 Fs for other students (failing 25.4% of their courses).

Table 2.5
Percent Students Whose Attendance Deteriorated

	Seniors	*Juniors*	*Combined*
Academic Team	60.0%	75.0%	66.7%
Other Students	64.0%	75.0%	69.4%

Table 2.6
Changes in TAP Scores, 1985-1987

		Seniors			*Juniors*	
	Dropped	*Same*	*Improved*	*Dropped*	*Same*	*Improved*
Other Students	34.9%	36.4%	28.7%	44.0%	36.6%	19.4%
Acad Team, '85-'86	47.9%	43.7%	8.5%	50.0%	35.7%	14.3%
Acad Team, '87 Fall	10.5%	52.6%	36.8%	23.8%	57.1%	19.0%

Better Attendance Patterns for Team Members

The attendance pattern of academic team members was better (five absences per semester, on average) than that of nonparticipants (eight absences per semester), but attendance deteriorated for about two thirds of each group between fall semester 1985 and spring 1988 (Table 2.5).

Variations in TAP Score Changes

TAP (Tests of Achievement and Proficiency) scores deteriorated for both groups of students between the fall of 1985 and 1987. When scores on all subsections were compared, more nonparticipants improved on TAP tests than those first making the academic team as freshmen and sophomores. However, the greatest improvement was seen in those first making the academic team in the fall of their senior year (Table 2.6).

DOES ATTITUDE CHANGE IMPROVE ACHIEVEMENT?

The current research literature reports that the use of motivational approaches rarely has a direct impact upon student achievement. Attitudinal approaches have been found to be effective and valuable only in their impact on attitudinal aspects of the school environment such as morale, motivation, self-esteem and school pride. Our findings in this assessment of the AAS program at South West were consistent with this literature.

LeCompte and Dworkin (1988) have summarized the literature on the impact of innovational educational programs on student achievement of disadvantaged students. They maintain that educational success in American schools should be measured by the reduction of student dropouts and teacher turnover. They suggest that short-term goals of increasing test scores, decreasing violence, and reducing the absenteeism rates of teachers and students are irrelevant if those involved become alienated and drop out. Given the assumption that education is a necessity, and that educational skills are directly linked to the potential economic well-being of students, LeCompte and Dworkin argue that success must be measured by the ability of the system to 1) maintain a competent and motivated staff, 2) bring disadvantaged students closer to their nondisadvantaged peers, 3) decrease the dropout rate, and, by doing so, 4) facilitate viable employment for these students (LeCompte & Dworkin, 1988, p. 136).

The tendency of those involved in trying to improve education has been to measure the success of motivational programs only by their impact on standardized test scores. As noted by LeCompte and Dworkin (1988, p. 139), "It is important to bear in mind that, despite the many efforts to improve the context, climate, and support systems of the schools, the only programs shown to have any *direct* effect on student achievement are those that directly link instruction to desired outcomes." Therefore, programs such as NDF's Adopt-A-School should be evaluated according to their effect on only those arenas that have been directly targeted by the program objectives. The AAS programs were designed to create a *new attitude;* therefore, the standards of measurement should be consistent with objectives pertaining to attitudinal effects. When measured by standards that review the program's impact on areas such as morale, motivation, self-esteem, and school pride, there was no doubt that the AAS programs had been a success. However, as we have seen, there had not been significant increases in the levels of student achievement. LeCompte and Dworkin indicate that such improvement should not have been expected.

The experience of National Diversified Foods at South West High is instructive about the effort to improve inner-city schools. The educational situation in these schools is dire. At the high school level, these schools have been negatively affected by the educational triage that funnels better students away from neighborhood high schools and leaves those schools with only the lowest-achieving freshmen. Even the best of efforts of a firm like NDF, which contributed more than $100,000 per year to improve the climate at South West High School, were not sufficient significantly to improve the achievement levels and graduation rates at its adopted high school. The programs were successful in improving the climate at the school and in improving the morale of faculty and students alike. But other, more directly instructional efforts would be required to improve the prospects for South West's students. The perception of administrators, faculty, and students that the Adopt-A-School programs had boosted achievement were incorrect. But the improvement in the atmosphere and attitudes of students was a hopeful sign to the assessment team that the school community would be receptive to future programs geared toward improving achievement.

3

Mobilizing a Movement for School Reform: Citizen Initiative

On October 11 and 12, 1989, 313,000 persons voted to elect 5,420 members of Local School Councils to begin school-based management at 542 Chicago Public Schools. This election was the climax of a movement to restructure the Chicago public school system radically.

The Chicago School Reform Act (P.A. 85-1418) set forth a list of school improvement goals (focused around bringing Chicago students to the national norms in achievement, attendance, and graduation), reallocated funds within the system to provide additional school-level resources in schools attended by disadvantaged students, and gave Local School Councils at each school the right to adopt a school improvement plan, determine the budget from a lump-sum allocation, and influence the staffing of the school through the right to select and terminate the principal. The legislation was designed, debated, and given final shape by a coalition of citizen activists, parents, and business executives. Legislator input was restricted to those relatively peripheral areas where compromises were necessary to secure enough votes for passage.

This chapter provides a chronology of the major events that led up to the establishment of this particular form of school reform in Chicago and analyzes the major elements of the effort that produced such a stunning result.

THE CHICAGO PUBLIC SCHOOLS: IN NEED OF REFORM

The Chicago School Reform Act builds upon the unique history of the Chicago Public School system. In 1985, the Chicago schools enrolled some 435,000 students, down from a high of 585,000 in 1968 (Chicago Board of Education, 1985). The school system was recovering from a fiscal crisis in 1979-1980 when it failed to meet its payroll and had required a state financial bailout. The school system was also operating under a desegregation consent decree and had virtually eliminated all predominantly white schools, but the vast majority of minority students continued to attend completely segregated schools and were not benefiting significantly from desegregation (Hess & Warden, 1987).

The system, however, was not being very successful in educating the children enrolled in its schools. In 1985, Designs for Change and the Chicago Panel revealed that only one in five entering freshmen graduated from a Chicago high school reading at the national norms (Designs for Change, 1985; Hess & Lauber, 1985).

A CHRONOLOGY OF REFORM

The Designs for Change and the Chicago Panel research reports provided fuel to the effort in Illinois to adopt statewide school reform as the state's response to *A Nation at Risk* (National Commission, 1983). Illinois school reform legislation, enacted in 1985 (P.A. 84-126), was built upon school reform proposals from a legislative commission, the governor's office, the Illinois State Board of Education, a citizen-business alliance, and the Chicago Teachers Union. The legislation, which the Panel's analysis described as being "long on accountability, but short on programs which will significantly alter the way schooling is done in Illinois" (Nelson, Hess, & Yong, 1985), contained programmatic initiatives in only three areas: early childhood, dropout alternatives, and enhanced elementary reading programs. The bill established annual school district report cards and a teacher accountability measure along the lines of the Toledo peer review and remediation plan.

An effort was mounted to divide the Chicago school system into 20 semiautonomous school districts, similar to the New York City decentralization plan. This effort was deflected at the last moment by an amendment sponsored by the House Speaker, which established Local School Improvement Councils at each Chicago school with the power to disapprove discretionary spending at the school and conduct hearings on ensuing year budgets. If local councils objected to their budgets, the school system was supposed to alter the budget to meet those objections, to the extent possible. A separate piece of legislation, backed by Designs for Change, encouraged local schools to create school improvement plans. The first round of school budget hearings in the spring of 1986 resulted in more than 60 schools rejecting their budgets, but not a single objection was met by a changed budget proposal from the Chicago Board of Education (Lauber & Hess, 1987).

School reform in Chicago picked up steam in the fall of 1986 when Mayor Harold Washington convened an education summit to address what he called the "learn-earn connection." The summit included about 40 representatives of the business community, civic agencies, area universities and junior colleges, the teachers union, and the board of education. The summit, designed to create a set of agreements modeled on the Boston Compact (Schwartz & Hargroves, 1986; Cippolone, 1986), was focused on improving the quality of graduates from Chicago Public Schools and guaranteeing that jobs would be available for qualified graduates. A white paper provided the basis for opening discussions about the number of dropouts and the lack of jobs for youth (Hess & Sandro, 1986). Six task forces produced reports on ways to improve schools, guarantee jobs, and improve adult literacy. However, negotiations between the business community (supported by the activist educational civic groups) and the board of education broke down during the summer of 1987.

During the first year of the education summit, the Chicago Panel released a follow-up dropout study, which revealed that Chicago high school students were systematically being shortchanged in daily instructional time by the use of phantom study halls (Hess et al., 1986). The daily newspapers presented the story on their focus pages, and the television stations featured the story on the nightly news (Banas, 1986; Lenz, 1986). While the school board president agreed to investigate the findings of the report, the general superintendent condemned the report for "trashing" the public schools. Both Chicago newspapers responded with stiff editorials upbraiding the general superintendent (*Chicago Tribune,* December 17, 1986; *Chicago Sun Times*, December 27, 1986) and later suggested that his response was indicative of the problems in the school system (*Chicago Tribune,* March 5, 1987). Not long after its editorials, the *Chicago Tribune* began a year-long series of articles examining the problems in the school system (eventually edited and published as a single volume, *Chicago's Schools: Worst in America?,* 1988).

During the spring of 1987, several pieces of legislation were introduced in the General Assembly to require more change in the Chicago Public Schools. Bills to establish four pilot decentralized districts were passed in each house of the legislature, but the same bill was not passed by both. A pilot project in school autonomy for 46 of the system's 596 school units was drafted by the Chicago Panel, sponsored by the House Speaker, publicly supported by the mayor, and passed the House, but failed in the Senate, when opposed by the city and the teachers union. Despite the defeat of the individual proposals, the legislature was showing its readiness to consider radical measures to restructure the Chicago school system.

On the last scheduled day of the spring legislative session in 1987, the teachers union and a local business group, Chicago United, jointly sponsored a conference on school reform in four other urban school systems. The conference featured collaborative reform efforts within several systems experimenting with school reform. The conference featured the head of the local American Federation of Teachers affiliates and the school superintendents or board presidents from Dade County (Miami), Rochester, Cincinnati, and Hammond, Indiana. Several of these systems were experimenting with school-based management as a vehicle for school improvement.

During the summer of 1987, the first year of the Mayor's Education Summit culminated in a series of negotiations between representatives of the business community (supported by activist educational groups) and the school system. These negotiations were expected to result in a set of agreements similar to the Boston Compact. The talks foundered when the general superintendent required $83 million in additional revenue as a condition of any serious effort at reform.

In the fall of 1987, a 19-day school strike mobilized widespread demonstrations of parents and community activists, demanding both the reopening of schools and the end of "business as usual." The strike created severe political problems for the black political and civic leadership in the city. For the first time, all of the major actors were black: the mayor, the general superintendent, the school board president, and the president of the teachers union. These leaders had fought together for civil rights and social justice for more than 30 years. The mayor was reluctant to impose his will to settle the strike. Black community leaders were reluctant to take sides against any of their former colleagues. Finally, after four weeks, black community leaders met in private sessions with the board and the union and imposed a settlement. The mayor coerced both sides to agree to reinvigorate the education summit to seek long-term answers to improve the schools.

The second year of the education summit abandoned the Boston Compact approach and focused on restructuring the school system. Both the school administration and the union had lost political credibility as a result of the strike. The momentum shifted to the parents (through a mayorally appointed Parents Community Council), civic groups, and the business community. In March, the summit adopted a tentative agreement that accepted the reform goals articulated by the previous year's task forces. The agreements included a commitment to expand early childhood and other remedial programs, to establish school-based management councils at every school, and to pursue several avenues to enhance teacher professionalism. A month later, a series of amendments was adopted that would greatly strengthen the powers of the local councils, reduce the size of the bureaucracy, and reallocate funds toward schools with the heaviest concentrations of disadvantaged students. The amendments passed over the objections of the school administration and the principals' association.

Meanwhile, separate pieces of legislation had been introduced by three civic groups (a new parents' coalition, the Chicago Panel, and Designs for Change, on behalf of a larger coalition called CURE, Chicagoans United to Reform Education). In the Senate Education Committee the three bills were merged into one, which eventually passed the Senate, on a partisan division, by only one vote. In the House, the Democrats were caught in wrangling between the black caucus, representatives tied to the unions, and the supporters of school reform. Finally, the Speaker called together a group of 50 activists, most of whom had participated in the Mayor's Education Summit. Out of four days of continuous, line-by-line negotiation, the final 115-page bill was crafted. Further political wheeling and dealing prevented passage of the bill until after the June 30 deadline for immediate implementation. The bill, as sent to the governor, would be implemented starting on July 1, 1989.

The governor, soliciting input from the reform activists, the teachers union, and the board of education, used his amendatory veto to correct several technical problems in the bill, and to phase in aspects of the funding reallocation. However, he stirred legislative opposition by eliminating some minimal job protection for teachers. A compromise resulted in the passage of a slightly rewritten bill with nearly unanimous, bipartisan support on December 2, 1988. The governor signed the bill into law 10 days later. During the Spring 1989 legislative session, the implementation date was moved forward to May 15, and an income tax increase was adopted that provided enough additional funds to open school on time without a teachers' strike.

There were three major components to P.A. 85-1418. The bill contained a set of 10 school improvement goals that focus on raising student achievement, attendance, and graduation rates to national norms in five years. The bill established a cap on administrative expenses (no more, proportionately, than spent for administration in the average of all other school districts in the state) and required that funds be reallocated to schools with the heaviest concentrations of disadvantaged students. The bill mandated elected Local School Councils (LSC) at each school as the vehicle for establishing school-based management. It gave the LSCs the power 1) to adopt a school improvement plan, 2) to adopt a budget, based on a lump-sum allocation, that would implement the improvement plan, and 3) to decide whether to terminate the present principal and select a new one or to extend a new four-year performance-based contract to the incumbent.

THE MAJOR ELEMENTS OF SUCCESSFUL REFORM MOBILIZATION

There were a number of critical components of the movement for school reform in Chicago, including independent research on the public schools, state reform and its lack of implementation in Chicago, national reform efforts creating an expectation and judgment, local training and organizing efforts, the attention of the media, philanthropic support, and interaction with city and state political events.

Independent Research on the Chicago Public Schools

Mention has already been made of several research reports that had a major effect on the school reform effort. Designs for Change's *The Bottom Line* and the Chicago Panel's *Dropouts from the Chicago Public Schools* (Hess & Lauber, 1989) had defined the educational problem in Chicago in 1985. Breaking with the past tradition of denial, the then-new general superintendent acknowledged the depth of the educational deficit experienced by Chicago pupils. However, 18 months later, denial and excuse-making characterized his response to the panel's report of phantom study halls and other policies that shortchanged the educational programs of Chicago high school students (Hess et al., 1986). Assessments of the implementation of the reforms embodied in the 1985 state reform act showed that the Chicago Public Schools were unwilling to make even legislatively mandated changes (Lauber & Hess, 1987; Warden, Lauber, & Hess, 1988). Budget analyses by the Chicago Panel showed the continued growth of the bureaucracy, while resources at local schools were being cut (Hess, 1987b). An assessment of the refusal to implement earlier management reforms recommended by a businessman's group (King, 1987) was the occasion for Bennett's visit. Finally, the Chicago Panel's analysis of the illegal diversion of $42 million in state compensatory funding into support of bureaucrat's positions in the central administration (Chicago Panel, 1988b) was a critical element in the agreement to include a resource reallocation section in the reform act.

State Reform Efforts

Statewide educational reform was mandated in 1985 legislation (P.A. 84-126), which was focused more on accountability than on providing new educational opportunities for the state's students. However, the passage of the act did not end the legislature's interest in improving schools in the state, especially those in Chicago. The 1985 act did mandate Local School Improvement Councils in all Chicago schools, a step toward school-based decision-making. The failure of the Chicago Public Schools to modify any school budgets as a result of budget hearings also mandated in the 1985 legislation further irritated legislators. A 1983 legislative commission (Bakalis, 1983) had recommended breaking Chicago into semiautonomous school districts, similar to the system in use in New York City (see Chapter 4), a recommendation that was embodied in annually proposed legislation by the commission's chair, Representative Douglas Huff. In 1988, the state superintendent of schools made such a proposal the keystone of his plan for reforming the Chicago Public Schools (*Chicago Tribune,* December 11, 1987), and Senate Republicans drafted such legislation and pushed it through the Senate on a 44-9 vote, while Democratic leaders in the Senate were shaping and building support for the bill that was to become the Chicago School Reform Act.

One aspect of the 1985 state legislation as the requirement that school districts across the state prepare a report card on the achievement levels of students in each school in the state (at the third, sixth, eighth, and eleventh grades, along with ACT and SAT test results). These report cards were widely covered by the local media, including the listing of the median scores for each grade of each school in Chicago by both of the major daily newspapers. It was the October 1987 report card, showing the first percentile placement of 33 of Chicago's 64 high schools, that provided the basis for Secretary Bennett's "worst in the nation" charge (*Chicago Sun Times,* November 7, 1987). Thus, components of the 1985 reform act gave impetus to the movement for reform in 1987 and 1988.

The General Assembly was also involved in other reform proposals. In 1985, it had adopted an Urban School Improvement Act that encouraged Chicago's Local School Improvement Councils to create school improvement plans. In addition to the regular reintroduction of some version of the Huff plan to break up the district, in 1987 Speaker Madigan introduced and pushed through to passage in the House the Chicago Panel's pilot program in local school autonomy (H.B. 935, which later died in the Senate Education Committee). Thus, legislators were constantly confronted with the failings of the Chicago Public Schools and with proposals for restructuring the system.

National School Reform Efforts

Events in Chicago and Illinois were taking place in a national context in which public education was drawing more media attention than it had since the mid-1960s. I will describe the national reform efforts more fully in Chapter 4, but a brief summary may be useful here. In addition to *A Nation at Risk,* released in 1983 (National Commission), a number of other prominent groups published reports on how to improve America's schools. Academic research was focusing on the refutation of excuses for low academic achievement by low-income students generated in response to the Coleman report (Coleman, Campbell, Hobson et al., 1966). Edmonds (1979), Brookover and Lezotte (1979), and others were demonstrating that inner-city schools could be "effective schools" and were identifying the characteristics of such schools. On the more pragmatic front, national education activists such as Carl Marburger (1985), were widely advocating the school-based management approach to school improvement. Major city school districts, such as Dade County (Miami), Rochester, and Pittsburgh, were undertaking major changes to improve their schools. These various reports, research efforts, and school district experiments were routinely reported in the city's major newspapers.

Training and Organizing Efforts

Parent and community resident training has a long history in Chicago. Since the 1960s, organizers have periodically focused on the public schools. In the early and mid-1960s, the focus was on desegregation (Hess, 1984). During the later 1960s and 1970s, the focus was more on community control. However, for a decade, from the mid-1970s on, there was little school-focused organizing in Chicago. There was some citizen involvement in various desegregation plans that were created during the late 1970s (Hess, 1984), but this was limited to the relatively small group of citywide activists from the established educational advocacy groups or the system's local school and district advisory councils.

With the release of the 1985 research reports and the passage of the 1985 reform legislation calling for the creation of Local School Improvement Councils, school budget hearings, and school improvement planning, new attention was given to training parents and community residents in the opportunities that were now developing for improving their schools. Designs for Change initiated its School-Watch program, based on the effective schools research, and began organizing and training parents at a number of inner-city schools. The Chicago Panel, which had been providing budget training to parents' groups for several years, collaborated with the Chicago Region PTA to conduct 45 workshops across the city, reaching more than 3,000 members of the newly formed Local School Improvement Councils with training on their rights of involvement in school decision-making and budgeting. Community-based groups such as the Chicago Urban League and the United Neighborhood Organization (a coalition of four constituent neighborhood organizations focused on Spanish-speaking neighborhoods) began to organize around school issues and invite trainers from the citywide agencies to assist them. On the city's northwestside, predominantly Hispanic groups, such as Aspira and other members of the Network for Youth Services, were mobilizing behind the dropout concern, with torchlight parades and political lobbying, which resulted in several legislative commissions and legislation in support of dropout reduction efforts in Hispanic areas of the city (Cf., Kyle, Lane, Sween, & Triana, 1986). Local philanthropies began to examine and raise their level of funding for training, organizing, and research related to the public schools (Hess, 1987a).

Intense organizing really emerged during the 19-day teachers' strike. Several new organizations sprang up, focused for the most part on different parts of the city. On the northside, one group calling itself PURE, Parents United for Responsible Education, organized several rallies of 300 to 400 protestors, at one point encircling city hall, demanding the mayor's involvement in resolving the strike. In the inner city, the People's Coalition for Educational Reform organized "freedom schools," which served about

30,000 students during the strike and became a channel for the participation of a number of social service agencies in the school reform effort. Another group, a combination of Hyde Park liberals from the southside lakefront and magnet school parents from the northside, even drafted legislation that became one of the three reform bills eventually merged into the Senate version of the reform act. These strike-generated organizing efforts, which resulted in numerous demonstrations throughout the duration of the strike, culminated in a major meeting sponsored by Mayor Washington a week after the end of the strike. Designed for 500 invited participants, the meeting drew 1,000 persons who showed up and raucously demanded a voice in the process of radically reforming the Chicago Public Schools. The mayor responded by creating the 54-person Parents Community Council, which would become part of a renewed education summit. The existence of the PCC gave inner-city parents and community organizers a voice in the summit process, thereby broadening community involvement far beyond the traditional black and Hispanic community leadership.

However, it was an unforeseen event that dramatically changed the organizing dynamics of the reform movement. On the day before Thanksgiving 1987, Mayor Harold Washington succumbed to a massive heart attack. After a week of political jockeying, Eugene Sawyer, a black alderman supported primarily by white politicians, was elected acting mayor, splintering the black-Hispanic reform coalition put together by Washington. The PCC, rebuffing the new mayor, dedicated itself to creating school reform as a memorial to the late mayor. In doing so, it set itself in opposition to the more established black leadership, which was more accustomed to going along with the political establishment. The PCC pushed hard for reform that would empower local parents rather than protect the existing power structure. School-based management was an ideal vehicle for this parent empowerment.

One final component was organized that was to prove critical to passage of reform legislation: the business community. Businessmen had been an integral part of the first year of the Mayor's Education Summit. That first year's effort was designed to produce negotiations and an agreement between the school system and the business community, in which the business community would offer support for the public schools and jobs for their graduates in exchange for a commitment to improvement by the system. This approach foundered on the failed negotiations during the summer of 1987. In the renewed summit following the teachers' strike, business leaders took a far more aggressive and less sympathetic approach with school personnel, both administrators and union. During the critical efforts to reach a set of summit agreements, these business leaders aligned themselves with the parents' groups and the educational activists. Together, these groups realized they had the votes to impose agreements that would not be acceptable to either the union or the school administration. Under political pressure, both the board of education and the Chicago Teachers Union reluctantly became signatories to the summit agreements. The business participation was also to be critical as the scene shifted from Chicago to the state capitol in Springfield. Chief executive officers and presidents of some of Chicago's largest businesses (e.g., Amoco Corporation, Helene Curtis, First National Bank, and Harris Bank) descended upon the capitol to lobby personally for the school reform bill.

As mentioned above, the Chicago Teachers Union was a somewhat reluctant participant in the mayor's summit. Some reform groups fastened on that reluctance to show that teachers were part of the problem in the Chicago schools. But the union's reluctance was not because it did not favor moving toward school-based management. It had cosponsored, with Chicago United, the June 30, 1987, conference featuring the shared decision-making models operating in Hammond and Dade County and had advocated such an approach in their reform agenda, *Perspectives from the Classroom* (Chicago Teachers Union, 1986). However, the mayor's summit, in the second year, was structured in such a way that individual items were debated in six different task force groups, preventing viable negotiations and trade-offs. This put both the board and the CTU in the disadvantageous role of rejecting suggestion after suggestion, about which they would have been willing to negotiate, but which they could not accept without a corresponding safeguard in another area. Since the safeguard was being debated in a different task force, there were no grounds for negotiation. Some have suggested that the summit was intentionally structured this way to make the board and the union look bad. More likely, it simply reflected the weak management skills of the mayor's staff, who did not anticipate or understand this problem.

The CTU did sign on to the final summit agreements. It was an active participant in the Speaker's minisummit at the state capitol, and it did not fight eliminating tenure as the basis of teacher selection at the school site or reducing the remediation time for unsatisfactory teachers from 180 days to 45. Subsequently, the union incorporated into its contract with the interim board of education all of the major provisions of the legislation involving working conditions, removing any threat of legal action from that quarter. While it is safe to say that the CTU would have preferred a professionalized shared decision-making approach to school-based management, it is unfair to imply that the CTU was opposed to school reform in Chicago.

Media Involvement

Critical to the organization of a school reform movement and to the eventual passage of the Chicago School Reform Act was the involvement of the media. Several dimensions of the media role have already been discussed. It was the media that turned the research of two independent nonprofit agencies into citywide awareness of the shortcomings of the Chicago Public Schools. On the afternoon of the release of the Chicago Panel's 1985 study, the *Chicago Sun Times* (April 24, 1985) carried the story in a three-inch, front page banner headline, "SCHOOL DROPOUT RATE NEARLY 50%!" But the media did more than just cover the reports of others.

In 1987, following the editorial rebukes to the general superintendent for his accusation that *"Where's Room 185?"* (Hess et al., 1986) was "trashing" the public schools, the *Chicago Tribune* assigned a team of reporters to begin an in-depth series on the problems of the Chicago Public Schools, including months of daily, in-school observations. The series, eventually reprinted as *Chicago's Schools: Worst in America?* (Chicago Tribune, 1988), focused attention two or three days a week for almost a year on the problems in the school system.

The media were also aggressive in covering opportunities for school improvement. Following the June 30, 1987, Chicago United-CTU conference, teams from both major newspapers and several television stations provided coverage of other large cities that were trying radically to reform their school systems, including Boston, Rochester, Pittsburgh, Dade County, and the nearby city of Hammond, Indiana. This coverage of reform efforts in other major urban areas lent an air of respectability to the reform proposals coming from the activist educational agencies in the city, which were providing the basic grist for the reform deliberations of the Mayor's Education Summit and for the drafting of reform legislation for consideration by the General Assembly. The reformers' ideas were still seen as "radical," but they were no longer considered "extreme." After the 19-day strike, most citizens and most legislators were ready for a "radical" solution.

The media played another role in connecting the school reform effort to the changing political scene in the city. Mayor Washington's death ended his predictions that he would be mayor for 20 years. It also splintered the fragile coalition he had built as the base of his power. The daily media devoted extensive coverage to the subsequent interplay of race-based political maneuvering in the months following Washington's death. This was also the critical period for formation of the school reform plan. The two became inextricably intertwined, with Acting Mayor Sawyer's reluctance to support school reform providing ammunition to its supporters, both among the reform elements of Washington's coalition and among the traditional white political leadership. In all likelihood, Washington's death and subsequent memorialization by the school reform efforts of the Parents Community Council produced a far more radical school reform plan than he would have been willing to allow to emerge, had he lived. Interestingly, the plan that ultimately emerged from the General Assembly was a more radical plan than the PCC was willing to support.

Philanthropic Support for School Restructuring

Critical to any movement is acquiring the funding to support the research and organizing effort. Chicago is fortunate to be the home of a number of innovative and farsighted foundations and corporations willing to support advocacy research and organizing. In the forefront are several larger foundations, some with a regional or national perspective, some more locally oriented, and a group of smaller foundations and corporate giving programs more focused on Chicago and its neighborhoods. These foundations had a history of funding many different downtown advocacy groups. One group of foundations, led by Wieboldt, Woods Charitable Fund, Joyce, and MacArthur, provided ongoing support for community groups across the city. These funders provided the support critical to the school reform movement, but they also played an important role in providing Chicagoans with access to educational leaders from across the nation.

In 1986, only a year after the release of the Designs for Change and Chicago Panel research reports, a group of about 18 representatives of foundations and corporations with giving programs in education came together to create an education task force under the Donors Forum of Chicago. The group emerged from discussions that had started in 1984 as an effort of funders to inform themselves about local education issues. The task force decided to survey the Donors Forum membership to analyze the support provided to education in Chicago. The committee asked me to design and analyze a survey of Donors Forum members. The survey (Hess, 1987a) showed that about 20 Chicago foundations and corporations contributed $7.5 million, 4.6% of their total giving, to precollegiate education in Chicago, which was about at the national average for all philanthropies. Most of the giving was focused on supporting direct service projects such as after-school programs, tutoring, and extracurricular activities like the city's science fair. A small portion went to advocacy groups and parent organizers.

Task force members, concerned about a more effective way to improve public education in Chicago, decided, on the basis of the survey results, to begin to work together on educational improvement efforts and to encourage their boards to support efforts to affect the basic structure of the school system. Representatives from the regional and national foundations, like Bill McKersie (Joyce Foundation), Nelvia Brady (Chicago Community Trust, previously director of equal educational opportunity programs at the Chicago Board of Education and shortly to become chancellor of the City Colleges of Chicago), Linda Fitzgerald (Spencer Foundation), John Laubenstein (Amoco Foundation), Ken Rolling (Woods Charitable Fund), and Peter Gerber (MacArthur Foundation), and some of the smaller foundation staff who had backgrounds in education like Anne Hallett (Wieboldt Foundation), Ben Rothblatt (Fry Foundation), Nick Goodban (Tribune Charities), and Ted Oppenheimer (Oppenheimer Family Foundation) were well aware of the national education reform efforts, and particularly of the focus on school restructuring. Although not widely circulated in Chicago, the MacArthur Foundation published one of the summaries of education reform efforts in the first half of the 1980s (Chance, 1986).

Together, these foundations significantly increased their funding in support of advocacy efforts to improve the Chicago Public Schools. They were joined by other foundations like the Prince Charitable Trusts and the Field Foundation of Illinois. Some corporations, like Borg-Warner and the Field Corporation, also increased their educational funding. Bill McKersie estimates that education funding in Chicago in 1989 exceeded $12 million, with much of the increase targeted toward the major research and advocacy agencies, the organizing effort, and support for systemic institutional change.

These foundations also committed significant staff time and expertise to the reform effort. The president of the MacArthur Foundation, John Corbally, formerly dean of the College of Education and chancellor of the University of Illinois, Urbana, was one of the cochairs of the Mayor's Education Summit. He also later chaired the Mayor's School Reform Authority, which, prior to implementation of the School Reform Act, acted as a monitor of the board of education's compliance with the summit agreements. A number of foundation staff people, like McKersie, Rolling, and Hallett, worked diligently in less visible ways on the various summit task forces.

The city's foundations provided the support to the organizing and advocacy efforts of the citywide nonprofit agencies involved in the reform movement. But they also played an active role in supporting innovative efforts at the school level. The Chicago Community Trust had traditionally provided significant support to large-scale projects at the board of education. It continued that policy during the reform effort. Several foundations contributed to the support of the Mayor's Education Summit. Martin Koldyke and several of his colleagues launched the Foundation for Excellence in Teaching, which began its Golden Apple Awards program to feature and support 10 of the best teachers in the area each year. The foundation's programs have broadened into an Academy of Scholars made up of former winners and a scholarship program for future teachers entering college. The Joyce Foundation launched its Educational Ventures Fund to supplement its larger educational support by providing minigrants to individual schools planning for school improvement. A number of corporations also provided support to the reform effort as their chief executives began to be involved in the reform movement. Richard Dennis, a singularly successful commodities broker who had been active in supporting the 1985 statewide reform effort, provided significant support to Designs for Change and the CURE coalition as they put together the draft of the bill that would form the core of the reform act.

After passage of the act, the philanthropic community became even more active, both with support and with staff involvement. Several funders, rallied by Anne Hallett of the Wieboldt Foundation, provided support for a retreat for the reform activists in December 1988. These funders stayed active in the citywide coalition, attending meetings, urging the reform groups to broaden their membership and include groups that had not been active in winning enactment of the legislation. They emphasized the need to continue the common effort as reform was being implemented. Particularly active were staff from Joyce, MacArthur, the Community Trust, Woods Charitable Fund, Field, Wieboldt, Amoco, and the Harris Bank. After a second retreat a year later, the citywide coalition formally organized representation on its steering committee of two representatives of the philanthropic community.

Foundations expanded their grants to individual schools and their staff. In addition to the Joyce Foundation Educational Ventures Fund, the Whitman Corporation began a Principal's Awards program that gave 20 winning Chicago principals each $5,000 grants for use in their schools. In 1990, Illinois Bell launched its Local School Council Awards program to provide grants to LSCs with innovative school improvement plans. The Beatrice Foundation began adding cash grants to a long-standing principals' award made by Citizens Schools Committee.

But the foundations and corporations also provided direct support to implementation efforts. In Chapter 8 I will discuss the corporation funding of Leadership for Quality Education's community organizers, focused on getting out a sizable vote for the LSC elections. Foundations also supported this program. The Chicago Community Trust contributed $250,000. In addition, staff from funders experienced in supporting community groups (Wieboldt, Woods, Joyce), although not contributing funds, served on LQE's grant-making committee.

LQE also provided direct support for activities like a principal's convention during the summer of 1989, prior to the first year of reform implementation. It funded the search for new top administrators at the board of education. The MacArthur Foundation provided funding for the interim board's summer transition task forces in 1989. The Joyce Foundation provided support for the

School Board Nominating Commission as it prepared slates of nominees for the mayor's choices in appointing the permanent board of education. In an innovative effort with possible long-term funding implications, 20 funders created a joint funding effort known as the Fund for Educational Reform, which makes small grants to schools and local organizations.

In addition, the philanthropic community has worked to expose Chicagoans to national experts and other models of reform. Early in 1987, several foundations cooperated to bring representatives from the Boston Compact, Pittsburgh's Schenley Teacher Training Center, and the Baltimore Commonwealth to meet with summit participants, the foundation community, and community organizers from across the city. In 1988, representatives from Dade County and St. Louis, two systems experimenting with school-based management, together with reform scholars from the Center for Policy Research in Education (CPRE) again met with Chicago reform advocates. In November 1989, the Joyce and MacArthur foundations sponsored a conference with a number of out-of-town experts discussing issues related to gauging the success of the Chicago School Reform Act. The Joyce Foundation also contracted with the Educational Excellence Network, now directed by former Assistant Secretary of the Department of Education Chester E. Finn, to bring a series of national experts into Chicago to assess different aspects of the reform effort and report back to reform leaders about their findings and their concerns.

In order to keep the nation apprised of the reform effort in Chicago, MacArthur, Joyce, and the Community Trust initiated and provided support to launch *Catalyst,* a journal sent free to 15,000 persons nationwide.

The list of supportive activities by the city's philanthropies is quite extensive, and this account only hits some of the high spots. Many other contributions could be added to this list, but I have tried to provide the reader with a sense of the major role in the reform efforts played by the philanthropic community, both in providing financial support and in active staff leadership.

Leadership Dynamics

During the spring of 1988, the focus of school reform efforts shifted from Chicago to the state capitol. Shortly after the mayor's summit agreements were forged, it became obvious that Mayor

Sawyer was not going to be an active advocate for school reform legislation. (Washington had also resisted a legislative solution to the school crisis, as noted in the city's opposition to H.B. 935, the pilot school autonomy bill in the 1987 session of the General Assembly.) However, three reform bills had already been filed by educational activist organizations represented in the summit. These bills were wending their way through the legislative process as the summit agreements were originally forged and then strengthened in its March and April meetings.

Although the reform groups had originally intended that legislation should be a bipartisan effort, Democrats in both houses of the legislature took control of the legislation and denied the Republicans any significant participation. This partisan approach meant individual pressure groups within the Senate and House Democratic delegations could have inordinate influence on aspects of the developing bill. The merged legislative proposal, S.B. 1839, finally passed the Senate on the last possible day with only one vote to spare. In the House, similar legislation was defeated. When the House took up the Senate's bill, wrangling within the Democratic caucus—between the black caucus, union-oriented legislators, and the Speaker's reform-oriented forces—threatened to prevent passage of any bill. The Speaker convened a minisummit in his office in late June to iron out a bill he could push through the House. This bill passed with only Democratic votes, but could not muster enough senators for passage before the June 30 deadline for immediate implementation. It finally passed on July 2, 1988, with a July 1, 1989, implementation date. The narrow partisan support for the bill, however, gave the governor immense leverage in redesigning aspects of the bill through his amendatory veto, which he announced in September. Following the Fall 1988 statewide elections, a bipartisan agreement on a new bill was forged during the legislature's fall "veto" session. This new bill was passed on December 2 and signed into law by the governor on December 12, 1988.

CONCLUSION

The Chicago School Reform Act has put in place an historic experiment in decentralizing authority in a major urban school system. The act was designed to create the conditions for the development of "effective schools" in every part of the city. During the first year of implementation, the basic elements of the reform plan have been successfully put in place. Local School Councils have been established at every school. In half the schools, a principal selection process has been undertaken with a turnover of at least one third of the affected principals. School improvement plans have been designed and lump-sum budgets fashioned.

The next chapter reviews the national interest in school improvement, the effective schools literature, and the various efforts at school improvement that are being implemented or proposed across the nation. In Chapter 5, the specific provisions of the reform act are examined.

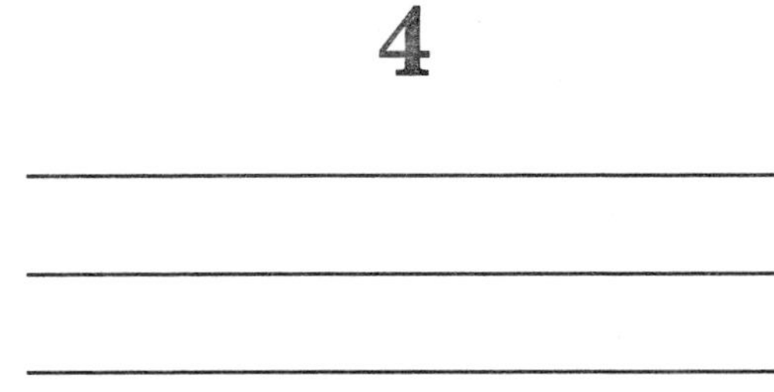

Basis for Restructuring Schools

The Chicago school reform movement, while focused on the Chicago Public Schools, took place within a national movement to improve our public schools. The leaders of the reform movement in Chicago were highly conscious of this national effort and of the school improvement literature that was being generated. In small ways, the Chicago leaders were contributing to that national literature (cf. Moore & Hyde, 1981; National Coalition of Advocates for Children, 1985; Hess, 1986; Hess, Wells, Prindle, Kaplan, & Liffman, 1987).

The ideas that were shaping the reform discussions in the Mayor's Education Summit and in the press were ideas that were present in the national debates about school improvement. The Chicago School Reform Act was based upon ideas and practices that were being discussed widely, particularly in the literature about effective schools and in the literature about restructuring schools. The reform act was also designed to avoid some of the problems encountered in the New York and Detroit experiments with decentralization to the subdistrict level. This chapter seeks to provide some perspective on the roots of various measures in the Chicago School Reform Act, which is described more fully in the following chapter.

THE GROWTH OF THE EDUCATIONAL BUREAUCRACY

In their pugnacious critique of the structure of American public education, John Chubb and Terry Moe (1990) point out that the current structure of public schooling is rooted in the "progressive" reforms of the early part of this century. Those reforms created, for the first time, a true system of public education. Prior to that time, they contend, schools were simple, local, tied to family and community, and focused on teaching. But with the advent of the progressive era, all that changed.

> Reformers and educational leaders, dedicated to the goal of effective education and possessed of the best scientific knowledge about how to achieve it, succeeded in building a rational system of schools for the nation as a whole, triumphing over the parochialism, fragmentation, and party machines of an unenlightened past. The system they created was bureaucratic and professional, designed to ensure, so the story goes, that education would be taken out of politics and placed in the hands of impartial experts devoted to the public interest. (Chubb & Moe, 1990, p. 4)

Thus emerged what one scholar has ironically labeled "the one best system" (Tyack, 1974).

During the first half of this century, this system grew and centralized and became more pervasive. Isolated schools were forced into districts. Districts were forced to consolidate. State funding mechanisms were established to assume part of the costs of education, and to offset some of the largest inequities in school-level funding. With state funding came statewide regulation controlling personnel certification, minimal curricular offerings, building safety, and a host of other issues. The number of school districts decreased from more than 40,000 to fewer than 16,000 nationwide today. And school districts, particularly urban school districts, became more bureaucratic.

As we have seen, the Chicago Public Schools fit this pattern exactly. It is hard to imagine, observing the school system in Chicago today, that a century ago there were 51 school systems in what is now the city. Mary Herrick (1984) has nicely traced the history of the Chicago Public Schools and emphasized the rational management argument in her focus on the qualities of superintendents and the central role of the chief administrative officer. Paul Peterson (1976) takes a different approach, emphasizing the negotiations among various power factions in control of the school system, an approach much more akin to Chubb and Moe's description of the democratic governance of the public schools. But in both cases, the picture that emerges is that of a large urban, bureaucratic system. It is that system I have tried to describe in the foregoing chapters.

DO SCHOOLS MAKE A DIFFERENCE?

During the first two thirds of the twentieth century, educational research was focused primarily upon individual schools and classrooms and the performance of individual students. As Chubb and Moe point out, the presumption was that "schools made a difference." James S. Coleman and his colleagues (1966) made a direct challenge to that assumption with the release of the Report of the Commission on Equal Educational Opportunity, *Equality of Educational Opportunity.* The Coleman report, as it came to be known, was based on a massive study of schools across the United States. Its central finding was that only the social and economic status of the family of a student and of the other students who attended the same school was significantly related to the achievement levels of students. From their data, Coleman and his colleagues argued that school-level factors, at least those that were easily quantifiable, were not important to student achievement. Schools with more money did not do appreciably better than schools with less money. Students did not necessarily learn more in well-equipped schools than in ill-equipped schools if students' background characteristics were taken into account. Coleman's research was substantially supported by Christopher Jencks and his colleagues (1972) and by other subsequent research.

There were at least two practical effects that followed the issuance of the Coleman report and of other independent research of that period. Adopting many of the recommendations of a research conference on educational and cultural deprivation organized by Benjamin Bloom and others (Bloom, Davis, & Hess, 1965), as a part of President Lyndon Johnson's War on Poverty the federal government enacted legislation to provide compensatory educational and nutritional opportunities to deprived youngsters. The largest of these school programs became known as Title I and became quite significant for large urban school systems. The Coleman report provided added justification for maintaining this compensatory effort for students whose disadvantage seemed to be the most important factor in their lower levels of school achievement. During the 1989-1990 school year, the Chicago Public Schools received $113 million (5% of its total revenues) in federal Chapter I aid, as the program was renamed under the Reagan administration. Chapter I aid is based upon the assumption that students from disadvantaged backgrounds need extra assistance, and the federal government has a role in providing that assistance.

A second effect of the Coleman report was unintended but far more insidious. By challenging the notion that schools make a difference, the report provided an easy excuse for the low performance of school systems that enrolled large numbers of disadvantaged students. Confronted in graduate school educational administration courses by the Coleman report, and bolstered by their own disappointing experiences in inner-city schools, a whole generation of school administrators grew up believing there was little school people could do for inner-city urban schools. Superintendent Byrd frequently drew on this excuse in responding to criticism of the performance of the Chicago Public Schools. Principals and teachers throughout the system, following the superintendent's example, expressed similar convictions.

But the claim that schools do not make a difference did not square well with the first-hand experience of many educational researchers. While not necessarily disputing the associations revealed in Coleman's large-scale data base, they did not accept the assumption that the relationships were causal. A group of scholars set out to demonstrate that there were differences between schools and that these differences did have an impact on student achievement (Purkey & Smith, 1983). More particularly, some of those scholars (Edmonds, 1979; Mortimore & Sammons, 1987) were concerned to show that there were inner-city schools that were particularly effective with students from low socioeconomic backgrounds. From their observations, they were convinced that low expectations for low-income kids reduced the chances of success for these kids, while schools with high expectations were much more effective (Edmonds, 1979). Eschewing large-scale, sociological approaches, these scholars focused on comparisons between a limited number of schools that could be studied in depth, using both quantitative and qualitative measures. In this way, they felt, they could more accurately address the question of causality. Cumulatively, this body of research came to be known as the "effective schools" literature.

Purkey and Smith point out that the effective schools studies arose at a time when research was showing that the elements of schools that could be changed by adding more money (class size, salaries, buildings, add-on programs) had little relationship to achievement.

> In contrast, the new literature on the determinants of achievement is concerned with variables relating to (1) how schools and school districts are structured and make decisions; (2) the process of change in schools and school districts; and (3) how classrooms and schools can be changed to increase the time spent on productive instruction. Although these variables are less susceptible to mechanical changes in policy, they are alterable (Bloom, 1981), generally with difficulty, but often for little money. (Purkey & Smith, 1983, p. 428)

Purkey and Smith go on to review four categories of research on effective schools: 1) outlier studies, which examine the differences between the best and worst schools (cf. Lezotte, Edmonds, & Ratner, 1974; Edmonds & Frederiksen, 1979; Brookover & Schneider, 1975); 2) case studies of an individual school or a small number of schools (cf. Brookover & Lezotte, 1979; Rutter, Maughan, Mortimore, Ouston, & Smith, 1979); 3) program evaluation studies examining successful and unsuccessful innovations (cf. Armor et al., 1976; Trisman, Waller, & Wilder, 1976); and 4) other studies such as Coleman, Hoffer, and Kilgore's study (1982) of private versus public schools. Purkey and Smith note that these research studies do not necessarily refute the earlier statistical findings of Coleman and Jencks and their colleagues. They do, however, including Coleman's 1982 study, attack the assumption that "schools don't make a difference."

Purkey and Smith refer to two other organizational perspectives that are important to note. They use Barr and Dreeben's (1981) conception of schools as systems of "nested layers" in which the context for each level of activity is set by the next larger dimension of the system. So, schools are the context for classrooms, districts are the context for schools, etc. In approaching the dynamics of change, they note the organizational research that describes schools as "loosely coupled systems" that do not respond very well, at the lower levels, to mandates from above (March & Olsen, 1976; Weick, 1976).

Purkey and Smith summarize the characteristics of effective schools identified in the literature they reviewed into two categories: organizational and structural characteristics and process characteristics. They suggest that process characteristics should be conceived of as nested within the context of the structural characteristics and only able to grow and develop within changed structural characteristics; that is, they cannot be mandated from above in loosely coupled systems, but must be developed from the bottom up. Their list of characteristics includes:

Organization-structure variables

1. School-site management; autonomy in addressing local problems.
2. Instructional leadership from the principal.
3. Staff stability.
4. Curriculum articulation and organization to cover achievement goals.
5. Schoolwide staff development related to the instructional program.
6. Parental involvement and support as a positive influence on students.
7. Schoolwide recognition of academic success.
8. Maximized learning time.
9. District support for fundamental change at the building level.

Process variables (defining school culture and climate)

1. Collaborative planning and collegial relationships.
2. Sense of community.
3. Clear goals and high expectations commonly shared.
4. Order and discipline.

The authors note that the effective schools literature was singularly lacking in direction on how to implement change in schools so that these characteristics might be present. They note that a wide diversity of studies has resulted in a surprising coherence in describing effective versus ineffective schools, but that there is little evidence in that literature about implementation. Purkey and Smith provide their own strategy for creating effective schools, focused upon the notion of school culture.

Starting from an assumption about the loosely coupled nature of schools, they reject the notion that school effectiveness can be mandated by fiat from the top, whether at the district or at the school level. Instead, they assume that the key is in building staff consensus about the goals and mechanisms of improvement. Citing the literature on innovation (McLaughlin, 1978; Elmore, 1978, 1979), they stress the necessity of teacher "ownership" of any improvement efforts, and therefore recommend a general strategy built upon "collaborative planning, collegial work, and a school atmosphere conducive to experimentation and evaluation" (Purkey & Smith, 1983, p. 442). Given this approach, they suggest first putting in place the structural characteristics and then allowing the process variables related to school culture to grow and develop. Somewhat optimistically, they note that such an approach demands "an organic conception of schools and some faith in people's ability to work together toward common ends" (Purkey & Smith, 1983, p. 445). Unfortunately, their strategy, like that of the effective schools researchers upon whom they are building, also stops short of answering some critical "how to" questions, such as, "How does a school get a principal who will exercise instructional leadership?" or "How does a school secure district support for fundamental change if the current district leadership is unalterably opposed to granting schools autonomy?" In part, the Chicago School Reform Act seeks to provide answers to those, and other, implementation questions. Its critics suggest it is still based on the naive optimism Purkey and Smith express about the organic nature of schools and the ability of people. I shall return to this theme later.

DECENTRALIZATION IN NEW YORK AND DETROIT

During the 1960s a movement for community control and community empowerment swept across the country, fueled by concerns over desegregation and the war on poverty. Daniel Patrick Moynihan (1969) has nicely retold the debates within the federal government as the legislative basis for "maximum feasible participation" was forged. He also showed how it was inevitable that community control would not survive in federal programs. But the movement did have some specific import for urban school systems.

First in New York City and then in Detroit, there was pressure to decentralize the school system to bring the locus of control closer to the community. In New York City, the movement grew out of the unrest surrounding desegregation. In language similar to that which could be used about Chicago, David Rogers described the situation in the 1960s in his study named for the school board's central offices at *110 Livingston Street*:

> In New York City public schools, one out of three pupils is a year or more retarded in arithmetic, and the gap between a pupil's achievement and national standards widens as he remains in school. In the past ten years reading scores have gone down, dropout rates have gone up, community protest has increased, and the middle class has been steadily withdrawing its children from the public schools. . . . Teacher strikes, deteriorating community relations, and increasing criticism from business of student unpreparedness are further indications of the schools' failure. In 1967, Superintendent Donovan made a public statement of hope that soon all high school graduates would be reading at or above eighth grade level. Many businessmen in the city were reportedly shocked at such a statement; they are angry at the school system's failure to produce an employable black and Puerto Rican population. (Rogers, 1968, p. 6)

Parents in the Ocean Hill-Brownsville section demanded that a new intermediate school (I.S. 201) either be integrated, as the board had planned originally, or that local parents and community residents be granted greater control over hiring the staff and running the school. At the same time, the state legislature requested that the New York City board prepare a plan for decentralization by December 1967. Rogers then recounts the complaints parents and community citizens had about the inaccessibility of officials of the board of education:

> Parents and other interested citizens, with few if any channels of access to the Board of Education, face a large, amorphous, distant bureaucracy that seldom responds to citizen demands. Many parents with legitimate complaints have no place to take them. Their local school boards are powerless. The principal and the district superintendent often pass the buck to headquarters. And headquarters officials, in turn, often pass it on to other headquarters colleagues, to state officials, or back down to

> the field. PAs and PTAs are sometimes of help, but there are many ghetto and white parents whom they don't reach.
>
> In short . . . many parents feel they are dealing with a faceless bureaucracy which is not accountable to the public. (Rogers, 1968, p. 86)

New York City eventually created 32 elementary school districts governed by community school boards elected in local elections. As the Chicago school reform movement was developing, those districts had been functioning for nearly two decades. Opinions about their success were clearly mixed. In 1983, David Rogers, with a colleague, Norman Chung (1983), produced a follow-up study of the New York City school system called *110 Livingston Street Revisited.* While noting the divergent views about the value of decentralization, Rogers noted that the reading test scores of New York students were higher at every grade in 1981 than they had been in 1971, ranging from +0.1 to +1.5.

Rogers concluded, "There was improvement in all 9 grades. Thus, the critics who predicted harmful consequences, at least on this particular measure of effectiveness, were wrong, and the proponents appear to be right" (Rogers & Chung, 1983, p. 196).

But other problems in New York were evident. The daily media were filled with stories of corruption on several community school boards. The record of union domination of many of the school boards was well known. These were problems to which the critics of the school reform movement in Chicago constantly referred, and they were problems the reform activists did not want to emerge in the Second City. The Chicago School Reform Act, by minimizing employee participation on councils elected at each school instead of at the subdistrict level, was designed to take advantage of the benefits of decentralization as experienced in New York, while avoiding the corruption and union control present in that city. Following the enactment of the Chicago School Reform Act, the New York legislature made employees of the New York City School system ineligible for membership on the community boards of education.

Also in response to desegregation pressures, but significantly impacted by white resistance to desegregation, Detroit initiated a decentralization plan of its own, which divided the city into eight regions. In the initial elections, in 1970, whites dominated the regional boards, winning majorities in six of the eight regions and control of the citywide board. Four years later, blacks gained control, winning 26 of the 40 regional seats. In many cases, these blacks had been active on local school advisory councils and had become well known in the community areas (Glass & Sanders, 1978).

The racial disharmony at the center of the establishment of decentralization in Detroit was also at the heart of its failure. Jeffrey Mirel (1990) cites a divisive 43-day school strike in 1973, at least in part focused on the ability of community school boards to appoint teachers, and thereby introduce faculty racial quotas, as poisoning the atmosphere between the community and the teacher force, thus undermining any significant improvement in school achievement. Mirel spells out the doom of the Detroit decentralization effort quite succinctly, "By 1976, virtually every major interest group in the city declared that decentralization was a failure so far as improving the quality of education in Detroit. In 1981, the city voted by a four-to-one margin to recentralize the system" (Mirel, 1990, p. 45). Reformers in Chicago did not see the Detroit case, involving regional decentralization rather than school-based management, as at all comparable to their effort, and have largely denied it has any significance for Chicago.

1980s SCHOOL REFORM: ACCOUNTABILITY, THE FIRST WAVE

In 1983 the National Commission on Excellence in Education released its report, *A Nation At Risk: The Imperative for Educational Reform.* In somewhat overblown rhetoric, the report announced that the nation's public schools were being inundated by a "rising tide of mediocrity" and that, had an outside power done to our educational system what we have allowed to happen, it would have been considered an act of war. However, the report did have its desired effect; it focused the attention of the nation on the problem of an inadequately performing public education system. More than a dozen other major reports criticizing America's public schools were issued during the early 1980s.

Some states, such as Arkansas and California, had already undertaken a number of school reform efforts, but many more responded to this national attention during legislative sessions in

1983, 1984, and 1985 (an early summary of state actions was distributed by the United States Department of Education in 1984, titled *The Nation Responds*; see also Doyle & Hartle, 1985; Chance, 1986). Illinois enacted statewide reform measures in 1985, which were similar to those enacted in a number of other states, though they were funded at a significantly lower level (Nelson, Yong, & Hess, 1985).

The key word in these early school reform efforts was "accountability." The central theme of these reforms was higher requirements to assure excellence: higher certification standards for teachers, higher graduation standards for students, and higher visibility for school performance levels in school districts. In a number of states, higher teacher salaries went along with those higher standards.

School report cards were constructed in a number of states to inform the public of how schools and school districts were doing. Illinois was one of those states. The 1985 state reform act required every school district in the state to begin distributing to every parent of an enrolled student a report card on that student's school, which compared the school's performance with that of the entire school district and of the entire state. The state set out to develop its own standardized test, which it would administer to all third, sixth, eighth, and eleventh graders in the state. Such a common test would allow valid comparisons from one school to the next across the state. Tests would be developed in reading, math, and language arts, and would be phased in over a 10-year period. In the meantime, quartile rankings on standardized tests already utilized by school districts would be reported for the required grades. Educators protested that such comparisons would be unfair and inappropriate, since school districts across the state used seven or eight different tests, none of which was properly equated to the others. Still, the state pushed forward and, in October 1986, released the first set of report cards, which showed what percentage of a school's third (and sixth, eighth, and tenth/eleventh) graders scored in the lowest quarter of all students taking whatever test they took and what percent were in the highest quarter. A school approximating the national norms for the test given would have 25% of its students in the lowest quarter and 25% in the highest. Schools with more than 25% in the highest quarter and fewer than 25% in the lowest quarter looked good. Those with more in the lowest quarter and fewer in the highest looked bad. In addition, the report card carried information on attendance rates, graduation rates, college entrance test scores (for high schools), and a series of descriptive characteristics about the schools' students (race, mobility rate, percent low income).

Illinois also raised its requirements for teacher and administrator certification, adding a testing requirement prior to certification for new applicants. In addition, universities with approved teacher education programs were required to begin testing teacher candidates to assure that they were proficient in reading, mathematics, and language arts. Those holding administrative certificates were to be retested and recertified every five years. Teacher evaluation standards were also changed to make it easier to dismiss low-performing teachers, but only after a year's remediation period. To support educators under these new requirements, the legislation increased staff development efforts for both teachers and administrators and provided scholarship assistance for minorities and teachers willing to retrain in subjects experiencing teacher shortages. The bill contained only a few provisions to improve educational programs in reading, preschool education, and dropout prevention. As noted previously, the Chicago Panel's assessment of the legislation at the time was that it "was long on accountability, but short on programs which will significantly alter the way schooling is done in Illinois" (Nelson, Yong, & Hess, 1985).

Accountability measures in other states were frequently similar to those enacted in Illinois. Some states went further and required all existing teachers to be tested for basic skills competency. In Arkansas, nearly 10% of the teachers tested failed the test the first time they took it. Half of those who failed passed the test on their second try. But such testing immediately raised the question of what the test was capable of showing and whether it was biased in its construction. Such tests give little information about the effectiveness of teachers in a classroom with children, but they satisfied politicians who now felt they could assure at least minimal competence in the classroom.

Some states incorporated report card scores into a set of state incentives for improvement and sanctions for diminished results. Perhaps attracting most attention is the South Carolina system, which categorizes school districts into five relatively similar "bands" on the basis of socioeconomic and educational factors and then rewards the districts with the greatest improvement in each band in each year. The state system acknowledges the different educational tasks faced by districts with different types of students enrolled, but rewards those who seek to make a difference in what they do with the students they have. Few states have enacted similar incentive systems.

At the other extreme, a few states have enacted "educational bankruptcy" provisions. New Jersey was the first state to use such a provision to judge the performance of one of its school districts as so inadequate that control of the district should revert to the state. In 1988, the state declared that the Jersey City school system was educationally bankrupt and took over the system (Jennings, 1988a, 1988b). The power of the board of education to manage the system was stripped away. The top administrative leadership of the system was removed and the state installed four top administrators of its own choosing. The new administrators were vested with nearly dictatorial powers to run the system and make improvements on behalf of the state. It is still too early to see any significant improvements from this radical action. Still, the idea of protection against the complete failure of a school board to improve its schools was appealing to Chicago reformers considering school-based management but worried about an adequate response to schools that do worse under local autonomy. The Chicago School Reform Act includes its own educational bankruptcy provision.

THE SECOND WAVE: RESTRUCTURING SCHOOLS

It was soon evident to educators that, while higher accountability might make the public more aware of how schools were doing, alone it would not fix the problems inherent in American education. Raising graduation requirements would not ensure that more students graduated with higher capabilities. In fact, several scholars argued the result was likely to be just the opposite, that fewer students would graduate, and that the disadvantaged students would suffer this fate more often than more affluent students (Bastian, Fruchter, Gittell, Greer, & Haskins, 1985). Attention had to be given to the means of improving the nation's public schools.

Richard Elmore (1988) has suggested that there are three competing models for how our nation's schools might be improved: 1) the technical transfer model, 2) the professionalization model, and

3) the client empowerment model. Under the technical transfer model, academics claim to have a body of knowledge about teaching and learning that would meet the need for improvement, if only they could get professionals adequately to implement what is already known. To the extent that public schools do not practice what is already known, it is because school bureaucracies or individual teachers are rejecting better ways of doing schooling. Under this model, the issue is how better to transfer the knowledge now in the possession of academics. It might be said that the ultimate test of this model is now occurring in Chelsea, Massachusetts, where Boston University is operating the school system under a 10-year management contract from the Chelsea School Committee.

The professionalization model emphasizes the expert knowledge of the teachers in the classroom, who know from first-hand experience what needs to be done to improve their schools. Academic expertise is seen to be complex and not always rooted in the realities of day-to-day classroom experience. Under this model, the reason that schools do not perform well is that they do not have the level of organization needed to sustain professional involvement. The locus of authority should be in the classroom, where teachers are in contact with children. If the bureaucrats would stay out of the way, the teachers would get the job done.

Under the client-driven model, schools are seen to be too professionally oriented, protecting the interests of the educators at the expense of the students. Technical knowledge is seen to be too distant from the real-life situations of enrolled pupils. School structures need to be ventilated through community governance or client choice of where to enroll. Ventilating the system is necessary in order to prevent professionals from coopting parents. Under this model, authority should be vested in the consumer of education or in a corporate representative of the consumers in a community.

Crosscutting these approaches to deriving strategies to improve schools is the effort to restructure schools and school systems. There are really three quite separate approaches that have been grouped together under the general category of "restructuring." The first is the effort to enhance teacher professionalization. The second and third are two different aspects of Elmore's client-driven model: enrollment choice and parent-dominated school-based management. Some scholars may prefer to link teacher empowerment and parent empowerment under the school-based management rubric, arguing that the shared decision-making aspect of professionalization is similar to school-based management under parent control, but it seems that this unduly narrows the scope of efforts to improve teaching and dilutes the importance of lay control.

Enhancing Teacher Professionalization

There are a number of different efforts that loosely hang together under the category of improving the quality of teaching in local schools. Two major reports have been issued in this arena. The first, *Tomorrow's Teachers,* issued by the Holmes Group (1986), focuses upon rethinking the preparation for teaching offered by schools of education. The Holmes Group is composed of leaders of major universities who have committed themselves to revamping their teacher education programs. This is restructuring of a part of the education system that is not always adequately considered in the school reform debates, but which could have long-range implications for one of the major "input" variables in the education equation. It can also be understood as an element in the technical transfer strategy of school improvement.

The second report, *A Nation Prepared: Teachers for the 21st Century* was produced by the Carnegie Forum's (1986) Task Force on Teaching as a Profession. To the concern about teacher preparation, this report adds efforts to empower teachers, advocating for greater teacher control over the teaching process and a share in school-level decision-making. It proposes a new category of lead teachers as the focus for more collegial responsibility by teachers for the entire school and its programs. It calls for significantly higher salaries and more paraprofessional support staff to enhance the professionalism of teaching. The report also calls for a national certification process to recognize outstanding teachers, similar to national certification in various medical specialties. With support from the federal government, a coalition of educators is currently laying the foundation to establish a national certification board by the mid-1990s.

Several efforts have been made to enhance the professional empowerment of teachers in large urban school systems. In each of these efforts, local units of the American Federation of Teachers have been instrumental. As part of the first wave of reform, teachers in Toledo agreed to a peer review process to enhance professional accountability. In Toledo, mentor teachers have been created to participate in the assessment of teacher performance and to guide a process of remediation for those teachers whose performance is judged to be unsatisfactory. Teachers who do not improve under the remediation program may be counseled out of the profession or ultimately dismissed. Other states, like Illinois, copied the Toledo plan in watered-down versions, thus far without demonstrable effect on teacher performance.

Much more successful has been Pittsburgh's efforts to improve the quality of teaching in its system. In a revolutionary staff development program adopted by the board of education in consultation with the teachers union, one high school was designated as a clinical training site (Wallace, 1986). Groups of 48 secondary teachers from across the system went to the Schenley Teacher Training Center for an eight-week sabbatical, during which they received updates on the latest developments in their own particular disciplines and in adolescent psychology, were exposed to related real-world contexts of employment (e.g., externships in an electronics laboratory for physics teachers or at a magazine for English instructors), and spent a three-week period under intense pedagogical mentoring from master teachers assigned to Schenley High School. Closely monitored by the system's research department, the program was evaluated as highly successful in improving the teaching abilities of the system's veteran faculty (Denton & LeMahieu, 1985). The program was replicated at both the primary and intermediate grades. Combined with a realignment of the curriculum across the system, the system's efforts were rewarded with regularly increasing median test scores on nationally standardized tests. To sustain the improvement, Pittsburgh entered upon a second phase, titled the Centers of Excellence Program (COE). The COE program was designed to "institutionalize shared decision-making and school-based professional development" (Johnston, Bikel, & Wallace, 1990).

Earlier experiments with shared decision-making had been launched in Hammond, Indiana, and Dade County, Florida. Hammond is a small city adjacent to Chicago, across the state line in Indiana. The Dade County public schools serve the students of Miami and its neighboring suburbs. The Dade County school system trails only New York City, Los Angeles, and Chicago in total enrollment. In both of these school systems, primarily at the instigation of the teachers' union president, school-based management, in the form of shared decision-making, was included in the contract negotiated between the union and the board of education.

Pioneered in Hammond, where all schools now participate (O'Rourke, 1987), the school-based management/shared decision-making model has been copied in Dade County, where nearly a third of the schools were voluntarily involved in the fourth year of implementation. Under the Hammond and Dade County models, schools that wished to volunteer were encouraged to create School Improvement Councils composed primarily of the principal and teachers. Some parents were involved. Originally, the faculty had to vote to participate (winning a two-thirds majority) and the principal had to be supportive. Schools were provided few new resources but were given permission to seek waivers of either contract provisions or board rules and regulations in order to implement approved school improvement plans. Liz McPike, editor of *American Educator,* introduced the 1987 O'Rourke interview with this description:

> The principles that underlie [the school improvement process] find strong support in both the literature describing the characteristics of effective schools—which says that each school is and must be allowed to be a separate culture—and in theories of modern management that emphasize the importance of decentralization, employee involvement in the decisions that affect their work, and the development of a feeling of "ownership" of those decisions. (O'Rourke, 1987)

The notions of rigorous staff development, higher expectations for student achievement, autonomous school improvement planning, and collaborative planning that run throughout the teacher professionalization efforts are themes that were struck by Purkey and Smith in their 1983 review of the effective schools literature. The programs reported here frequently were begun prior to the release of *A Nation At Risk* and antedated many of the accountability-oriented state reform laws. They came to fruition, however, and gained attention in the latter half of the 1980s, during the same period that the Chicago school reform movement was gaining strength. In particular, the efforts in Hammond, Dade County, and Pittsburgh all had direct impact upon the thinking of the reform activists who were instrumental in drafting the Chicago School Reform Act.

Using Market Pressures to Improve Schools via Enrollment Choice

During the late 1970s and early 1980s there was considerable agitation from some conservative political camps to change dramatically the formula for supporting public access to education. The key word in this debate was "vouchers." Drawing, in part, upon the experience of support for postsecondary education for veterans under the G.I. Bill following World War II, proponents suggested each child should be given a voucher, worth an appropriate amount of money, which he could use to attend any school of his choice. The school administration could then exchange the voucher for enough funds from the government to meet its tuition requirements. In this way, all children would be given the choice of what school to attend. Schools would compete for children. Bad schools would lose students, and good schools would grow. In this way, competition through the marketplace would generate a desire for improvement at the school level (cf. Friedman & Friedman, 1981; Lieberman, 1989; and Coons & Sugarman, 1978).

Public school advocates saw vouchers as an attack upon the public school system. They charged it was a subversive attempt to siphon public funds into parochial schools. They charged that the public schools would be left with students who required high-cost special services and with the poor who would not know how to find more adequate schools, while private schools creamed off the elite students from the public systems. Attempts to enact a federal voucher plan affecting Chapter I compensatory funding, amounting to about $600 per Chapter I eligible child, were soundly defeated in the U.S. Congress.

But the basic notion of market-driven motivation for school improvement has not died. During the latter half of the 1980s, the effort focused on creating enrollment choice among public schools. Advocates noted that many school districts permitted some limited choice of enrollment among schools within the district, either for special-purpose schools or for magnet schools. Magnet schools had frequently been associated with desegregation efforts. Schools were developed with special emphases to make them attractive to different groups of students. By controlling entrance, racially balanced schools could be created, based on student or family chores. Such voluntary desegregation programs often avoided the problems of forced busing. Critics pointed out, however, that such approaches not infrequently resulted in two-tiered school systems, which worked to the disadvantage of low-income and minority students.

Enrollment choice among public schools was given a big boost with the release, in 1986, of a report from the National Governors' Association titled *Time for Results: The Governors' 1991 Report on Education.* Among other reforms, the report urged that states should "expand opportunities for students by adopting legislation permitting families to select from among kindergarten to twelfth grade public schools in the state. High school students should be able to attend accredited public postsecondary degree-granting institutions during their junior and senior years" (National Governors' Association, 1986).

In 1985, Minnesota Governor Rudy Perpich introduced legislation allowing parents to choose what school their children might attend. That legislation did not pass, but juniors and seniors were allowed to attend postsecondary institutions for individual courses, with state support following them. In 1987, at-risk 12- to 21-year-olds were permitted to enroll outside their home district. In 1988, the original legislation was passed, phasing in the right of all parents to exercise enrollment choice (Perpich, 1989). Several other states have passed similar legislation, including Iowa and Nebraska.

Two local choice plans have received considerable attention. Perhaps best known is the District 4 plan in New York's Spanish Harlem. Starting slowly with three small alternative schools in 1974, one of which was specifically designed for troubled youths, the district expanded to some 24 specialized schools in 1985. In 1989, the district served 14,000 students through 16 regular elementary school programs, 9 bilingual schools, 23 alternative schools, and 2 high schools in 21 buildings (Fliegel, 1989). Parents in the district may choose to send their children to any school in the district. During the same period, the percentage of students reading at or above grade level is reported to have increased from 16% to 62%. While advocates of choice frequently point to these achievement increases as the result of enrollment choice, I believe a better argument can be made that program differentiation, resulting from collaborative planning and resulting in teacher "ownership," as described by Purkey and Smith in their review of the effective schools literature, might be a better explanation. This supposition is supported by the fact that the alternative programs began in 1974 and student achievement grew apace, while districtwide enrollment choice did not come until the end of the period.

The other widely noted district choice plan is from Cambridge, Massachusetts. The city had 15 elementary schools and one comprehensive high school in 1980 when a districtwide enrollment choice plan was initiated, primarily for desegregation purposes. All parents chose which elementary school their child would attend. But the system was a controlled choice system, governed by racial quotas to assure racial balance in each school. In 1984, new superintendent Robert Peterkin introduced a systemwide planning process for improvement called the Key Results Plan, which won gradual acceptance. At the heart of the planning process was Peterkin's commitment that *"all children can learn"* (Peterkin & Jones, 1989; italics in original). In the 1984-1985 school year, only 54% of Cambridge elementary students passed reading, math, and writing basic skills tests (California Test of Basic Skills); by 1987-1988, 87% passed all three tests. The Cambridge system involved controlled enrollment choice, intensive staff development, and collaborative systemwide planning augmented by individual school planning. Its results were just beginning to be widely recognized as the Chicago School Reform Act was being crafted.

In passing, it should be noted that there were two major interdistrict enrollment plans in midwestern cities through much of the 1980s. One was in St. Louis and the other in Milwaukee. In both, students were exchanged between the city and the suburbs, with students theoretically moving in both directions. In both cases, student desegregation was the primary goal in establishing the plans. In practice, in both cities, the primary movement was from the city to the suburbs. A voluntary exchange program had been included in the 1981 desegregation plan worked out for Chicago under a consent decree with the U.S. Department of Justice. However, the interdistrict transfer provisions of the plan were never more than words on paper.

There have been two other developments in the arena of enrollment choice since the passage of the Chicago School Reform Act that should be acknowledged, though they obviously played no role in shaping the reform plan. Beginning with the Fall term 1990, 1% of the lowest-income students in Milwaukee, just under 1,000 students, were eligible to receive vouchers worth $2,500, which can be used in any private, nonsectarian school. This plan was sponsored by Representative Polly Williams, a black Milwaukee legislator, and supported by Governor Tommy Thompson. The plan survived an initial court challenge, and was implemented in September 1990.

Also in 1990, a very provocative attack upon the fundamental structure of public education in America was released by the normally liberal Brookings Institution. *Politics, Markets, and America's Schools* is authored by John Chubb and Terry Moe (1990), who predict that all of the previously discussed reforms are bound to fail because they do not address the fundamental cause of the bureaucratization of our educational system, namely the process of democratic control. On the basis of a study of some 500 schools and surveys of over 200,000 students, principals, and teachers, Chubb and Moe contend that the single most important factor in the ability of schools to promote student achievement is the degree of autonomy with which they operate. They suggest the only place autonomy is seen extensively in public schools is in small suburban systems. The other place it is found is in private schools. Their proposal is radically to revise the way in which schools are funded by allowing the state to charter schools, both public and private, to delegate authority directly to local schools, to allow parents to choose which of these schools their children will attend, and then to fund these chartered schools on the basis of their enrollment, with higher funding provided for disadvantaged students or those requiring specialized educational programs. In short, Chubb and Moe are proposing to eliminate democratic control of the schools and replace it with a market-driven funding approach that will encourage autonomy and effectiveness. I will comment more extensively on the Chubb and Moe argument as it applies to the Chicago experiment in Chapter 9.

Parent Involvement Through School-Based Management

While the American Federation of Teachers has been advocating a version of school-based management that focuses upon teachers and principals sharing decision-making at the school level, other efforts have focused upon involving parents in decision-making about the programs and practices of local schools. In smaller school districts, parents have had easy access to school board members and have been able to influence decision-making informally. Parents have been quite capable of organizing caucuses to contest for school board seats when they felt board members were not being responsive to their concerns. However, in larger districts, parent power was not as easily exercised.

One of the themes of the War on Poverty was the empowering of the poor themselves. One of the architects of the poverty effort, Daniel Patrick Moynihan, produced a stunning critique of the effort to empower community residents, which he suggests was doomed from the start, in his essay *Maximum Feasible Misunderstanding* (1969). While Moynihan does not dwell on the education aspects of the poverty bill, he notes the contradiction between those who sought participation of the poor in planning how federal funds would be spent and those seeking to retain control of spending on the poor. One of the outgrowths of this effort was the mandatory establishment of parent advisory councils at schools receiving federal compensatory education funding. While in many places these advisory councils became rubber stamps for program decisions made by principals or other administrators, they did create a pattern of parent advisory councils in the urban centers of America.

Parent advisory councils grew up in a number of cities. Perhaps the most extensive utilization of these councils was in Salt Lake City. There Superintendent Donald Thomas encouraged advisory panels at every school and focused their attention on making collaborative decisions that would lead toward school improvement. On nonsubstantial items, the councils seemed to work quite smoothly. But on critical issues, parent influence was considerably diminished, according to those who studied the system closely (Malen & Ogawa, 1988).

Perhaps the most cogent argument for school-based management, with significant parent involvement, is made by Carl Marburger (1985), formerly commissioner of education for the state of New Jersey. Marburger quotes a representative of the Broward County, Florida, school system which was already engaged in school-based management:

> School based management is a form of *district* (and state) organization and management in which the school-community system is the *key unit* for educational change and improvement. . . .
>
> Administrative decentralization, in general, is marked by moving authority for certain functions to different parts of an organization, while retaining power centrally. Political decentralization involves

> changing the power distribution. While relinquishing power appears to be giving up total power, experience indicates that the total system gains in power, and those at the top can get more results. (Marburger, 1985, p. 25)

Marburger advocated the establishment of school management councils that were equally balanced between parents and school professionals. In his view, school-based management was based on a collaborative approach entered into voluntarily. Support from the superintendent of schools was a requirement. Marburger was actively involved in promoting his ideas about school-based management, working, among others, with schools in St. Louis and New York City. *One School at a Time* was a primer for encouraging more school districts to embark upon this effort. School reformers in Chicago met with Marburger several times to discuss possibilities for Chicago, but ultimately rejected the voluntary approach and eventually designed councils in which lay members would hold a substantial majority.

IMAGES FROM THE WORLD OF BUSINESS

Although not incorporated directly into the Chicago School Reform Act, an important aspect of the mobilization of the business community behind the school reform effort was the correspondence between the decentralization implicit in school-based management and business postulates of decentralization of authority, lean central office staffs, and worker participation theories. These ideas have dominated the thinking of businessmen as they have sought for higher profitability in their own companies. The school reform effort struck responsive chords with this literature, and the resistance of administrators at the board of education to calls for downsizing the central office seemed ludicrous to business leaders in Chicago. As one representative of the business community put it, "We've all had to do this over the last 10 years. Why should the board of education be exempt?"

In 1982, Thomas Peters and Robert Waterman's book, *In Search of Excellence: Lessons from America's Best-Run Companies,* burst upon the business world. Peters and Waterman were featured in business magazines and then in the popular press. They were everywhere on television. Their book was widely read and even more widely cited. Several chapter headings are significant for the decentralization theme: "Close to the Customer;" "Autonomy and Entrepreneurship;" "Productivity Through People;" "Simple Form, Lean Staff;" and "Simultaneous Loose-Tight Properties." While the responsiveness to the customer emphasized in the first of these chapters undergirds notions of choice and market-driven solutions, other dimensions are more relevant to the school reform effort Chicago business leaders came to support.

Peters and Waterman are salesmen. Their book is a very loose analysis of case studies. They are out to make their points by telling stories about successful businesses. Quantitative researchers would shudder, reading the book. But their stories are compelling and their points are well made. They start their concluding chapter this way:

> Organizations that live by the loose-tight principle are on the one hand rigidly controlled, yet at the same time allow (indeed insist on) autonomy, entrepreneurship, and innovation from the rank and file. They do this literally through "faith"—through value systems, which . . . most managers avoid like the plague. . . .
>
> Carlson [United Airlines] doesn't blush when he talks about values. Neither did Watson [IBM]—he said that values are really all there is. They lived by their values, these men—Marriott, Ray Kroc, Bill Hewlett and Dave Packard, Levi Strauss, James Cash Penney, Robert Wood Johnson. And they meticulously applied them within their organizations. They *believed* in the customer. They *believed* in granting autonomy, room to perform. They *believed* in open doors, in quality. But they were stern disciplinarians, every one. They gave plenty of rope, but they accepted the chance that some of their minions would hang themselves. Loose-tight is about rope. (Peters & Waterman, 1982)

Peters and Waterman made businessmen believe in the principles they were describing. Their stories were exciting. They were about hugely successful men, men of a type most businessmen wanted to be. But their stories would not be as effective if they were not being reinforced by other "hot" business gurus.

One of the hottest business consultants in the latter half of the 1980s was W. Edwards Deming. Deming has long been associated with the turn-around in Japanese industry that has allowed their companies to be known for their quality products. Deming is a supersalesman for the Japanese approach. He starts by lecturing top management that they must stop managing for short-term results and look at long-term success. He warns that drastic changes are required to achieve greater quality and productivity, and that they will not result from "everyone doing their best," but that there must be new ways to work to accomplish quality, which is everyone's job. Finding those new ways is management's job (Deming, 1982). After reading, or more likely listening to, such injunctions, and beginning to utilize some of Deming's approaches to quality improvement, business people would not take kindly to excuses for nonperformance from the top administrators of a school system. Further, they found proposals for giving more authority to site-based personnel in line with other Deming proposals.

Deming's approach is never to blame the workers, but to involve them in solutions to problems. He tells the story of a manager in a motor freight company:

> "Bill," I asked of the manager of a company engaged in motor freight, "how much of this trouble (shortage and damage) is the fault of the drivers?" His reply, "All of it," was a guarantee that this level of loss will continue until he learns that the main causes of trouble belong to the system, which is for Bill to work on. (Deming, 1982, p. 117)

Deming tells the story of QC-circles (quality control circles) and their introduction by K. Ishikawa in Japan. QC-circles are cross-cutting groups of employees who work to solve problems existing between various dimensions of a company's operations. He suggests that such circles would best be instituted in management for most American companies, and allowed to grow spontaneously at other levels. The notion of collaborative planning by constituents from various dimensions of an organization resonates nicely with the idea of local school councils composed of parents, residents, teachers, and the principal working together to solve problems at the school level. Most importantly, it encourages the worker to be proud of his own work.

These business "gurus" are taken seriously because they have their roots in the masters of management. So Peter Drucker's recent collection of essays (1986) features a chapter on "Slimming Management's Midriff" that is based more in the changing demographics of the middle management work force (baby boomers moving through, fewer graduates of business schools coming) than in sermonizing. It gives practical advice on how to reduce middle management (attrition: not filling vacancies; widening job responsibilities instead of promotions). But the message is the same: middle management bureaucracies have grown unreasonably and must be sharply curtailed. This is the same message business leaders in Chicago delivered to Superintendent Byrd during the failed 1987 negotiations to create a Boston Compact type solution. They could not understand why he would reject this position out of hand. His opposition to the common wisdom of the business world convinced them that radical change had to happen. The next chapter describes the change designed by the Chicago School Reform Act.

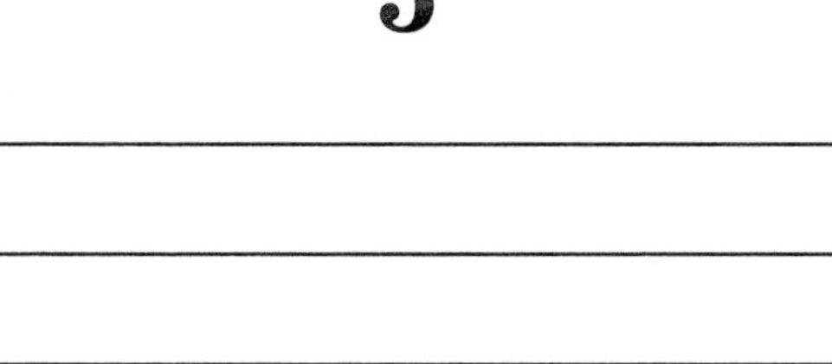

Restructuring the Chicago Public Schools

In 1976, Paul E. Peterson published his analysis of the intractable problems inherent in public schooling in Chicago in a book titled *School Politics: Chicago Style* (1976). Peterson noted, in great detail, the inequities in the Chicago Public Schools of the 1960s and the frustrations of efforts to bring about the desegregation of that school system. He noted the importance of the political influences that shaped the destiny of the school system, even though those political leaders were not exercising direct control over the schools. He predicted that little of a creative nature would happen in the Chicago Public schools until the controlling political forces were altered.

For 20 years, Peterson's assessment was accurate. Desegregation was one explicit example. At the time Peterson wrote, white student enrollment had just fallen below a majority. A desegregation lawsuit had just been settled out of court, and promises to implement a desegregation study plan were seen to be hollow even as they were accepted. It was not until 1980, when white enrollment had fallen to 18%, that the system entered into a court-approved consent decree (Hess, 1984). Even then, the plan adopted proved to benefit white students more than it did the continuing victims of segregation (Hess & Warden, 1988).

But the problems in the Chicago Public Schools were far deeper than who attended school with whom. At one level, it mattered little with whom students attended school, for even the best of Chicago schools were little more than mediocre. The worst schools were the worst in the country! But at another level, of course, it mattered greatly with whom a student went to school, for few white or affluent minority students attended these worst schools. They were reserved, in a system of educational triage (Hess, 1986), for poor, inner-city black and Hispanic young people. This distinction became even more invidious with the implementation of the magnet school enrollment choice component of the desegregation plan that resulted from the consent decree (Hess & Warden, 1988). Among other things, the Chicago School Reform Act was designed to address this problem.

THE CHICAGO RESTRUCTURING PLAN

The restructuring of the Chicago Public Schools is mandated by P.A. 85-1418, the Chicago School Reform Act. This act was adopted by the General Assembly of Illinois on December 2, 1988, and signed into law by the governor 10 days later. There are three major components to the act: 1) a set of goals, 2) a requirement to reallocate the resources of the system toward the school level, and 3) a system of school-based management that is centered upon the establishment of Local School Councils at every school.

School Reform Goals

The 123-page Chicago School Reform Act contains 10 goals to serve as the measures of school improvement over a five-year period. In essence, these goals require that students perform at national levels in achievement, attendance, and graduation rates and that the school system provide an adequate and well-rounded education for each enrolled student.

The specific goals are as follows:

1. Assuring that students achieve proficiency in reading, writing, mathematics, and higher-order thinking that equals or surpasses national norms.
2. Assuring that students attend school regularly and graduate from high school at rates that equal or surpass national norms.

3. Assuring that students are adequately prepared for further education and aiding students in making a successful transition to further education.
4. Assuring that students are adequately prepared for successful entry into employment and aiding students in making a successful transition to employment.
5. Assuring that students are, to the maximum extent possible, provided with a common learning experience that is of high academic quality and that reflects high expectations for all students' capacities to learn.
6. Assuring that students are better prepared to compete in the international marketplace by having foreign language proficiency and stronger international studies.
7. Assuring that students are encouraged in exploring potential interests in fields such as journalism, drama, art, and music.
8. Assuring that individual teachers are granted the professional authority to make decisions about instruction and the method of teaching.
9. Assuring that students are provided the means to express themselves creatively and to respond to the artistic expression of others through the visual arts, music, drama, and dance.
10. Assuring that students are provided adequate athletic programs that encourage pride and positive identification with the attendance center and that reduce the number of dropouts and teenage delinquents. (P.A. 85-1418, Sec. 34-1.01.A)

While these goals are quite wide ranging, it is generally agreed among the reform advocates and the monitoring agencies that the primary goals are the first two: raising student achievement to the national norms, and raising attendance rates and graduation rates to the national norms. To achieve these goals systemwide would be a tremendous challenge, and at least in terms of graduation rates, probably unreasonable, given what is known about the elementary school effects on student graduation rates (cf. Hess, Lyons, & Corsino, 1989). However, the act asks that these goals be met, not only at the district level, but *at each school in the district*!

The Reallocation of Resources

The Chicago School Reform Act was drafted to include two provisions to alter the disproportionate allocation of resources within the school system. The first requirement was to place a cap on administrative costs. The intent of the reformers was to limit the proportion of the school system's budget that could be spent in the administrative units (the central office and 23 administrative subdistrict offices). However, difficulty was encountered in finding a nonarbitrary criterion for assessing what was "disproportionate." The initial legislation required not exceeding the proportion of expenditures in the Fiscal Year 1985 budget (FY 1985 was the year during which the then general superintendent had assumed office). One legislator wanted to use the FY 1981 year as the base. The associate superintendent for finance of the Illinois State Board of Education proposed an alternative that seemed less capricious. His suggestion, which was adopted, was to limit the proportion of noninstructional costs in the system to the average proportion of all other school districts in the state for the preceding year. The advantage of this recommendation was the obvious fairness of the criterion. The disadvantage, in practice, is that the state's codes of noninstructional expenditures include a number of items at the school level, such as teacher retraining, which the reformers explicitly intended that additional resources should support. However, the state associate superintendent predicted that his recommendation would free up about $40 million through down-sizing the central administration; these funds would be available for redistribution to local schools. That figure was the key target figure for the second half of the reallocation design.

The Chicago Panel, along with two of its member organizations, the Chicago Urban League and the United Neighborhood Organization (a coalition of four constituent groups in primarily Hispanic communities), had been pressing the board of education to change the basis for its allocation of State Chapter I funds for several years (Hess & Warden, 1987). Although the general superintendent of the Chicago Public Schools acknowledged the propriety of the panel's recommendation, he claimed such a shift in resources would be too disruptive of the school system. His response came at the same time that he was increasing central office staff while proposing to cut teachers at the school level.

These reform groups were able to incorporate into the Chicago School Reform Act a provision to change the allocation procedures for State Chapter I aid. The first change was to prohibit the use of State Chapter I funds for any purposes outside local schools, except for 5% of the funds that had been used for desegregation purposes during the 1980s (the reform act, in numerous places, ensures that provisions of the act are not to be used to infringe on the system's desegregation efforts). This reallocation provision required that about $30 million of previously deducted "program support" funds be distributed directly to the schools, starting in the fall of 1989. In addition, another newly incorporated provision shifted the proportion of targeted funding from 60% to 100% over four years (70% in the fall of 1989, 80% in 1990, etc.). Finally, one Chapter I reallocation provision, phased in over five years, required that none of the Chapter I funds would be used to support basic programs present in all schools. The resultingly freed funds would be available for discretionary use at the school level.

The act also required that any newly targeted aid (i.e., the difference between the 60% level in 1988-1989 and the 70% level for 1989-1990) be considered discretionary. This "supplemental/discretionary" provision of the act required that an additional $10 million be shifted to the school level. As a result of these various provisions, the average elementary school received about $90,000 in new discretionary resources for the first year of implementation of school reform in Chicago. That figure should increase to about $450,000 in the fifth year.

School-Based Management Provisions

The primary vehicle for achieving the goals of the act and for utilizing the reallocated resources was the establishment of Local School Councils (LSCs) at each school site. These councils were to be the cornerstone of school-based management and decision-making. The councils were given three major responsibilities: to adopt a school improvement plan, to adopt a budget to implement that plan based upon a lump-sum allocation, and to decide whether to terminate the incumbent principal and select a new one or to retain the incumbent—in either case to sign the selected principal to a four-year performance-based contract.

Complementary to the establishment of the LSCs, a number of other provisions shifted the responsibilities and authority of other aspects of the school systems as described in the following pages.

Local School Councils

Local School Councils were mandated for each school site. These councils are composed of six parents, two community representatives, two teachers, and the principal. In high schools, they include one nonvoting student. The parent representatives are elected by a vote of the parents who have children attending the school; parents who are also employees of the system are not eligible to vote for parent representatives or to serve on LSCs as parent representatives. The community representatives are elected by residents living within the geographical boundaries of the school enrollment area who are neither parents of enrolled students nor employees of the school system; employees may not serve as community representatives. Two teachers are elected by all employees assigned to each school, exclusive of the principal. The principal is considered elected by his assignment to the school (P.A. 85-1418, Sec. 34-2.1).

This particular configuration of membership was designed during the Mayor's Education Summit, which had originally been convened by Mayor Harold Washington. It was designed to give parents a major voice in the educational decisions affecting their children. It was also designed to avoid the problems encountered in New York City where employees, for several decades, were able to dominate elections to the 32 community boards of education, which govern elementary schools in the city. Employees were given representation on each Local School Council, but only through the teacher and principal positions.

Subdistrict Councils

Subdistrict councils were established for each administrative district in the city (P.A. 85-1418, Sec. 34-2.5). The councils are composed of one parent or community member elected from each Local School Council in the subdistrict. The interim board of education reduced the number of subdistricts to 10 for the elementary schools and one for the high schools. Elementary subdistricts now each include 45 to 50 schools.

These councils were given powers similar to those of LSCs to retain, terminate, or select a subdistrict superintendent. The subdistrict superintendent was changed from a line officer with authority over principals and school employees into a monitor and facilitator of school improvement. The district superintendent (DS) is charged with facilitating the provision of training to the LSCs, with mediating disputes at the local school, with settling election disputes, and with monitoring the establishment and implementation of a school improvement plan at each school.

In a provision that echoes state-level educational bankruptcy plans, if the DS judges that a school is not progressing adequately in adopting or implementing its improvement plan, he can recommend to the district council that the school be put on a remediation plan, which he develops for the school. If the school continues not to improve under the remediation plan, the district council can place it on probation, under which a board of education improvement plan shall be established to correct identified deficiencies at the school. If no improvement in correcting the deficiencies is noted after one year, the board may:

1. Order new LSC elections.
2. Remove and replace the principal.
3. Replace the faculty.
4. Close the school.

The subdistrict council is to play a coordinating function for schools in geographical proximity to one another. It is composed of one parent or community representative from each school in the district. Each subdistrict council elects representatives to a systemwide board nominating commission.

The Board Nominating Commission

The nominating commission is charged with proposing three nominations to the mayor for each appointment to the newly composed board of education. During the initial year of implementation, an interim board of education was to be appointed by the mayor. The interim board contained seven members and was designed to serve only one year, until May 15, 1990. The new permanent board would contain 15 members on staggered four-year terms. Thus, the initial nominating commission would be charged with proposing 45 candidates to the mayor by mid-April, 1990. From the 15 slates of three nominees, the mayor was to select one appointee for each slot. If he found a slate that did not contain any satisfactory candidates, he could reject the entire slate and request a new one be recommended to him (P.A. 85-1418, Sec. 34-3.1). The nominating commission has 23 members elected from district councils (two from each elementary district, three from the high school district) and five appointed by the mayor.

The Interim Board of Education

As a result of an amendment to the Chicago School Reform Act, the interim board of education was appointed during May 1989. The interim board of education, in addition to providing governance to the district between the initiation of the implementation of reform and the installation of the new permanent board of education, was charged with five major responsibilities: to institute a nationwide search for a general superintendent, to adopt a systemwide set of reform goals and objectives, to reduce administrative expenditures to meet the cap on noninstructional costs, to adopt a budget reallocating resources in line with provisions of the reform act, and to negotiate a contract with the system's employee groups (P.A. 85-1418, Sec. 34-3).

The Permanent Board of Education

The new permanent board of education was given most of the powers of the previous board, with the exception of the powers granted to Local School Councils. To recognize the existence of these new, semiautonomous LSCs, the basic descriptive term for the board was changed from "*management of*" to "*jurisdiction over* the public education and the public school system of the city" (P.A. 85-1418, Sec. 34-18). Specific new responsibilities included assuring the proper reallocation of State Chapter I funds, the establishment of an open enrollment plan by school year 1991-1992, the establishment and approval of "system-wide curriculum objectives and standards which reflect the multi-cultural diversity in the city," assure the civil rights of special-education and bilingual pupils, reduce overcrowding, meet new university entrance requirements, encourage new teacher recruitment efforts, provide training for personnel for their new responsibilities, and establish a fund to meet special priorities the board might establish while distributing funds to attendance centers in an equitable manner. The powers and duties section (P.A. 85-1418, Sec. 34-18.1-28) concludes with the notation, "Nothing in this paragraph shall be construed to require any additional appropriations of State funds for this purpose."

Teacher Empowerment

While other school-based management efforts across the country have focused on giving teachers new participation in decision-making at the local school level, the Chicago plan gives more votes to parents and community representatives than to the professional staff. However, in most other school districts experimenting with school-based decision-making, there are few new powers given to the school improvement planning teams. In most cases, the new powers are restricted to individual case waivers granted by the board of education or the relevant employee union. In the Chicago plan, extensive programmatic, budgetary, and personnel control are granted to the LSCs. Since the intent of the Chicago reform act was to establish a new level of staff accountability for student achievement in the LSCs, it was deemed critical to assure that the councils were dominated by parents and community representatives.

However, the effort to establish participative decision-making was recognized in the relationships mandated between the councils and the professional staff. Primary responsibility for school improvement planning was vested in the principal, advised by a Professional Personnel Advisory Committee (PPAC). The PPAC is to be composed of "certified classroom teachers and other certificated personnel who are employed at the attendance center." The size and operation of the PPAC is to be determined by the certificated personnel at each school (P.A. 85-1418, Sec. 34-2.4a). The PPAC is established "for the purpose of advising the principal and the local school council on matters of educational program, including but not limited to curriculum and school improvement plan development and implementation."

The Principal

Although never stated explicitly in the description of the principal's powers and duties, the Chicago School Reform Act is built upon the assumption that the principal is the chief instructional leader in each school. The principal is given new powers and duties to enable his/her performance of that role. But principals were made directly accountable to Local School Councils for the effectiveness of their performance. At the point of contract renewal, principals who are judged ineffective may be terminated, with no tenure rights other than those they hold as teachers.

Principals are given the right to select teachers, aides, counselors, clerks, hall guards, or any other instructional program staff for vacant or newly created positions "based upon merit and ability to perform in that position without regard to seniority or length of service" (P.A. 85-1418, Sec. 34-8.1). For the first time, the engineer in charge and lunchroom manager are also made accountable to the principal, though still not completely under his/her control.

Principals are also given the responsibility for initiating, in consultation with the LSC and the PPAC, a needs assessment for the school, for designing and recommending a school improvement plan for consideration by the LSC, and for drafting a budget for amendment and/or adoption by the LSC. Thus, the principal is placed in the role of being the instructional leader of the school, charged with proposing ways to improve the school that will win the approval of the parents, community, and teachers who make up the school community. The principal is given additional powers in staff selection, planning, and budget flexibility, and given additional resources with which to work. In exchange, the principal's continued employment is dependent upon his/her ability to convince the Local School Council that he/she is being effective in exercising that leadership.

Expanded Choice

The reform act required the State Board of Education to conduct a study of enrollment options within the Chicago school district and report those options to the General Assembly by January 1, 1990 (P.A. 85-1418, Sec. 2-3.89). The state board's study essentially said the Chicago system should decide for itself what would be the best enrollment policy. In another section (Sec. 34-18.7), the board is required, starting in the 1991-1992 school year, to offer "the opportunity for families within the school district to apply for enrollment of their children in any attendance center within the school district." The board is given the discretion of how to phase in such a program, over what period of time, and under what circumstances. However, students living within a school's attendance area have first call on spaces in that school. In a district with more than 30 schools officially designated overcrowded, another 30 magnet or specialty schools oversubscribed, and available spaces primarily in schools with low achievement scores, the significance of this choice provision is unclear.

The Chicago School Finance Authority

Primary responsibility for monitoring the proper implementation of the Chicago School Reform Act was vested in an already existing oversight body, the Chicago School Finance Authority. The CSFA was established in 1980 to oversee the finances of the

Chicago Public Schools, but with the return to fiscal stability of the system, it had been reduced to annual reviews of the board's budgets to assure that they were balanced (they could prevent the opening of schools if the budget were not balanced) and to paying off the large bonded indebtedness incurred to bail out the system from 1980 through 1982. The Chicago School Reform Act requires the board of education to submit and gain approval of an annual plan for reforming the school system. The CSFA is charged with assuring that the major elements of the reform act are appropriately implemented by the Chicago Board of Education (P.A. 85-1418, Sec. 34A). However, since the sanctions available to the CSFA are largely limited to reporting inappropriate actions to the General Assembly and other public officials, its oversight function on reform is significantly less empowered than its charge to assure the financial stability of the system.

THEORETICAL BASIS FOR CHICAGO SCHOOL REFORM

The major components of the Chicago School Reform Act were not selected randomly or as the haphazard result of political compromises, though compromises were required on several lower-level issues. The primary theoretical bases for the reform act are found in the research results associated with the effective schools literature and in the participative management theories that find their educational manifestation in school-based management practices.

Effective Schools

As noted in the preceding chapter, the effective schools literature traces its roots to the efforts of a number of researchers, including Ronald Edmonds (1979), a professor and researcher at Michigan State and Harvard universities, and later a high-level administrator in the New York public schools where he tried to implement the findings from his research. Edmonds sought out successful inner-city schools in which disadvantaged students were learning at or above national norms. He then compared these schools with equivalent schools that were less successful. He and his collaborators were able to identify a series of characteristics of what they called "effective schools." Chief among these characteristics was the conviction, among the faculty, that all students can learn successfully. While such an assertion seems self-evident, as we have shown, inner-city educators had been making excuses for the poor performance of students in their systems based, in part, on the 1966 Coleman report. Edmonds was able to show that, when faculties held high expectations for the abilities of their students, the students were more likely to achieve at the national norms.

Edmonds also showed that the leadership of the principal is a key characteristic of an effective school. While, in Edmonds' studies, no particular style of leadership was associated with this effectiveness, effective leadership was related to the ability of the principal to establish a philosophical consensus about the educational program in the school. In addition, effective schools utilized frequent student assessments (testing) for diagnostic purposes, designing educational programs that were specifically geared to meet the educational needs of the enrolled students. These schools were also seen to have clearly defined and maintained discipline with an orderly educational climate.

The Chicago School Reform Act was designed as an effort to foster the development of these characteristics in every city school. The leadership of the school system had used the poverty level of its students as an excuse for low performance for years. In a letter to the editor of a major city newspaper, General Superintendent Manford Byrd cited the poverty level of the city's students as the reason dropout rates were so high and test scores so low (*Chicago Tribune,* January 18, 1987). He explicitly rejected the findings of a Chicago Panel research report that suggested the system was shortchanging the city's high school students by scheduling students into nonexistent study halls and using other scheduling mechanisms that reduced daily instruction to less than four hours (despite state law requiring five hours of instruction and a pattern of even higher average minutes of daily instruction across the suburbs).

It was obvious to the activists in the Chicago school reform movement that few school faculties would operate out of the conviction that all students could be successful learners as long as they, and their principals, were responsible to administrative leadership that was more concerned with eliminating threats to bureaucratic stasis than to assuring the high achievement of the system's students. This conviction was supported by research conducted a few years earlier by several University of Illinois: Chicago professors.

Van Cleve Morris, Robert Crowson, and their colleagues (Morris, Crowson, Porter-Gehrie, & Hurwitz, 1984) had studied a number of principals in the Chicago school system. They coined the term "creative insubordinates" to describe those principals whom they found to be particularly successful. These were the principals who were willing to break the rules "creatively" to see to it that their schools performed effectively for their students. To the reformers, it was evident that the multitude of sanctions, both explicit and potential, that were part of the Chicago Public Schools' bureaucratic chain of command produced a repressive effect on principal creativity and leadership at the school level. While the "creative insubordinates" ignored the potential for sanction by their superiors, most principals lacked the intestinal fortitude to ignore the threats of their immediate superiors (the district superintendents, as formerly constituted) and other central administration bureaucrats.

The Chicago School Reform Act broke the repressive control of principals under the bureaucratic chain of command and shifted the locus of their accountability from their administrative superiors to Local School Councils dominated by parents. It was assumed that the primary concern of parents and community representatives would be the achievement levels of their students enrolled in the school. The reformers believed that principals would be empowered to exercise the instructional leadership necessary for effective schooling by removing the potential for bureaucratic sanctions and by providing new capacity to shape the composition of the faculty of the school over time and by providing new flexibility and resources for school improvement planning.

Participative Decision-Making

A second basis for the design of the reform act is the theory of participative management, which, as described in Chapter 4, is sweeping across the American business community. The movement in business toward decentralization and site-based management is rooted in the conviction that employees will be more productive when they participate in the decisions that affect their effort. In public education, that theory was embedded in the notion of school-based management or school-based decision-making. Activists in the school reform effort had examined several particular manifestations of school-based management.

Carl Marburger (1985) of the National Center for Citizens in Education was consulted several times on his experiences with school-based management in school systems across the country, including St. Louis, Salt Lake City, and New York. In Marburger's experimental sites, school improvement councils were half parents, half staff. They enjoyed no additional powers at the school level over those previously experienced by the school staff. Their power at the school site was dependent upon the extent to which principals wished to share the power they exercised. Marburger emphasized that, as he conceptualized it, school-based decision-making was a voluntary sharing of power by the general superintendent and by principals at local schools. Given the intransigence of the Chicago general superintendent and the perceived number of ineffective principals, the Marburger approach was rejected.

The approach taken by several local affiliates of the American Federation of Teachers, the parent of the Chicago Teachers Union, was more promising. Under experimental implementation in Hammond (Indiana) and Dade County (Miami), school improvement councils were formed at participating local schools. They were given permission to develop school improvement plans that might violate individual restrictions of either board of education regulations or provisions of the union contract. By agreement between the board of education and the union, waivers could be granted for potential violations of those regulations or provisions.

Elements of the AFT approach were incorporated into the Chicago School Reform Act. Although the Local School Councils are not dominated by teachers and professional staff members, as they were in Hammond and Dade County, teachers do have a role on the LSCs. However, the major parallel with the AFT approach is vested in the PPAC, the Professional Personnel Advisory Committee, which is designed to work collaboratively with the school principal on designing a school improvement plan, on matters of curriculum, and on other instructional matters. The reform act explicitly calls for the provision of waivers from both board of education policies and employee collective bargaining agreements (P.A. 85-1418, Sec. 34-2.3). Since the Chicago Teachers Union had initiated the discussion of contract waivers, it is not surprising that waiver language was added to the contract negotiated during the summer of 1989 to reflect the provision of the reform act.

Educational Bankruptcy

One other important provision was included in the reform act on the basis of experiments in school reform elsewhere in the nation. In New Jersey and several other states, so-called "school bankruptcy" laws had been enacted, under which the state board of education could declare a school district educationally bankrupt and move to take over control of the district from local officials. In response to concerns that LSCs would not become accountable for lack of improvement at their schools, a similar provision was incorporated in the school reform act, as already described under the subdistrict councils. However, reformers placed their primary reliance upon the accountability of biannual elections for members of the Local School Councils. As in most other jurisdictions in this country, the primary responsibility for effective LSCs lies with the electorate.

THE NECESSITY OF A LEGISLATIVE APPROACH

After describing the major components of the Chicago School Reform Act and detailing the theoretical bases on which it rests, the question still remains: Why was a legislative approach necessary? The answer to this question lies in the particular history and context of school reform in Chicago. Some dimensions of the answer have already been described above.

As just mentioned, in other locales, less radical school-based management approaches have been undertaken voluntarily. In St. Louis and in several community elementary districts in New York City, school-based plans were being implemented, with the consultation of Marburger and his associates. In Salt Lake City, under Superintendent Donald Thomas, school councils were in operation for a dozen years, though their effectiveness was questioned by outside researchers (Malen & Ogawa, 1988). In Hammond, Dade County, and several other cities with AFT locals, school-based management was incorporated in the union contract.

In each of these situations, the key ingredient was the willingness of the superintendent of schools to engage in some dimension of power sharing. Similarly, at the local school level, a required element was the willingness of the principal to enter into a power-sharing arrangement. Only in Hammond, after years of implementation, was there any requirement that principals be willing to engage in power-sharing or face removal.

In Chicago, these conditions simply did not exist. As has already been demonstrated, the general superintendent was focused on power accumulation, rather than power sharing. His budget proposals progressively drained resources from the schools while expanding the bureaucratic empire. He accused those who questioned his priorities of "trashing" the public schools and, referring to their support by foundations, of "pimping off the miseries of low income students." In sharp contrast to his counterparts in Dade County, Hammond, Rochester, or Cincinnati, his approach to the teachers' union and other employee groups was confrontational, rather than collaborative. (The general superintendents and AFT local presidents from these four cities were guests at a conference in Chicago on June 30, 1987, just two months prior to the longest teachers strike in the city's history. The conference was jointly sponsored by the Chicago Teachers Union and Chicago United, a coalition of major business and civil rights groups in the city. Superintendent Byrd refused the invitation to attend or even to bring greetings to his colleagues from these other major urban school systems.) The confrontational relationships between the administration and the unions culminated in the 19-day school strike in the fall of 1987. The school reform effort gained significant momentum as a result of that strike.

In the obvious absence of any inclination for voluntary agreements that might lead toward improvement of the Chicago Public Schools, an effort was mounted through the mayor's office to coerce the school system and its employees into a set of agreements patterned after the Boston Compact (Schwartz & Hargroves, 1986; Cippolone, 1986). In October 1986, Mayor Harold Washington convened an educational summit focused on what he called "the learn-earn connection." Washington, facing a reelection campaign the following spring, perceived potential vulnerability in two related areas: high minority youth unemployment and high dropout rates/low qualifications of graduates of the public schools. He called together some 40 representatives of the business community, the school system, the teachers' union, area universities, and civic groups to address these issues.

The first year of the education summit was built upon the false premise that the school system would be willing to take steps to reform itself if it was offered jobs for its qualified graduates. The assumption was that promises of expanded job opportunities for qualified graduates would induce the administration to take steps to expand the number of its students who both graduated and had higher achievement levels. The fallacy involved was the assumption that school administrators would be primarily concerned with what happened to their students after they left high school. School systems receive no inducements for the success of their students after they leave the system. As long as pupils are enrolled, the system receives state aid tied to some student-based formula. But even this aid is no inducement to retain students, for the aid formula in Illinois provides less than half of the per-pupil costs of education, while property tax support is not affected by enrollment declines (e.g., declines resulting from high dropout rates—cf. Hess & Lauber, 1985). The fallacy was in assuming that school administrators would be willing to undergo the pain of restructuring and resource reallocation (i.e., firing or reassigning their friends and colleagues) in order to secure a benefit for former students for whom they were no longer responsible. Needless to say, during the summer of 1987, summit-sponsored negotiations between the business community and the school system failed. They foundered on the general superintendent's demand for $83 million in additional support before the system would agree to any significant effort to improve its schools.

In the second year of the Mayor's Education Summit, after the disastrous 19-day school strike, the fears and desires of system administrators and union representatives were largely ignored. Under immense political pressure following the strike, neither the system administrators nor the union leaders were willing to refuse to participate in agreements that were dominated by the desires of parent and business representatives. However, it was also obvious to most participants that school administrators and board of education members had little intent to implement any significant aspects of the summit agreements. Mayor Washington had died during the second year of the summit and had been replaced by a weak acting mayor, who showed little capacity or interest in trying to pressure the administration to adopt significant reform.

Thus, it became apparent that mandating legislation would be required if school restructuring and reform were to be implemented in Chicago. The Chicago School Reform Act, P.A. 85-1418, was the vehicle to require that reform in the city's schools. The next two chapters examine the changes required for the various constituencies empowered under the reform act.

6

Changing Roles of Principals and Teachers

During the spring of 1987, the then vice president of the Chicago Board of Education, William Farrow, and I participated, with others, in a panel at the annual convention of the Chicago Principals Association. The panel was focused on school reform efforts then underway. Both William Farrow, who had served on the 1981 Chicago United Task Force, and I called upon the principals of the school system to take an active leadership role in calling for and enacting efforts to improve the Chicago Public Schools. We were both astounded by the vehemence of the responses of individuals in the audience who informed us, in no uncertain words, that they could not do what we were asking. To be a leader for reform, participants told us, would mean they would be identified as troublemakers, would be upbraided by their subdistrict superintendents, and would forfeit any prospects of promotion to a larger school with a larger salary. With one exception, they were unwilling to wear on their breasts the scarlet "R" for reformer, even with the support of the board's vice president. The one exception was a young, Hispanic principal at Sabin Magnet School, Lourdes Monteagudo. She was the most outspoken principal, urging a radical restructuring of the Chicago Public Schools. She worked closely with the United Neighborhood Organization to develop a model school staffing pattern and actively lobbied the legislature as the reform bills were being debated. When Mayor Daley, in May

1989, appointed the interim board of education to implement the reform legislation, he also appointed Monteagudo as his deputy mayor for education (see Chapter 8 for a report on initial implementation of the reform act). However, at the time of this principals' association convention, she was just a young upstart principal, goading her older colleagues.

At the end of the panel, William Farrow pledged his support to any principal who was willing to take risks to improve his or her school. He asked them to call him if they encountered any trouble with their superiors in such an effort. The final response, however, was, "We can't call you! Staff regulations do not permit us to communicate with board members."

Principals in the Chicago Public Schools saw themselves as the ultimate victims in the struggles over school improvement. They were the highest-ranking school officials at the local school, so they were blamed, locally, for all of the problems at the school. But within the system, they felt they had little capacity to change things. They could not get rid of nonperforming staff. Except for a select few, principals had little input into policy decisions made at the central office. In short, they were middle managers charged primarily with passing on the decisions of their superiors, with keeping their schools orderly and out of the news, and with managing the personnel who worked in their schools. Their own personal advancement was in the hands of their district superintendents, who evaluated their work and through whom favors and extra program resources were dispensed.

All of these points were made regularly by the new president of the Chicago Principals Association, Bruce Berndt. Berndt was a member of the Mayor's Education Summit and the only summit member to vote no on the Summit Reform Agreements adopted during the spring of 1988. It was his contention that principals were being made the fall guys of school reform. In shifting from lifetime tenure to four-year performance contracts, principals were the one group, according to Berndt, who were losing something significant. He discounted the new opportunities that would be open to principals.

But principals were seen as a key element for reform. The reform groups pointed to some outstanding principals who were having a key impact on their schools. Robert Crowson described to the principals' association his experience shadowing principals for a number of days (Morris et al., 1984). He told them how he and his colleagues had coined the term "creative insubordinates" to describe effective principals. In urban bureaucratic school systems, principals have to be creatively insubordinate to get anything done to improve their schools.

The designers of school reform for Chicago said to themselves, this has to change. A key ingredient of effective inner-city schools is an effective principal. The restructuring of the lines of responsibility for principals under the Chicago School Reform Act was a deliberate attempt to eliminate that long list of sanctions and oppressive oversight that required a principal to be insubordinate in order to be creative.

The reformers were also convinced that lack of leadership from shopworn principals, even those with compassion for their pupils, could keep a school bogged down and its children achieving at unacceptably low levels. The *Chicago Tribune* profiled one such principal from Goudy School during its 1988 series on the Chicago schools. The profile begins by describing the principal's dedicated effort to visit the family of a problem student in a run-down part of the city, but then goes on to catalogue the chaos in the school.

> "You can't send a kid to the office for punishment," said 4th-grade teacher David LaRue. "They like to go to the office because they know they can play with Doc" [the principal]. . . . McDonald does not require that his teachers chart out lesson plans. . . . He does not ask them to follow school board policy and assign homework, so not all of them do. (Chicago Tribune, 1988, p. 30)

The article goes on to describe the principal interrupting classrooms on a whim with questions over the loudspeaker and chronicles his petty tyranny in assigning an overweight teacher he wants to get rid of to a third-floor classroom. These are all behaviors avoided by principals in "effective schools" (Purkey & Smith, 1983). The reformers believed some principals would simply have to be replaced if such schools were to become effective.

Teachers, also, were acknowledged to play an important role, particularly in their expectations for their students. In 1988, as staff from the Chicago Panel conducted the assessment of the Adopt-A-School programs at South West High described in Chapter 2, we interviewed about a quarter of the school's teachers. In anticipation of school-based management and its accompanying school improvement planning process, as part of the interview we asked teachers, "If you could do anything you wanted, what would you do to improve the achievement levels of students in this school?" There was almost unanimous agreement about the answer: "Change the kids!"

These teachers, working in an inner-city school where two students have been killed since we conducted the assessment, had lost any vision they might ever have had about how to make our system of public education work for inner-city young people. All they could see was that their compatriots in the suburbs had easier kids to work with, and that it was unfair to think they themselves could be as successful with less advantaged kids. Brainwashed for the past 20 years by schools of education and educational researchers who tout the Coleman report's (Coleman et al., 1966) findings that only the family's socioeconomic status correlates with student achievement levels, these teachers, like other urban educators, blame the victims (Ryan, 1976) for the failures of urban school systems.

Who is to blame for the sad plight of the Chicago Public Schools? Traditionally, administrators blamed the teachers; teachers blamed the parents; and parents blamed both the teachers and the administrators. When a principal received complaints about lack of supplies or a poorly performing teacher, the typical response was to throw up one's hands and say, "I can't do anything about it. I've tried, but that's controlled by the central office."

The Chicago School Reform Act was built upon the assumption that there was no one group of individuals who were to blame for the sad shape of the public schools. It assumed that it would be necessary to change the basic relationships between groups of individuals to create a new spirit and a new set of opportunities and a new conviction that all children in the Chicago schools can learn. Since school reform focused new attention upon the local school level, the professionals at the school level, principals and teachers, have been seen as a primary focus for change.

The Chicago version of school-based management can be described in two different ways, both of which are accurate. On the one hand, some of the reform groups, such as Designs for Change, the United Neighborhood Organization, and the Parents Community Council, emphasized that reform means lay control of the schools. They focused upon the constitution of the Local School Councils, with 8 of the 11 members being parents or community representatives, none of whom can hold other jobs with the board of education, thereby diminishing the likelihood of union control. They emphasized the principal's accountability to the parents and community residents as the key to turning local schools around. Confrontation between professionals and lay people would not be unexpected from such an interpretation.

Other reform groups, such as the Chicago Panel, have emphasized more the delegation of authority from the central and district offices to local decision-makers. From our perspective, the critical issue is that local folks, who understand the needs of the children trying to learn in their schools, get to make the decisions about how best to assist those children. While disagreements are likely to arise in any deliberative body with 11 members, the focus here is on collaboration, utilizing the expertise of each constituency.

Given these two possible interpretations of the legislation, which are not necessarily contradictory, it should be expected that different schools will focus their efforts in different ways. In some schools, confrontation may be necessary to move a school staff seriously to attempt to improve the education they are offering. In others, principal, teachers, parents, and residents had already forged a smooth partnership dedicated to providing the best possible educational program. In most Chicago schools, however, new relationships had to be forged under the mandates of the legislation. In some schools, these new relationships were confrontational; in others they were more collaborative. But in all, local school professionals experienced new demands upon their time, expertise, and skills.

NEW ROLES FOR PROFESSIONALS

The roles for educational professionals at the school level have changed dramatically under Chicago-style school restructuring. There are many different connotations to current efforts to increase the professionalization of teaching. The Carnegie Forum (1986) report contains one set of expectations, with implementation undertaken with great fanfare in the Rochester public schools and, more quietly, in planning between the University of Cincinnati and the Cincinnati public schools.

The report describes the shortcomings of the nation's public schools as they impact upon its global economic competitiveness.

In a fairly simplistic argument, it makes the obvious point that only teachers are in direct contact with students, so they are the key to changing the education system. The weakness of the argument can be seen by analogy. Few would seriously argue that since social workers are the key contact with persons on welfare, the key to changing the welfare system in America is to focus on better training and empowerment of social workers. Still, there is an obvious persuasiveness in the argument that teachers must be intimately involved in the reform process or little is likely to change in classrooms.

The report then lays out in some detail a plan for dramatically changing the role of teachers in our entire educational system. One of the advantages of the plan is that it includes both teacher preparation and school-level functioning. Another is the flexibility for diverse implementation. A serious weakness is in the inadequate attention paid to retraining the existing teacher force, which, despite the demographic turnover the report predicts, will still dominate schools for the next several decades. The main elements of the plan are:

1. Create a national board for professional teaching standards, organized with a regional and state membership structure, to establish high standards for what teachers need to know and be able to do, and to certify teachers who meet that standard.
2. Restructure schools to provide a professional environment for teachers, freeing them to decide how best to meet state and local goals for children while holding them accountable for student progress.
3. Restructure the teaching force, and introduce a new category of lead teachers with proven ability to provide active leadership in the redesign of the schools and in helping their colleagues to uphold high standards of learning and teaching.
4. Require a bachelor's degree in the arts and sciences as a prerequisite for the professional study of teaching.
5. Develop a new professional curriculum in graduate schools of education leading to a master's degree in teaching (M.Ed.), based on systematic knowledge of teaching and including internships and residencies in the schools.
6. Mobilize the nation's resources to prepare minority youngsters for teaching careers.
7. Relate incentives for teachers to schoolwide student performance, and provide schools with the technology, services, and staff essential to teacher productivity.

8. Make teachers' salaries and career opportunities competitive with those in other professions. (Carnegie Forum, 1986, p. 55f.)

The Schenley Teacher Training Center in Pittsburgh presents a different model (Wallace, 1986). In Pittsburgh, the public school system and the teachers' union collaborated to create a series of clinical teacher retraining centers (see Chapter 4). Every teacher in the system was given a sabbatical (five weeks at the primary and intermediate grade levels, eight weeks at the high school level) to attend the appropriate grade center, be updated on latest developments in his or her field, and receive mentoring on the system's commonly adopted curriculum goals and teaching methodologies. In Pittsburgh, curriculum realignment and upgrading teacher capacities was at the heart of the reform effort. While such an approach was included in the Mayor's Education Summit, it was omitted from the Chicago reform plan due to lack of funds. Some advocates, including the Chicago Teachers Union, continue to press the board of education to implement voluntarily a similar approach in Chicago.

Shared decision-making approaches, such as those undertaken in Dade County and Hammond, present yet another model. In these cities, school improvement teams were established in individual schools, composed primarily of the principal and teachers. Some parents were included, but relatively few. Teachers were given the opportunity to share in solving problems that they identified. If the solutions required waivers from board regulations or union contract provisions, such waivers could be secured. Under such participative democracies, teachers gained in managerial participation, while principals gained faculty support and collaboration.

In the Chicago case, there are dimensions of each of these approaches and other responsibilities that are unique to this city. The roles of principals and teachers are both significantly altered.

CHANGES IN THE ROLE OF PRINCIPAL

With the establishment of Local School Councils, the basic employment relationship of principals has been fundamentally changed. Principals are no longer middle managers, passing on the demands of their bureaucratic superiors to the lowest level of professionals (the teachers) for whom they are the immediate supervisors. In fact, there are no longer any bureaucrats to whom principals are directly responsible at all. There are administrators with whom principals must negotiate for resources or whom they must satisfy on compliance matters. But the relationship of principals to central office staff is now fundamentally changed and is more like the relationship of school district superintendents to state board staff than to the old images of line authority flowing downward through the hierarchy from the general superintendent.

Principals are now primarily responsible to their Local School Councils, a fact some principals only learned the hard way, as the first round of principal dismissals took place. The reform act established a two-stage process for principal evaluations and contract offerings. Half the principals were to be evaluated and selected or terminated during the first year, half the second. In the first half of the schools, principals were to be selected by April 15, 1990, for the next four-year term, which was to begin on July 1. The board of education requested that the selecting LSCs make a decision about the incumbent by February 28, so that nonrenewed principals could become candidates at other schools. While the dismissal of white principals at four minority schools claimed the national headlines for one full week, the turnover went more smoothly at most schools. One group of principals, including the principal at Goudy School, retired rather than face adapting to the new system. New principals were installed in about 40 branch schools, which were given independent status under the school reform act. Another 20 principals were not rehired for the next four years. A study by Designs for Change, reported in *Catalyst* (Andreoli, 1990), showed that, altogether, 154 new principals were installed between July 1988, when the act first passed the legislature, and April 1990. With additional changes anticipated during the second year of principal selection, more than one third of the local school leadership will have changed.

Under school reform, the major new dimension of the role of principal is that of chief executive officer working with a managing board. For nonprofit and business reformers, that role was quite familiar. For the first six years of my tenure as executive director of the Chicago Panel, my board met twice a month. As a coalition, we had to have the unanimous consent of our members for every policy position we adopted, a far higher requirement than any vote required of the LSCs. And, like most nonprofit managers, I serve at the pleasure of my board.

But for Chicago principals, working with a board and depending upon them for their employment was a major role change. Previously principals had enjoyed lifetime tenure. They had been primarily responsible only to please their subdistrict superintendent. Under the prior arrangements, they had had the freedom to ignore parent advisory councils if they so desired. With the 1985 imposition of Local School Improvement Councils (LSIC), with rights of disapproval of discretionary spending, parents took on new importance, but many principals continued to ignore them or stacked the council so that it was a rubber stamp. Now they had to work with an independently elected council that could terminate their contract and could command budgetary responsiveness. This is a role for which their educational administration graduate training had not prepared them.

Four years' experience under the 1985 statewide reform mandates should have prepared principals for their new relationships with Local School Councils under the 1988 act. Under both pieces of legislation, principals were moved out of the presiding role. Under the 1985 legislation, Local School Improvement Councils were to elect their own president, who would formally preside over council meetings and annual communitywide hearings on the proposed budget for the following year. Under the Chicago School Reform Act, the office of president was restricted to one of the parent members, who was to preside at all meetings of the Local School Council. In fact, since 1985 many principals had continued to preside over council meetings and found it hard to relinquish the gavel as the new LSCs were convened. Similarly, under the 1985 legislation, principals were to have been prepared to explain the school budget to annual budget hearings and to present proposed expenditures of discretionary funds to the LSICs each month. Most principals, however, had never really understood their school budgets, and the board had so narrowed the definition of discretionary spending that the financial decisions under the 1985 legislation were often not taken seriously. Similarly, since there were no real sanctions under the 1985 legislation, principals, if they so chose, could and did refuse to answer the questions of parents and teachers. However, under the new legislation, such arrogance could result in the loss of employment.

Immediately following the elections of the Local School Councils in October 1989, some principals continued not to take the new councils seriously, attempted to act as presiding officers, and refused to cooperate with information-seeking and planning efforts of the LSCs. As it became evident that some principals were going to lose their jobs, that they would not be extended a new contract, or that they would be required to compete with other candidates to retain their positions, principals began to abide by the new relationships required under the legislation: to present planning and financial proposals, to respond to questions, and to be one voting member among 11.

In some schools, this transition was made more difficult by conflicting loyalties with previously existing parent groups. In some of these schools, the PTA or other parent organization represented only part of the parent community. The Chicago Region PTA expressed many reservations about the reform act, and some local PTAs actively opposed it. In some of those situations, the PTAs did not run successful council candidates, and tensions developed between the PTA and the new LSC. In other schools, the PTAs had had good working relationships with the staff, and PTA members dominated the newly elected councils. In these latter cases, collaboration was likely, but in the former cases, principals could easily be caught with conflicting loyalties: those to their traditional parent support group and those to the new officially constituted governing council. In some schools, this conflict was heightened by racial polarization. In at least one high school, this conflict led to the principal's termination and an eventual suit charging the dismissal violated his civil rights. At the end of the first year of implementation, the suit had not been upheld and a new principal had been installed.

A second change in role involves the new responsibility of principals to take a leadership role in conducting a needs assessment and developing a school improvement plan. While some principals have developed some skills in creating a strategic plan for their schools, most have never done so. Particularly in large urban school systems, principals have not been encouraged to think strategically, and when they have done so, their options for action have been severely constrained. When it has been done at all, planning in large urban school systems has frequently been done at the top of the system, with individual principals simply told about the decisions that affect them. In some instances, token principals may have been included on planning teams to foster some input from their ranks. This is one of the differences between large bureaucratic systems and most smaller school districts in which the several principals are more likely to be part of the planning team for the school district. More frequently in urban systems, principals experience the constraints, the long list of sanctions and of reasons why they cannot undertake any serious initiatives.

Throughout the 1980s, Chicago principals had been encouraged to engage in some strategic planning. Under Superintendent Ruth Love (1981-1985) they had been required to develop and turn in their goals and strategic objectives for improving their schools. This continued to be the case under her successor, Dr. Byrd. While some principals utilized faculty input in their planning process, for most, this was simply a paperwork exercise. As Goudy School's principal told the *Chicago Tribune,*

> "All principals are liars," he says. "If anyone wanted to find out what I'm doing, they'd have to go through my desk." He laughs, looking down at the mishmash of papers, reports, and the ever present stack of books. . . . "In the public school system," McDonald explained, "you can fake almost anything." (Chicago Tribune, 1988, p. 31)

With the passage of the Chicago School Reform Act, principals are required to draft a school improvement plan after consultation with the members of the Local School Council and with the advice of the Professional Personnel Advisory Committee and other members of the faculty. The principal is then to bring the plan to the council for thorough discussion, possible amendment, and eventual adoption. In many cases, LSCs established a planning committee to work with the principal in developing the draft plan. Such a collaborative planning process was far different from the prior experience of Chicago principals. In fact, during the spring of 1989, after the reform act had been signed into law but before its official implementation date, Superintendent Byrd required all principals to develop their own three-year improvement plans. With only four weeks allowed for the development of the plan and a deadline several months prior to the election of the Local School Councils, this requirement was widely understood to be an effort administratively to undermine one of the three major responsibilities granted to LSCs under the reform act. It put principals into a real conflict between obedience to their then still legally constituted supervisors and faithfulness to the spirit of the reform act, which was about to take effect.

Principals must now assume responsibility, not only for doing strategic planning, but for leading teachers and educational laymen in a planning process for their school. The skills required to lead a corporate planning process are not the skills most principals developed, either in the classroom or in graduate schools of education. Good strategic planning requires the capacity to be visionary, to be creative, and to bring to bear information about improvement options being utilized elsewhere. These are exactly the capacities that were discouraged under the bureaucratic, middle-management mode of operations. As former Undersecretary of Education Chester Finn and his colleague Stephen Clements (1990) discovered, many principals brought little imagination and creativity to their new planning responsibilities. If the new school improvement plans created by LSCs simply replicate the previous operating procedures, it is unlikely that school reform will have much impact on the teaching and learning process in the classroom. It is for that reason that Finn and Clements worried that this lack of imagination might be the Achille's heel of Chicago school reform.

Similarly, under school reform, principals are charged with administering the school budget and with proposing a budget for the succeeding school year. The reform act assumes the improvement plan will be developed first and the budget then shaped to support the plan. In the past, principals paid little attention to their school budget because they had little control over any items in it, and the printed budget often did not include positions provided through categorical funds or special grants. With little control, principals often had little understanding of the rationales for the positions they received. Frequently, they benefited from or were hurt by their relationships with their immediate supervisors, the district superintendents, or with grant-administering central office bureaucrats. An audit of staff positions, mandated to meet the reform act's requirement to equalize basic program levels across the system, disclosed that more than 1,000 teaching positions had been inequitably established in various schools while other schools, in aggregate, had been shortchanged by more than 400 staff. With this history of arbitrariness in staff allocation, it was difficult for some principals to realize the extent of their new authority to change and reshape the budget of their local school.

In school after school, LSCs reported that principals made only minor revisions to the school budget, explaining that they were constrained by law, regulations, and contracts from making any significant changes. In reality, these constraints frequently did not exist.

A third responsibility of principals, under the reform act, is the evaluation of existing staff and the interviewing and selection of new staff. While such activities are not unusual for suburban and small-town principals, these are skills not widely utilized in urban school systems. It is true that the accountability dimension of the school reform movement nationally has resulted in an expansion of the evaluation role of principals, and Illinois, in 1985, was one of the states adopting stricter rules for evaluating teachers (P.A. 84-146). To meet the new evaluation requirements, the state mandated additional training in evaluation for administrators through administrator academies established through 18 educational service centers located statewide. In addition, the state required all certified administrators to be tested for recertification every five years. However, in 1990, just as the first group of administrators would have been due to be tested, the state quietly removed the testing provision from the recertification process, relying now entirely upon annual and biannual training experiences.

Urban school systems, with their restrictive teacher union contracts, had effectively abandoned significant teacher evaluation efforts. Similarly, with most teacher assignments rigidly controlled by seniority provisions in union contracts, staff selection was equally beyond the control of school principals. Unlike their colleagues in smaller school districts, Chicago principals were never involved in the original decisions to hire staff into the system. Their choices were restricted to choosing among already employed personnel, and those choices were severely constrained by seniority provisions. The net result of these provisions, largely ignored in most studies of urban principals, was that many principals in Chicago had abandoned any significant role in faculty selection. The conscientious principals would interview widely for new positions and would inquire of their colleagues about the performance of teacher candidates. They would also work to get rid of bad teachers, not by the formal removal procedures, in most cases, but by securing administrative transfers for nonperforming teachers, which simply shifted them around the school system. One of our early studies at the Chicago Panel (Hess & Meara, 1984) showed that some of these teachers were transferred as often as seven times in a single school year. Many principals, however, took whoever was sent to their school, and thereby had a handy, built-in excuse for nonperformance by the faculty.

Under the Chicago School Reform Act, selection of staff to fill vacant positions or newly created positions is now the responsibility of the principal, not the personnel department, and is to be accomplished on the basis of merit, not seniority, a change to which the union acquiesced. This means that principals are now accountable to their Local School Councils for the quality of staff coming into the school and for faculty performance. Similarly, the act shortened the remediation period for unsatisfactorily performing teachers from 180 to 45 days. Thus, principals now have a new responsibility to identify low-performing teachers, establish a remediation plan to improve their performance, or move to dismiss teachers who do not respond to the remediation effort. Administratively transferring a poorly performing teacher should become more difficult as receiving principals realize their vulnerability with their own LSC if they willingly accept other schools' problems. Principals' jobs now depend, in part, upon their abilities to motivate staff and to coordinate the school's educational program around a consistent theme or philosophy. The reader who is familiar with the descriptions of effective principals in the effective schools literature (cf. Purkey & Smith, 1983; Edmonds, 1979) will recognize corresponding dimensions of the newly defined role of principals in Chicago.

Some commentators have worried that these new staff responsibilities for principals could return the system to the days of arbitrary principal tyranny. It was that arbitrariness that gave credence to union demands for job security provisions in their contracts. Most Chicago reformers, however, felt that the pendulum had swung too far in favor of teacher and principal job security through tenure, to the extent that some professional educators were insufficiently motivated to perform satisfactorily in educating the city's children. Greater principal responsibility in the selection, remediation, and removal of teachers was seen as a necessary corrective, moving the pendulum back toward a balance point. It carries with it, however, the threat of renewed arbitrary leadership at the school level.

To the extent that centralized budget controls are further relaxed to allow local purchasing of supplies and services, a similar arbitrariness is risked. Some critics have suggested that local purchasing will inevitably degenerate into favoritism in contracting and will have a negative impact on the board of education's affirmative action purchasing plans. This risk is balanced with the inefficiencies and delays associated with the current pattern of centralized purchasing, which has frequently resulted in higher costs for items purchased through the bidding process than for those same items in neighborhood discount stores near the purchasing school. The combined purchasing practices of large school bureaucracies frequently produce contract specifications that are so large or cumbersome that only the largest suppliers find it practicable to submit bids. These are the diseconomies of scale often ignored in the discussions praising the efficiencies of large systems.

CHANGES IN THE ROLE OF TEACHER

Teachers too are being asked to play new roles under school restructuring reforms. Teachers have been the focus of efforts in other large urban school systems to improve their schools. The Carnegie report (Carnegie Forum, 1986) focused on the role of teachers. Teacher professionalization has been a theme in the school restructuring efforts in Dade County and Hammond. Pittsburgh's Schenley Teacher Training Center focused on the need to retrain and improve the capacities of that city's teachers. There has been widespread acknowledgment of the low ranking of graduates of schools of education.

In 1984, Professor Gary Orfield (1984) of the University of Chicago released a paper in his Metropolitan Studies series that showed that the Chicago Board of Education drew most heavily upon two Chicago-based state universities for its supply of new teacher recruits. He noted that these were the two state universities with the lowest average ACT (American College Test) scores for entering freshmen. He noted that these freshmen were overwhelmingly graduates of the Chicago Public Schools. He then concluded that a vicious cycle exists through which underprepared Chicago high school graduates enroll in these two state universities, matriculate in their schools of education, eventually emerge with teaching certificates, secure employment with the Chicago Public Schools, and further perpetuate the underachievement of

Chicago school children. This study underlines the later conclusions of the Carnegie report, which notes that future teachers tend to graduate in the bottom quarter of their college classes.

In addition to their relatively low graduation ranking, future teachers are frequently unprepared to deal with the problems of educating high concentrations of disadvantaged students. Too frequently their college texts and courses assume they will be teaching the "average" student when discussing curriculum and pedagogy. Adjustments for teaching high concentrations of inner-city kids are relegated to courses in educational psychology. While a graduate teaching assistant in one state teacher-training university in Chicago, my wife taught the one 50-minute period about disadvantaged students in the basic "ed psych" course that future teachers were required to take. Thus, preparation for 30 years of teaching disadvantaged students in Chicago schools was packed into one period taught by a graduate student. With that kind of preparation, new teachers in Chicago are thrown into the classroom and left to sink or swim on their own.

Teachers in the system had been particularly demoralized under a previous superintendent, Ruth Love. Dr. Love's assessment was that Chicago teachers were not adequately prepared or skilled to teach inner-city students. Therefore, she installed a system that reduced the teaching role to rote drilling of a set of discrete skill elements identified as the key components of reading and mathematics. As a bastardization of Benjamin Bloom's mastery learning approach, the Chicago mastery learning program was touted by Dr. Love as being "teacher proof"! Akin to the industrial production line, each worker worked only with a limited set of required tasks that could easily be monitored by a supervisor. Lost in the mechanization of the teaching process were both the creativity of the teacher and the facility of the student to put together all of the discrete skill exercises to achieve a love of reading. In fact, under the Chicago mastery learning approach, students worked primarily with worksheets and rarely with whole stories or books.

The reformers understood that teachers would have to play a critical role in improving Chicago's schools and that the city had to depend upon the currently employed teachers and could not wait for the results of reforms to the teacher preparation institutions. The Chicago School Reform Act assumes that teachers will respond creatively to the needs of their students, both in schoolwide planning and in classroom curricula. It assumes that teachers will be willing to forego protections incorporated in their own contract in order to accomplish some agreed-upon goals that will benefit their students. The law includes the opportunity for teachers to vote to endorse waivers of provisions of their contract when such waivers would allow the local school better to serve its students. Responding to this confidence by the reformers, the Chicago Teachers Union, which had originally proposed the idea of waivers, incorporated such a provision into its next contract with the Chicago Board of Education.

Two members of each faculty serve on the Local School Council. They, like principals, have to develop new skills in working collaboratively with parents and residents, as well as with the principal. Other members of the faculty may be drawn into committees working on various dimensions of the school's programs. These roles require a degree of respect and trust in the judgments of parents and other laymen that is often not fostered in schools of education and in large urban school systems.

There is a class difference in teacher-parent relations in inner cities and suburbs. Teachers in inner-city school systems are not infrequently the first professionals in their families. Many first-time college graduates have trouble respecting the opinions of parents and residents who are not equally educated. In many suburbs, the dynamics are reversed as parents may possess more education than the teachers and may hold what they perceive to be more powerful jobs. In these suburban situations, teachers are often more deferential than in the inner city. But, under the new Chicago governance structure in which each LSC parent and resident has an equal opportunity to affect decisions about the school, teachers have to develop new capacities for working cooperatively with these laymen, and with the principal.

The Chicago School Reform Act, due in large part to the advocacy of my organization, created at each school a Professional Personnel Advisory Committee (the PPAC). The PPAC is charged with working cooperatively with the principal to develop a school improvement plan for final adoption by the LSC. It is also charged with advising the principal on all other instructional matters in the school. It is designed to give teachers a voice in the decisions that will affect them. It is the shared decision-making or participative democracy dimension of school-based management that has been given a larger role in other site-based decision-making experiments, such as in Dade County or Hammond.

Each school faculty was empowered to decide for itself who would be members of the PPAC and what the group's structure would be. In some schools, the PPAC was constituted with only three members and it functioned in a way that could not easily be distinguished from the local union grievance committee. In other schools the entire faculty was empaneled as the PPAC. In some of those situations different faculty members appeared at different meetings, depending upon what issue was to be discussed. Principals, in that situation, found it frustrating to deal with an ever-changing PPAC. In the absence of a core group, with a comprehensive charge to consider the best interests of the entire school, each recommendation made by a principal would be greeted by a turnout dominated by those teachers whose special interest would be threatened by the recommendation. In such situations, it was very difficult for the principal to gain faculty support for the reallocation of school resources better to address the special needs of the students enrolled in that school.

For school-based management to work, teachers must be ready to break out of the parochialism of "my classroom." Schools of education focus their students' attentions upon learning how to teach a group of students. They are taught about the curriculum that is appropriate for the particular group of students that they are being prepared to teach. They are taught the pedagogical methodologies that are most likely to be successful with such a group of students. They are taught the classroom management skills appropriate for particular aged students. But it is only infrequently that they are taught much about schools as organizations, as planning units, as collaborative communities of teachers and learners. And the culture of teaching encourages noninterference in the teaching efforts of colleagues. School restructuring requires a more cooperative and collaborative approach by all members of a faculty.

Participation in the PPAC, just as on the Local School Council, requires corporate planning skills for teachers. As with principals, teachers have not been prepared, in college or in graduate school, for such corporate planning endeavors. As in most American education, corporate or cooperative effort is more frequently regarded as "cheating." Under school-based management, Chicago style teachers are expected to be active leaders and participants in the corporate planning process of the school. It is assumed they should have a major voice in curriculum decisions, text book selections, and the shaping of the entire instructional program of the school.

But to exercise that voice, they must be able to plan together with other adults and be willing to invest the time that such corporate planning requires.

One dimension of corporate planning is the ability to interact smoothly among adults. One of the surprising things, to me, is the relative unease of teachers, particularly elementary school teachers, in interacting with adults. In the last two years, as I have attended parent orientation sessions at my daughter's school, I have been astounded at the nervousness, hesitance, and insecurity of my daughter's teachers as they addressed the parents. I was surprised because both Sarah's prekindergarten and kindergarten teachers are excellent in the classroom, where I have seen them in action. Under school-based management schemes, teachers are going to need better adult interaction skills.

A second requirement for corporate planning for school improvement is some knowledge of the things that have the promise to improve schools. While this point seems fairly self-evident, most teachers in the Chicago system have not read widely in the school improvement literature. Similarly, few have explored the various proposals for altering classroom instruction to emphasize the active role of students as learners (except for the usefulness of this concept as an excuse for low achievement by students in their school or classroom). Under a rigid bureaucratic system that emphasized sanctions for any behavior out of the ordinary, it is not surprising that most teachers were not very venturesome. But a reform proposal that relies upon the readiness of professionals to change their behavior better to meet the needs of their students must include provisions to inform, encourage, and support teachers who are willing to take those pedagogical risks.

Finally, as members of the Local School Council, teachers now have a role in the formal evaluation of the principal. This, too, is a new role. Teachers have always evaluated the person under whom they worked. But when they could do little about that person other than gripe or file grievances, objectivity was not required. Now, in more formal evaluative positions, they must also learn the basics of personnel evaluation.

Unfortunately, little attention has been paid to providing training for teachers in the new roles they must assume under school reform. Teachers have participated in the training offered to Local School Council members in general, which will be discussed at greater length in the next chapter. Some Chicago universities have offered special courses or programs focusing on the new roles of principals and teachers. Most notably, Northeastern Illinois Ui versity converted a project it had originally designed as a suppo and upgrading program for principals into a project fosteri collaborative leadership at the 30 schools involved. This outstan ing endeavor is called Project Co-Lead. But the scope of su projects falls far short of the needs of 542 schools.

The Chicago Teachers Union has proposed a training progra for the PPACs at 10% of the system's schools. Despite the urgi of review committee members such as myself and the director Northeastern's teacher center, the training provided by the CT project, if funded by the city's philanthropic foundations, wou focus on teacher empowerment rather than on school improv ment. The training will provide teachers with some of the afor mentioned strategic planning skills, but unfortunately will igno the opportunity to provide participating teachers with mu insight into the new efforts to improve classroom teaching a learning. As such, it may serve to increase the local-site pow confrontations rather than enhance collaboration on restructuri classrooms as well as governance.

Largely missing in the effort to assist school-level professiona with the new skills they need to make school restructuring wo is the administration of the school system itself. Originally led a superintendent who strongly opposed the imposition of the Cl cago School Reform Act, the administration's training efforts we spotty and inconsistent. Their staff development efforts proceed blithely along the same patterns established years earlier. St development in the Chicago Public Schools utilized two prima patterns, half-day "in-services" at the school or district level a after-school or Saturday "lane placement" offerings sponsored the central administration and frequently taught by other teac ers. During the year of preparation for and the first year implementation of the reform act, the staff development progra of the Chicago Public Schools was maintained virtual unchanged.

IMPLICATIONS FOR SCHOOLS OF EDUCATIO

Restructuring schools, Chicago style, is not a model of schc reform for all communities. It is an approach that was careful crafted for the Chicago situation. It is built on a number of unique aspects of Chicago's school history. But beyond the particular fit to the Chicago situation, it is a type of school reform that is particularly suited to large urban school systems and to states with countywide school districts. While there are dimensions of the Chicago plan that might apply in small school districts, the real virtues of the plan are in addressing the problems of bureaucracy and rigidity of approach that are more evident in large school districts. In smaller communities, where parents have easy access to the superintendent and to the members of the board of education, many of the elements of the Chicago plan are unnecessary. But in large urban or county school districts, those with 10,000 or more students, the Chicago plan might quite beneficially be adapted.

If other large school districts follow Chicago's lead, or adapt the Dade County approach to school-based decision-making, new demands will be placed upon schools of education that are producing teachers and administrators for those systems. Quite apart from the specific reform measures adopted, the new attention to the problems of urban and rural public schools will require changes in schools of education. These schools must start to distinguish which types of students various educational strategies or curricula are most likely to benefit. Professors of education are going to have to stop assuming that their students will be teaching "average students." These professors must reexamine their own lesson plans for the hidden assumptions about the target students implicit in their present patterns of teaching. This is particularly true for those in curriculum arenas. But it is also true for those teaching courses in administration and in the social foundations of education. This is probably the hardest part of refocusing a school of education, for it requires a reexamination of the unthought-about biases that each of us brings to our own work.

Secondly, schools of education that serve urban or rural areas must reexamine the courses that are part of their curricula. Are there enough courses to help prepare future teachers for their roles in school districts that are distinctly "not average"? A reexamination of course offerings is much more straightforward than reexamining the hidden biases implicit in current courses. But it, too, carries political concerns. Will the college be willing to commit itself and its resources to meeting the real needs of the future teachers in our urban schools. Will it continue to provide these courses if enrollment in them is low? How committed is the school of education to helping improve urban school systems? Individual scholars have been willing to work with individual urban schools for a long time. But how willing is a whole school of education to commit to improving a whole urban school system?

The implications for graduate schools of education in the preparation of principals should be quite evident from the new roles described above. Educational administration courses must now be focused on training future urban principals in the basic skills of democratic leadership. They must include work on leadership in corporate program analysis, planning, and strategizing. Finally, they must teach principals how to keep abreast of new developments in efforts to improve schools. One of the most frightening aspects of talking with many principals in Chicago, who are probably not much different from their colleagues in other big cities, is that they have no knowledge of the many ideas now circulating about how to improve inner-city schools. Faced with the demand to be leaders in school improvement planning, too many are bankrupt themselves on ideas about this subject.

The implications for teacher education of the kind of restructuring of the school system taking place in Chicago are fairly straightforward. Teachers, too, need new skills in assessing the educational problems they confront in educating inner-city children. Unfortunately, as has already been implied, most likely they received little training in this area as undergraduates, as teachers in preparation. Secondly, they need training in thinking about the whole organization of the school, not just their classroom. This is the obvious shortcoming manifested by the teachers with whom we were working at South West High School who wanted to change the kids first in order to improve the school.

Both teachers and principals must be prepared to deal with parents and community residents in new ways that treat these lay people as collaborators in school improvement rather than as potential troublemakers. But for this collaboration to take place, parents and community members must themselves be ready for new roles. The next chapter addresses these changed roles for educational laymen.

Parents and Community Residents in School-Based Management

Local School Councils of one kind or another have existed in Chicago for more than 20 years. The establishment of decision-making councils did not suddenly appear out of some theoretical void. Their powers were not dreamt up in a professor's study, nor did they emerge from a political speechwriter's word processor. Local School Councils were built on a long history of advisory councils, which acquired some real power, at first informally, and then in the years just prior to the adoption of the Chicago School Reform Act, through legally mandated powers.

A HISTORY OF ADVISORY COUNCILS IN CHICAGO

Although Chicago, like other school systems, has had PTAs at its local schools for decades, the real history of advisory councils with intended impact on school programming dates to the advisory councils established to accompany federal funding of programs for the disadvantaged in the late 1960s. These councils, in Chicago, were similar to those established elsewhere around the country, with results that were predictably similar. (Daniel P. Moynihan [1969] nicely analyzes the inconsistencies in public support for citizen participation while undermining any real influence for citizen panels in *Maximum Feasible Misunderstanding.*) When the Reagan administration eliminated the requirement for such advisory councils (then primarily related to Chapter I programs for the economically disadvantaged and for bilingual education), the Chicago Board of Education voluntarily voted to continue their existence.

However, in 1970, the Chicago board also voted to establish Local School Advisory Councils (LSAC) at every school in the system (Cibulka, 1975). In about 300 schools, the existing PTA was recognized as the advisory council. In about 200 schools, no PTA existed and new councils were organized, at least on paper. In a small number of schools, Local School Advisory Councils were established in opposition to an existing PTA. Subdistrict advisory councils were also established, with two representatives from each school. Board policy dictated that where both a PTA and an advisory council existed, each would have one delegate to the district council. In some schools, the opposition between the PTA and the advisory council represented a racial split among the parents of the school.

Local School Advisory Councils had two primary duties. The explicit rationale for the existence of LSACs was to advise the principal on the education program of the school. For the most part, these advisory councils provided a context for parents and school activists to discuss with the principal developments at the school. It also provided the principal with an opportunity to encourage parents to support the school with fund-raisers and volunteer efforts. Subdistrict advisory councils had a similar function relative to the district superintendent, but, with both principals and lay members attending their meetings, played the additional role of facilitating coordination discussions between high schools and their feeder elementary schools until 1985 when Superintendent Byrd established separate high school districts. In some parts of the city and in some schools across the city, these advisory councils fostered genuine collaboration between principals and parent groups. In a few places they were the site of confrontation and a place to organize marches on the board of education to get an unwanted principal transferred, a tactic that seemed to be effective for one or two schools every year. At a number of schools, the LSAC existed only on paper.

At some schools, the advisory councils, just like the federal advisory councils, were rubber stamps for the principal. This was particularly notable in those schools where the federal advisory councils, which were still supposed to sign off on program decisions involving federal funds, were served by officers who were also employed out of those federal funds as aides or community relations staff. Under those conditions, advisory council presidents were known to sign off on anything a principal requested.

The second duty of Local School Advisory Councils was to be involved in the process of selecting a principal when a new one was needed. When a vacancy occurred in the principalship, the Local School Advisory Council was instructed to establish a principal search committee. The position would be advertised in the general superintendent's weekly bulletin, and candidates who had already been certified by the board of examiners would apply. Usually a school would receive 15 to 20 applications. The search committee would interview each of these candidates and would frequently visit the schools of the highest-ranked candidates or would interview their current supervisors if they were not already acting as a principal in another school. The committee would then recommend their top three choices; these recommendations were usually approved by the Local School Advisory Council, though they need not have been. The recommendations were submitted to the general superintendent who then made his choice for formal recommendation to the board of education. Although the board's rules indicated that choices were not to be ranked, in practice, search committees almost invariably submitted their choices in rank order. The last superintendent to operate under this procedure, Dr. Byrd, indicated that in most cases, schools received their first choice as the new principal. Still there were a number of well-publicized cases in which a favorite of the general superintendent or of the local district superintendent was installed despite the extensive search and recommendation process.

Thus, it is important to note that, although some unknowledgeable critics have questioned the capacity of parents to select their educational leader, in fact, parents had been doing just that for a number of years in Chicago. The *new* power they were to assume, through the Local School Councils, along with their community resident and teacher colleagues, was the ability to *terminate* a principal at the end of his or her employment term. While not formally the case, in the sense of ability to make a binding choice, advisory councils, in practice, previously had had the capacity to select their principals. Their new power was to be able to correct a mistake in the selection process or to respond to changing conditions that indicated new leadership would be preferable to a continuation of the old leadership. It was the capacity to change educational leadership that was new, not the initial selection power.

In 1985, the General Assembly of Illinois enacted a statewide school reform measure (P.A. 84-126). In the last week of the legislative session, which had been combining various provisions from at least five major statewide proposals (cf. Nelson, Hess, & Yong, 1985), the Speaker of the House of Representatives inserted a provision in the bill to create state-mandated Local School Improvement Councils in every school in cities with a population exceeding 500,000. Since Chicago is the only such city in Illinois, LSICs were being mandated for every Chicago public school.

Along with the establishment of Local School Improvement Councils, the legislation mandated two new budgetary procedures in the Chicago Public Schools. The bill required that a hearing be conducted at each school during the spring to consider the projected budget for the school for the coming year. The hearing was to be conducted by the president of the LSIC (who could not be the principal) and the budget was to be explained to those gathered by the principal. School budgets were to be sent home to every parent before the budget hearing. At the end of the hearing, a vote of parents, community representatives, and teachers was to determine if the budget was acceptable. If it was not acceptable, the board of education was charged with making "a good faith effort" to meet objections to the budget, which voters could list on their ballot. As has already been noted, in two years operating under this provision, the board did not change a single school budget, though more than 100 were rejected during that period. However, parents, staff, and the principal at each school had had several years of experience with examining, discussing, and voting upon the adequacy of their school budget prior to the passage of the Chicago School Reform Act in 1988. Its budgetary provisions were built upon this foundation of experience.

In addition to considering the budget as a whole, the 1985 legislation also mandated that the LSICs have the power to disapprove planned discretionary spending by the principal. The principal was enjoined from authorizing any discretionary spending without having submitted it for consideration by the LSIC. This mandate was phrased in the negative mode so that LSICs could not prevent necessary spending by inaction. If they did not take action on requests made by the principal within 30 days, the principal was authorized to continue with the spending. In effect, this aspect of the legislation required that LSICs meet monthly during the school year and in each meeting some portion was devoted to making decisions about discretionary spending at the school. In order to frustrate the intent of this provision, the then-sitting board of education severely narrowed the definition of "discretionary" so that very few dollars were really covered under this mandate, but once again, the procedure of regular monthly spending deliberations was established and council members were accustomed to exercising these powers.

The LSICs also assumed the principal nomination powers that had been exercised by the preceding advisory councils. They continued to create nominating committees to screen potential principal candidates and to recommend, in priority order, their choices for a new principal to be assigned.

LSIC membership determination was left to the decision of people at the local school, but it was mandated that at least 70% of the members must be parents. In addition, the LSIC president was required to be a parent. A long and fairly torturous process was undertaken by the deputy superintendent to develop guidelines for the implementation of the 1985 legislation. This process included representatives of the previous advisory councils, of the PTA, and of various groups advocating more public involvement in school decisions. In a number of schools, the LSIC simply replaced the preceding advisory councils, with little noticeable difference, except for the new budgetary responsibilities. In other schools, the PTA created a committee that became the LSIC. This relationship was a bit contorted in that the LSIC committee had the actual power to act on the budget and to select the principal, but the committee was usually dominated by the PTA officers, so that in effect, the PTA controlled the LSIC. This convoluted arrangement was adopted because a provision in the legislation prevented the LSIC from raising funds and most PTAs wanted to be able to continue that practice. To honor that restriction, PTA meetings would be formally adjourned before the LSIC would be convened. Sometimes the LSIC would then adjourn and the PTA meeting would be reopened. In other schools, entirely new organizations were created with broader parent and community representation.

The 1985 session of the General Assembly also adopted a second piece of legislation aimed entirely at the Chicago Public Schools. Called the Urban School Improvement Act, it contained some provisions that were somewhat contradictory with the Chicago-only provisions of the main statewide reform legislation. The main ingredients of the improvement act allowed Local School Councils to opt to create school improvement plans that must then be considered for approval by the board of education. If adopted by the board, the improvement plans would preempt administrators' decisions about the programs of those schools. This bill opened up the debate about school-level program planning, but delays and misdirection by school system administrators effectively prevented any significant efforts to implement school improvement planning under this bill. The Chicago School Reform Act repealed both the LSIC provisions of P.A. 84-126 and the Urban School Improvement Act.

Goaded by the activists seeking to implement both pieces of the 1985 legislation fully and pressured by the sessions of the Mayor's Education Summit, the board of education finally created and adopted a formal policy on community involvement in the local schools in March 1987. (The policy was adopted March 11, 1987, as board report #87-0311-RS1.) This policy was developed at the instigation of one board member, who had formerly been active in the PTA, but was adopted only after extensive negotiations between myself, on behalf of a coalition of groups convened by Chicago United to follow up its 1981 management study, and the board's law department. The policy stated, "The Chicago Board of Education welcomes and solicits the ideas, suggestions, and cooperative efforts of parents and community organizations with the administration and staff of the Chicago Public Schools and pledges to cooperate with them in seeking to improve the quality of our children's education." The policy indicated that, to facilitate this cooperative relationship, it would embark upon a public information campaign, inform parents of their opportunities to affect school decisions, and communicate parents' rights to be involved in their children's education. It directed staff to:

- engage in cooperative planning with parents and community residents to improve the quality of education offered at each school,

- seek the assistance of parents and community residents in resolving problems at all levels,
- facilitate open and honest communication between the Chicago Board of Education and parents and community groups, including the timely release of relevant information about the schools and the school system's performance, management, and finances following written requests for such information, and
- participate in hosting meetings at local levels to vote on the school site budget by April 15.

The policy enjoined staff to act cooperatively with the community in the LSIC's mandates to vote on the discretionary budget of the principal, make recommendations about the employment of staff at the school level, and to make recommendations about school curriculum. However, the board rejected any provisions for disciplining staff who ignored or violated this policy. Instead, it substituted a simple statement that "Consistent with this policy staff shall be accountable for interaction with parents and community representatives." In a milieu in which the general superintendent had already indicated his own resistance to parent and community influence, and in which the board had itself refused to adopt any changes to rejected school budgets, little credence was given to this new policy. Still, it put the board of education on record about its official valuation of the importance of parental and community involvement in the schools.

Thus, the Chicago School Reform Act built upon a long experience with parent and community involvement in local school decision-making. This history of lay involvement had progressed through the stages of support, advising, principal selection, budget consideration, and expenditure control. The school reform act vested formal control in the new local school councils, turning them from being "advisors" with some power into being "deciders" with ultimate authority on most issues. It was a logical extension of the history of lay-dominated councils in the city.

NEW ROLES AS "DECIDERS"

The major authority for school-based management under the Chicago School Reform Act is vested in Local School Councils at every school site. The basic constitution of the LSCs was decided during the Mayor's Education Summit when it was established that the councils would be dominated by parents and community representatives. LSCs have six parents, two community representatives, two teachers, and the principal as their membership. In high schools, a nonvoting student member is also elected. Each member, except for the principal, was elected by others of the same constituency group. In November 1990, this voting pattern was declared unconstitutional by the state Supreme Court and must be changed.

Neither the parents nor the community representatives elected to the LSC may be employed by the board of education. This provision was included to curb two potential abuses. In the New York City decentralization to elementary subdistricts, Local Community Boards frequently became dominated by school union personnel. They had a direct self-interest in the actions of these boards, and they had the political and financial organization to mount credible campaigns for election. This domination by employees was seen to foster political corruption, reports of which were extensively carried in both *The New York Times* and the Chicago papers during the Mayor's Education Summit. Second, the practice of hiring presidents of Chapter I advisory councils as school community representatives was seen to have turned these advisory councils into rubber stamps for dictatorial principals. Since the intent of the legislation was to reorient the accountability of principals from the hierarchy of administrators to those assumed to be more concerned about the achievement of enrolled students, it would be counterproductive to allow LSCs to be dominated by persons responsible for their income to the principal.

As with the earlier LSICs, the president of the Local School Council must be one of the parent members. This provision was included to militate against the perceived likelihood that the principal and teachers might unite and attempt professional domination of the councils. This was a major concern for those groups in the reform effort who focused on lay control as the primary value in school-based management. It was of less concern for those focusing primarily upon the devolution of authority from the central administration. Out of the same perspective, the LSC representative to the subdistrict council was required to be either a parent or community resident member.

As has already been articulated, the major responsibilities of the Local School Councils are the adoption of a school improvement plan, the adoption of a school budget, and the employment of a principal. The Chicago School Reform Act is quite specific on what is involved in creating a school improvement plan. The legislation says:

> A 3 year local school improvement plan shall be developed and implemented at each attendance center. This plan shall reflect the overriding purpose of the attendance center to improve educational quality. The local school principal shall develop a school improvement plan in consultation with the local school council, all categories of school staff, parents and community residents. Once the plan is developed and after the local school council has approved the same, the principal shall be responsible for directing implementation of the plan, and the local school council shall monitor its implementation. After the termination of the initial 3 year plan, a new 3 year plan shall be developed and modified as appropriate on an annual basis. (P.A. 85-1418, Sec. 34-2.4)

The act goes on to list the five priority goals of the school improvement plan: assuring that students achieve proficiency, attend school regularly and graduate at national norm rates, are prepared for further education and employment, and have a common learning experience of high quality. The act then spends two full pages describing the various components of the school improvement plan.

Thus, the primary responsibility for formulating and implementing the school improvement plan rests with the principal, and it has already been described how this changes the role and required skills of principals. But the plan is to be developed in consultation with the Local School Council and parents and community residents. In practice, LSCs have developed committees to work on the school improvement plan, in some cases with multiple subcommittees and with as many as 40 different persons participating.

In a similar fashion, the Local School Council is responsible for adopting an expenditure plan for the school. This budget, based upon a lump-sum allocation to the school from the board of education, should be developed by the principal, again in consultation with the LSC, the Professional Personnel Advisory Committee, and other school personnel. The budget must be "consistent with applicable law and collective bargaining agreements," but LSCs are given the right to seek waivers from board policy and collective bargaining agreements. This right of waivers was confirmed in the contract extension negotiated by the new interim board with the Chicago Teachers Union during August 1989. The lump-sum allocation from the board of education is to be based upon "the school enrollment and the special needs of the student body" (P.A. 85-1418, Sec. 34-2.3).

The third major power of the Local School Councils is the decision about whom to employ as principal of the school. Half of all schools in the system would make that decision in the first year of implementation of the act and half in the second year. The division of schools was to be determined by lot. LSCs had to evaluate their current principal and first decide if they wished to retain that person. If they did not vote to extend the incumbent a new contract, they would create a selection committee and go through a process very similar to the one that had previously existed. However, their pool of available candidates was expanded through the legislation, which prohibited the Chicago Board of Education from enacting any further criteria for appointment as a principal other than that the candidate hold the appropriate administrator certificate from the State Board of Education. Thus, candidates from outside the Chicago system, even from outside the state, could be considered for the first time.

An additional responsibility of the Local School Councils is to reach out to the entire community, parents, residents, and staff, to keep them informed of the actions of the council and to solicit their input. The LSCs are mandated to hold two public hearings to present their school improvement plans and budget, and to receive public comment during those hearings. Beyond that, the reformers saw that the parents on the LSCs would be logical persons to reach out and solicit the active involvement of other parents in the educational program of their children.

Critics of the reform act noted that, at many schools, there would be reduced parent participation in the decision-making body at the local school. They pointed out that under the previously mandated LSICs, 70% of the membership had to be parents, while only 55% of the LSC membership was composed of parents. Further, they noted, LSICs could be much larger than 11 members, and frequently involved 30 to 50 persons. On the other hand, at a fairly sizeable number of schools, perhaps as many as 100, LSICs had existed only on paper.

Therefore, in the training provided to potential candidates for election to the LSCs and provided to LSCs after they were installed, the reform groups regularly urged that LSCs create committees with extensive memberships beyond those of the elected members. In this way, participation of parents and community residents could be expanded beyond the eight who won election. The critics decried the power differential between the elected members and those who merely served on committees, but the reformers pointed out that the advisory capacity of those serving on committees was no less than the advisory powers the entire councils had previously enjoyed prior to the statewide 1985 legislation and that real local control was immeasurably enhanced.

Parents and community members have two responsibilities they do not share with the professional members of the LSC. First, the president of the LSC, as with its predecessor LSIC, must be a parent. Thus, at least one parent on each council must have the skills to conduct a meeting. In that many LSCs have established subcommittees, usually chaired by an LSC member, in practice more than one parent must develop these skills. Second, only parents or community members can be elected to the subdistrict councils. The subdistrict councils have three major responsibilities:

1. To promote dissemination of information and training, coordination of programs among district schools, and to provide voluntary dispute resolution.
2. To evaluate and select a district superintendent to serve under a four-year performance contract in a process similar to that of principal selection.
3. To respond to initiatives of the district superintendent when the D.S. finds a school within the district that is not progressing satisfactorily in implementing its school improvement plan.

The legislation spells out a remediation approach that the D.S., with the concurrence of the district council and the board of education, may utilize to assure that each school in the district makes appropriate progress in improvement.

Because they share power on issues before the Local School Councils, the new powers and roles of parents and community residents under Chicago-style school restructuring are very similar to the new roles and powers of the professional staff. The parents and community residents elected to LSCs are now policymakers at the local school level. They must identify problems faced by the school, examine alternatives (frequently proposed by the principal or other professional staff), and determine a course to be taken. Ideally, policymakers must be able to put aside prejudices and subjective responses to consider the objective facts and evaluate the competing proposed solutions. Critics of the Chicago School Reform Act charged that parents and community residents were not capable of taking such an objective stance. Interestingly, they did not make the same charge about other elected officials from the same communities, nor did they make that charge in reference to school board members elected in the other 970 communities across the state. In fact, policymakers frequently have great trouble meeting the ideal objectivity standard. The democratic process is designed so that when they do not meet that standard, they generally do so in the same direction as the subjectivities of the majority of their fellow citizens, that is, so that they reflect the thinking of their constituency and can win reelection.

A second role expected of parents and community residents serving on the LSCs is that they are the corporate "directors" overseeing the chief executive officer (CEO) of the school. The rhetoric of the business directorate and CEO was extensive during the debate over the Chicago School Reform Act, and Local School Council relationships with principals follow that basic model. The primary responsibility for initiating the school improvement plan and for drafting the budget is given to the principal. He or she is required to consult with the council and with other relevant persons in designing a recommendation to the LSC. The LSC is charged then with considering, amending if necessary, and adopting the plan or budget, responding to the principal's initiative. Similarly, the LSC is charged with evaluating the principal's administration and management of the school under the policies adopted by the LSC or applicable under law, bargaining agreements, or central board policy. Thus, LSC members must resist the temptation, on the one hand, to assume that they are involved in the day-to-day management of the school, and on the other, to assume that they should approve whatever the principal recommends. The directorship responsibilities of LSC membership require a delicate balance between responsibility for setting direction and evaluation of program implementation, both without day-to-day interference.

As has already been suggested for principals and teachers, parents and community residents must become strategic planners under school-based management. The most successful schools under such a governance scheme are those that collaboratively plan for the future. Parents and community residents must be able to participate in the process of goal-setting, designing of broad strategies, and deciding upon implementing tactics in order to adopt appropriate policy directives. For many parents and community residents, this is a new role. Under the previous primarily advisory structures, parents and residents were more frequently in "responding" or "critiquing" roles. They liked or disliked aspects of the school program; they commended or criticized. Rarely were they responsible for designing more appropriate alternatives. But LSC members must be willing to go beyond praising or decrying to create new directions, and to see to it that those new directions are given substance and form. They must participate in the strategic planning process.

The parent and community members of the LSC are seen to have primary responsibility for interpreting the desires of the wider constituency of parents and community residents about the school. This, of course, is at the heart of representative democracy, particularly in those structures with segmented constituencies. The simple answer to the questions "Who speaks for the parents?" and "Who speaks for the community?" is written in the law: their elected representatives. The ultimate judgment about how accurately LSC members have represented their constituency will be made at the next election by the voters from each constituency. LSC members who are judged not to have represented the school's parents or the residents of the community fairly will not be re-elected to office.

But the law requires the LSCs to take steps to be assured that they are aware of the concerns of the parents and the community. As has already been mentioned, they are charged with holding two hearings each year. In addition, in developing the school improvement plan, the LSC is enjoined to survey the concerns of the parents and the community. Thus, parents and residents of the community are given responsibility for seeking out the opinions of their peers and of assuring that those opinions are considered as the school develops policies and implements educational programs.

At the same time, the parent and community members of LSCs are expected to be interpreters to their own constituency of issues at the school. Frequently, issues arise in school communities because parents or residents do not understand actions that staff members have undertaken. In its oversight role, the LSC is the appropriate body to examine those actions. Frequently, the action may arise from policy directions established by the LSC. In those cases, it is the responsibility of the LSC parent and community members to interpret to their constituencies what is happening at the school and why. When the actions in question are the result of LSC decisions, LSC members should assume responsibility for the actions, rather than allow the staff to be criticized inappropriately. In many communities, this will be a new role for parents and residents, as partners in responsibility with the staff, and as interpreters of actions that may be unpopular among some of their constituency.

For LSC members, the role of interpreter may logically extend to that of negotiator. The last few paragraphs have been written as though differences would exist primarily between members of different constituencies: professionals vs. parents or community residents. Certainly this is the perspective from which some reformers have emphasized the lay control aspect of school-based management. In practice, many issues arise at a school that result in different positions by different members of the same constituency. Sometimes it is one group of teachers in conflict with another group, perhaps, one department against another or the extracurricular sponsors or coaches against the classroom teachers. At other times it may be one group of parents opposed to another group of parents, for example over textbook selection or support for athletic teams. The parents on an LSC may themselves be divided over issues or over whether or not to retain the principal. In such situations, these members must learn to be negotiators. They must learn how to discern the primary concerns of competing groups and attempt to find a common ground that can overcome the division. Not all LSC members will be equally adept at this role, just as not all legislators are equally adept at negotiation. Some will reject the role in favor of dogmatic partisanship. But some must emerge, if the LSC is to function smoothly, who can bring together divergent groups with divergent interests.

Finally, parents and community residents must learn how to be accountable for their actions. Critics of the Chicago School Reform Act, particularly the president of the Chicago Principals Association, have charged that "Local School Councils are accountable to no one." In fact, that charge is not true. The reform act explicitly spells out the accountability of LSCs: "All decisions made and actions taken by the local school council in the exercise of its powers and duties shall comply with State and federal laws, all applicable collective bargaining agreements, court orders and rules properly promulgated by the Board" (P.A. 85-1418, Sec. 34-2.3.13). And, as I have pointed out several times, LSC members, like all other elected members, are accountable to the electorate that voted for them and that will decide whether or not to reelect them. LSC members, like other elected representatives, have wrestled with the question of what that accountability means. At one school, which received extensive media coverage over the rejection of its principal, a teacher told me that she had voted to retain the principal against her own better judgment because a majority of the teachers at the school favored the principal's retention. Her own opinion had been formed in observing the principal's unwillingness to work with the new Local School Council. Caught in the conflict between representing her constituency's desires or following her own best judgment, she chose to represent the other teachers. Still, the LSC voted to replace the principal. In retrospect, the teacher told me that she would vote her own judgment in the future.

One concern frequently raised in the debate prior to passage of the reform act centered around the capabilities of parents and community residents who would be elected to Local School Councils. Would they be capable of successfully assuming these roles and responsibilities? The assumption, which was frequently articulated as though it were a fact, was that parents in more affluent neighborhoods would have these abilities, but that they would be sorely lacking in parents from the inner city.

A survey conducted at the behest of *Catalyst,* a school reform journal sponsored by the Community Renewal Society, found that the typical LSC member was a female about 40 years of age, with at least a high school diploma. The average age of parents was lower, at 37, than that of teachers (45), community residents (47), and principals (51). By definition, all principals and teachers are college graduates. The survey found that 25% of parents and 41% of community residents were college graduates. By contrast, only 15% of parents and 11% of community residents had not completed high school. The occupational profile was less encouraging. LSC members spanned a wide range of occupations from professionals to laborers, but 47% of parents and 38% of community members did not list their employment. The majority were experienced council members; 58% had been members of PTAs and 37% had been on an LSIC (Menacker, Herzog, Hurwitz, & Weldon, 1990).

The survey gives no information on the distribution of these various characteristics among different types or locations of schools. But the survey does indicate that the dire characterization of schools across the city being governed by councils of ignorant parents and community residents was, at minimum, overstated.

Further, the design of responsibilities of the Local School Council means that LSC members need not be educational experts. The basic structure of the LSC puts the initiative on educational and budgetary matters in the hands of the professionals: foremost, the principal in consultation with the advisory committee of teachers (PPAC). Thus, parents and community members on the LSC must decide if the professional initiatives will be good for the students enrolled at the school. The lay control of the LSC is designed to prevent the professionals from creating school improvement plans that primarily benefit employees. This is one way in which the Chicago School Reform Act differs significantly from the teacher professionalization approaches to shared decision-making in systems such as Dade County or Hammond, where such controls do not exist structurally. The basic dynamic in Chicago is that of professional initiation and lay-dominated evaluation, adjustment, and adoption.

TRAINING MANDATED FOR LSC MEMBERS

The framers of the Chicago School Reform Act anticipated the need for extensive training for LSC members. The act specifies that LSCs may contract with individuals or nonprofit agencies to provide up to 30 hours of instruction. Many LSCs chose to accept training from the central administration staff or free training provided by nonprofit civic agencies or universities. In any event, the legislation indicated that council members should at least receive training in school budgets, educational theory as it applies to their own school, and personnel selection (P.A. 85-1418, Sec. 34-2.3.10). It was anticipated that a widespread and massive training effort would be launched to support the initiation of Local School Councils.

The board of education did make available $1,500 to each LSC to fund contracts to provide training. The board also established a Parent Training Center to coordinate the training that its own staff would provide. The nonprofit reform groups who were instrumental in the drafting and passage of the Chicago School Reform Act also coordinated their training efforts to provide as wide a coverage as possible to fledgling LSCs. In the next chapter, I shall comment on the successes and failures of that training effort.

Just as for the professional staff, the Chicago School Reform Act has established a set of new roles and responsibilities for parents and community residents. As Anne Henderson and Carl Marburger envisioned, these are responsibilities *Beyond the Bake Sale* (Henderson, Marburger, & Ooms, 1986). Some 3,252 parents and 1,084 community residents are now elected officials, gaining training and experience in carrying out these new roles on LSCs. It does not take great vision to see that the sudden creation of such a body of newly elected, grassroots officials has implications for community empowerment far beyond the restructuring of the public schools in Chicago.

Initial Implementation

On December 12, 1988, Governor James R. Thompson signed the Chicago School Reform Act during the opening ceremonies at a brand new elementary school building in a regentrifying area near the West Side University of Illinois Medical Center. The bill was essentially the legislation negotiated during the four days of meetings in Speaker Madigan's offices late in June but contained the compromises worked out following the governor's amendatory veto. The bill had passed the legislature with commanding majorities in both houses; only one senator and nine representatives voted against the bill.

Reform activists had worked diligently to get the legislation passed prior to the June 30 legislative deadline for immediate implementation. They were sorely disappointed when the bill did not pass until July 2. During the weeks following the close of the legislative session, the leaders of the reform group met repeatedly with members of the Speaker's staff to strategize about securing the governor's signature on the bill. They were bitterly disappointed when the governor used his amendatory veto to correct some technical problems (which even they agreed needed to be fixed) and to add some controversial measures of his own. They had worked diligently to force the governor and the legislative leaders to reach a compromise on the governor's issues, which were seen to be of secondary importance to the main thrust of the bill. They were elated when the compromise was achieved and the bill was passed, now with overwhelming bipartisan support. But, they were still disappointed that the act had not been passed quickly enough to be implemented during the fall of 1988.

In retrospect, however, the half year of planning to implement reform proved to be critically important. The reform act was extensive and complex. Its 123 pages included changes in many dimensions of the operations of the Chicago Public Schools. While most of its provisions focused on new opportunities for decision-making and operations at the local school level, there were many changes in the overall structure of the system. These systemwide changes were outlined in the bill, but the specific means of implementation had to be planned locally.

Further, the framers of the legislation did not fully envision the complexity of integrating the new provisions of the act with the ongoing responsibilities of school-level administrators to comply with provisions of the school code that were not changed. The first year of implementation proved to be far more complex and confusing than the reformers had anticipated. Some reformers argued that the confusion was intentionally fomented by recalcitrant central office administrators, which was undoubtedly true to some extent. But it must also be acknowledged that the reformers underestimated the difficulty of the tasks set before the newly elected councils, and in their interest in preserving choices for these councils, compounded the situation by requiring councils to make quick choices about critical issues, such as State Chapter I spending, immediately after they were elected and before they had even received any training. The first year had been envisioned as a relaxed year of training and planning. It turned out to be a hectic and confusing year at most schools, and a very turbulent one at some schools. It was extremely fortunate that political wrangling delayed implementation until 1989.

EFFORTS OF THE EXISTING BOARD AND ADMINISTRATION

Under the reform act (P.A. 85-1418), the existing board of education was to be replaced when the act became effective, July 1, 1989. The board was also mandated to conduct a national search for a general superintendent. Superintendent Byrd's contract with the board was to expire on March 26, 1989. The current board had already authorized a national search and had secured the assistance of the Illinois Association of School Boards to carry out the initial stages of that search and to narrow down the initial list of candidates to a short list of five. Superintendent Byrd had been invited to be one of the finalists, if he chose to apply for reappointment. Eventually, in March, the board extended Dr. Byrd's contract for one year to allow the soon-to-be-installed interim board of education to select the general superintendent who would implement the school reform act.

After the act was signed into law, Superintendent Byrd became more conciliatory. He quickly announced that he intended to live by the provisions of the act, though he still disagreed with its basic thrust. "It's the law!" he proclaimed over and over. Some members of the board of education began to focus on preparations to implement reform. Others, such as Francis Davis, an employee of Operation Push, decried the bill as a "deform" act aimed at taking power away from the black superintendent and from black contractors.

Dr. Byrd quickly organized his administrative leadership to develop a plan to implement the legislation. He created a Reform Implementation Task Force. He entrusted the planning process to his director of operations analysis and planning, Maxey Bacchus. The task force established 18 subtask forces, through which nearly 400 district-, central office-, and school-level staff worked with parents, members of civic organizations, university faculty, and staff from the Illinois State Board of Education to propose guidelines and policies to implement the Chicago School Reform Act.

The soon-to-be-supplanted board of education also reacted aggressively to prepare the system for reform. It created an ad hoc school reform committee, which designed a rigid timetable for interim and then final reports from each of the 18 task forces, based on a timeline developed by Maxey Bacchus. The individual task forces met weekly, for the most part, to meet strict deadlines so that their recommendations could be reviewed by the overall task force and the superintendent before going to the board's reform committee. Initially, task force chairs were permitted to choose whether or not to include members who were not employed by the system, but after a protest from the Chicago Panel, parents and representatives from civic and community organizations were included on virtually every planning task force. In the final analysis, about 68% of the task force members were board of education employees, 15% were parent representatives, and 17% were representatives of independent organizations. These outside participants had significant effect on some task forces, while on others their participation was disdainfully tolerated and ignored in the submitted reports. Staff of the Chicago Panel or its member organizations served on 14 of the 18 task forces.

In March, the board's committee on reform began a series of twice-a-month meetings to review interim and final reports from each task force. A third of the task forces reported at each committee meeting. The reform committee members severely criticized initial task force reports for recommending bureaucratic growth as the way to implement school reform. Resistant and defiant administrators typically approached the planning process in top-down fashion, translating every mandate in the reform act into a requirement for new administrative positions responsible for its implementation, all this despite the provision imposing a cap on administrative expenses.

It was the intent of the board's committee on reform and the director of operations analysis and planning to push the planning process through to completion to produce a set of reports that would form the basis of the systemwide educational reform goals and objectives plan that the board of education was mandated to submit to the Chicago School Finance Authority by August 1, 1989 (P.A. 85-1418, Sec. 34A-412). The final report of the implementation task forces totaled over 600 pages of background information and recommendations.

In its newsletter of June 1989, participating staff of the Chicago Panel and its member organizations provided an assessment of the task force planning and noted that most of the task force recommendations met the requirements of the law, but only grudgingly. Frequently the recommendations did not go far enough to implement the law adequately, and some of the recommendations completely ignored the intent of the reform act. The newsletter summarized the report of each task force and assigned a grade in evaluation of its product. The report is reproduced here in its entirety to provide a sense of the range and extent of planning that was necessary to launch the reform effort.

	Grade
Elections and Operations of Local School Councils Produced a comprehensive guide for Local School Councils.	A
Local School Council Training Good use of volunteer trainers, but doesn't allow Local School Councils to screen outside trainers.	C–
Monitoring and Evaluating Local School and District Councils Totally distorted the reason for Local School Council monitoring.	F
School Improvement Plans Report shows no understanding of reason for improvement planning; undermines next year's school improvement plans.	F
Lump-Sum Budgeting Good fund allocation to schools, but doesn't really describe how Local School Councils can spend the funds.	B+
Principals and Teachers Generally a good report that could use more imagination and innovation.	B+
Personnel Training Unclear report that deals with passing along information rather than training personnel.	D
1993 College Entrance Requirements No discussion of curriculum modifications or role of Local School Councils; ignores research on retention.	D
System-Wide Curriculum Objectives and Standards Understands the role of the local school in shaping curriculum.	A–
Mandated Objectives Lets the central office dictate annual goals for each school rather than letting each school set its own goals as reform statute intended.	C
State Title I Only partially reflects the intent of shifting State Title I funds by failing to establish an equitable funding base for all schools.	D
Administrative Cap Openly recognizes the legislative intent, but looks for loopholes around it.	B+
Financial Support Straightforward estimates of cost.	A
Pre-School Education Too much reliance on standard operating procedures, and on extensive busing of four-year-olds.	D+

Facilities D
Failed to establish any policies; merely a plan to plan.
Too top-down in orientation.
Special Students D
Unclear report uses legislation to solve current problems.
Misses legislative intent.
Desegregation F
Report tries to stem the tide of reform rather than implement it.
Restructuring Decisionmaking C+
Well-done report, but doesn't shift decisionmaking far enough, namely to the local schools. (*Chicago Panel,* 1989a)

The participation in the board's planning task forces by members of the reform groups was coordinated through a more formal alliance created by the reform activists. A group of about 50 reform activists and other interested organizational representatives held a weekend retreat at a suburban conference center on the weekend between the passage of the reform legislation and its signing by the governor on December 12. At the retreat a Citywide School Reform Coalition was established, with task forces focused upon community organizing, parent training, reform monitoring, principals' involvement, and teaching and learning. The reform monitoring task force, cochaired by the Chicago Panel, recruited independent representation on each of the board's planning task forces and coordinated the assessment of the final report reproduced here. Other citywide coalition task forces began to develop a common curriculum for training programs conducted by the various reform groups, common organizing strategies in preparation for Local School Council elections, and strategies for involving progressive principals and teachers in planning for reform at the school level.

During the spring of 1989, the two major business organizations active in school reform announced the creation of a new organization that would unify the business voice on school reform and would signal its intent to be involved continuously in the implementation of reform, not just its legislative enactment. The new organization was eventually called Leadership for Quality Education (LQE), and it was to become a major player during the first year of reform implementation. Joseph Reed, a vice president at AT&T, was persuaded to take early retirement to become the president of LQE.

INTERACTION WITH MAYORAL POLITICS

As has already been noted, Mayor Harold Washington died only a few months into his second term as Chicago's first black mayor. He was replaced by another black, Sixth Ward Alderman Eugene Sawyer. However, Sawyer was elected as the nominee of Washington's former all-white opposition block. His election split the Washington coalition of blacks, Hispanics, and progressive (primarily lakefront) white aldermen. It also split the black political community into those who wanted to recreate the Washington legacy and those who were more interested in "keeping the seat." Washington's former floor leader, Alderman Timothy Evans, created a city council opposition block composed of the more progressive elements of the former Washington coalition. Black alderman whose roots were in the Democratic machine but who had virtually been forced to line up with Washington after his election in 1983, joined the white Washington opposition to elect and support Sawyer. Unified support for Sawyer, however, was short lived.

Because Washington died with more than half of his term remaining, a special interim election was required under recently enacted state law. Evans and his supporters brought suit against the board of elections to force them to conduct the special election, which was then scheduled for March 1989. By December 1988, as the reform law was being signed into law, it became apparent that State's Attorney "Richie" Daley, son of the former mayor, intended to run in the interim election. Daley had been blamed for splitting the white vote in the 1983 primary, when Washington won with a plurality of only 36% of the Democratic voters. Mayor Byrne received 34% of the vote, and Daley claimed 30% (Holli & Green, 1989). Now Daley stood to be the white candidate who would benefit from Sawyer and Evans splitting the black vote.

In January 1989, Daley announced that school reform would be a cornerstone of his campaign for mayor. He recruited a number of white and Hispanic reform activists to help shape his reform platform. Daley's adoption of the school reform platform was in line with his earlier adoption of other issues (e.g., improving mental health efforts) that were attractive to the progressive wing of the Democratic party, which was particularly influential along Chicago's lakefront. The white liberal lakefront vote had been key to Washington's narrow 1983 electoral victories and the more comfortable 1987 victory over Edward Vrdolyak (Holli & Green, 1989). Daley's campaign strategy appeared to focus on recapturing the Hispanic and lakefront vote, which could provide a margin of victory even against a united black vote.

Acting Mayor Sawyer had been less than enthusiastic about school reform from the moment he was elected in December 1987. His support of the mayor's Education Summit was lukewarm, at best. As the summit was moving toward its fruition, he stripped Washington's chief policy advisor, Hal Baron, of responsibility for managing the summit process and vested that authority in his newly appointed chief advisor, Erwin France. France, a prominent black consultant, had been politically well connected for decades, serving as Richard J. Daley's head of the model cities program in the 1970s. In a highly unusual move, Sawyer then appointed France to the board of education, where he served while continuing as the chief advisor to the mayor. France was well connected with the traditional black political and social establishment in the city, including Superintendent Byrd and groups like Operation Push. France represented the mayor and the board in the meetings in Speaker Madigan's office when the reform act was finally put together. His had not been an active voice for radical reform.

When Daley pre-empted the school reform issue, he injected racial politics into the reform effort. By attacking Sawyer for not being aggressive on reforming the city's schools, and by attacking the administration of the school system, then led by the first black superintendent elevated from the ranks of local administrators, he crystallized radical black political opposition to school reform. After his victory over Sawyer in the primary election and over Evans in the general election, Daley's every action on school reform was met by opposition in the black political community, who tried to use opposition to Daley's schools agenda to reunite the former Sawyer and Evans forces. Black political leaders, such as Robert Starks (Black Task Force for Political Empowerment), Conrad Worrill (Black United Front), and Jesse Jackson (Operation Push), sought to portray school reform as Daley's vehicle for reasserting white control of the school system and of school contracts (e.g., Starks, 1990). However, this confrontation over city racial politics eclipsed the genuine school reform interest of many groups in the black community and of many involved parents.

Daley's victory significantly affected the way school reform would be implemented. Shortly after his election, sympathetic legislators amended the school reform act to move forward its implementation date to May 1, 1989. This allowed Daley to appoint the new interim board before school closed for the summer, giving them an earlier start on shaping a reform plan and reshaping the system's budget. In addition, in the closing days of the legislative session, his forces pushed through the General Assembly a temporary income tax increase, half of which would be distributed to municipalities across the state (thereby eliminating a projected city budget deficit) and half of which would go to school districts. This extra state funding was to allow the interim board to extend the existing employee contracts with a significant raise and assure the timely opening of school.

On May 26, 1989, Mayor Daley announced the appointment of seven members as the new interim board of education. He also announced the appointment of a deputy mayor for education, Lourdes Monteagudo, the young, reform-minded principal of Sabin Elementary School. Daley had persuaded James W. Compton, president of the Chicago Urban League, to agree to lead the interim board. He also appointed William Singer, a former alderman and leader of the independent opposition in the city council. Prior to an ingloriously failed 1975 campaign for mayor against Richard J. Daley, the current mayor's father, Singer had published his own little-noticed study of the failings of the Chicago school system. Now he was to be Richard M. Daley's point man on the school board's budget and labor contracts. Daley further appointed Joseph Reed (the president of LQE), Joan Jeter Slay (a staff person for Designs for Change), and Adela Coronado-Greely (an Hispanic teacher active in Parents United for Responsible Education, known as PURE). These three new appointees had firm connections to the former school reform groups. The remaining slots were filled with a little-known Asian academic, William Liu, who was the only carry-over appointment from the previous board of education, and an even less-known black West Side preacher, Janis Sharpe. Thus the interim board was composed of three blacks (Compton, Slay, Sharpe), two whites (Singer and Reed), one Hispanic, and one Asian. Compton, Singer, and Reed were to emerge as the leaders of the interim board, though some black political activists immediately labeled Compton as merely a symbolic front for Singer and Reed.

THE INTERIM BOARD'S FOUR MIRACLES

The new interim board took office in a flurry of activity. Less than three weeks after being appointed, at its first meeting, the board responded to testimony from various reform groups and unanimously rejected both the proposed reform plan and the tentative budget for 1989-1990 put forward by Superintendent Byrd. In very direct language the board members instructed the superintendent that they would not do "business as usual," and they would not accept a plan or a budget that did not reflect the basic intent of the reform legislation. The interim board adopted a stripped-down committee structure with only three committees: budget and finance, reform implementation, and management and operations. Singer was appointed chair of budget and finance and was charged with developing a new budget that would reduce the size of the administration (Byrd's tentative budget would have increased the administrative staff!) and to negotiate new employee agreements. Slay was appointed chair of reform implementation to develop a new reform plan and prepare for the LSC elections. Liu was appointed chair of management and operations and delegated to keep the system operating while major changes were being fashioned. Compton appointed himself to chair a committee of the whole to conduct the national search for a new superintendent.

At the board's first meeting, Singer moved to defer action on any normal spending items in an effort to focus the board's attention on policy issues, not normal administrative trivia. The board's lobbyists quickly pushed a measure through the General Assembly that allowed the board to delegate to the general superintendent responsibility for most of the day-to-day appointments and spending decisions that had clogged the agenda of former boards of education. While some observers worried about giving such responsibilities to a general superintendent in whom the board had already demonstrated a lack of confidence, this legislation allowed the board to concentrate on what Singer referred to as the board's "list of miracles."

Following the board's initial meeting, Singer established a "transition budget task force" to reduce the size of the central and district office staff and to reallocate funds toward local schools, as mandated under the reform act. The task force was composed of selected administrative staff, some school-level staff, outside volunteers, and some "loaned staff." The John D. and Catherine T. MacArthur Foundation provided funds to several nonprofit agencies to support the loaned staff and to the board to underwrite reform planning costs. The task force was chaired by the Chicago Panel's assistant director, Diana Lauber. After weeks of exhaustive work, the task force provided the board with a revised budget that cut more than 500 jobs out of the central and district offices and moved $40 million to local school budgets, thereby funding the first year of reallocations toward schools with high enrollments of disadvantaged students under the State Chapter I provisions of the reform act. Another 1,000 positions were designated for eventual elimination or reassignment to individual schools. The reallocation of the $40 million meant that the average elementary school received $90,000 in new discretionary funding for the first year of reform (Chicago Panel, 1989b; a fuller analysis of the staff changes was published in the January *Panel Update,* Chicago Panel, 1990a).

During the same period, Compton and Singer were negotiating directly with the board's employee unions to secure a contract extension that would complete the budget process. In late July, union contract extensions were agreed to, guaranteeing a timely opening of schools in the fall. This early agreement was in stark contrast to the previous history of 9 strikes in 18 years. The contract with the Chicago Teachers Union also contained language confirming the reform act's provisions about teacher selection, remediation, and contract waivers, thereby eliminating concerns about labor disputes in these critical areas of reform. Under Singer's leadership, the board also settled two pending litigations, signing consent decrees with the federal government committing the board to more rapid assessment of students recommended for special education placement, and committing the board to rectifying discriminatory underfunding of athletic programs for females. Each of these actions underscored the interim board's intent to serve students better as it moved to implement reform.

During October 1989, the interim board finally completed work on its two other "miracles." After a tension-filled struggle with Superintendent Byrd, the board converted his contract into a consulting relationship in August and appointed another long-time black administrator, Charles Almo, as interim superintendent. Board members were embarrassed when Almo took the opportunity of his introductory press conference to blast the board for dumping Dr. Byrd. It was obvious that Almo's days were also numbered. However, the board was finding that its national search was not as productive as it had expected. Due to the unexpected death of Chancellor Richard Greene of the New York City public school system, several large urban districts were seeking minority superintendents at the same time. At least one of the board's primary candidates did not pass a background check, forcing a reopening of the search. In October, the board settled on Ted D. Kimbrough, then superintendent of the Compton, California, schools. Kimbrough had worked in the Los Angeles schools for 26 years prior to moving to Compton as superintendent in 1983; he had risen to assistant superintendent in the L.A. district, the nation's second largest. Unfortunately, however, Kimbrough was not available to assume his Chicago duties until January of 1990, leaving the board dependent upon Interim Superintendent Almo, with whom relations were already strained.

Finally, as has already been reported, on October 11 and 12, 1989, Local School Councils were elected at 542 schools. More than 313,000 persons voted in the elections at the elementary schools on the first day and at the high schools the second. While 65,000 of these voters were high school students voting for nonvoting members on the secondary school councils, the remaining voters still represented 16% of total registered voters in Chicago, as compared to voter turnout for Cook County suburban board of education elections of only 12%. Fewer than 2% of the LSCs did not elect a full slate of members, a problem easily corrected at the first meeting of these LSCs (Faulkner, 1990). All of this occurred amid dire predictions in the daily media that shortages of candidates could appear at more than half of the city's schools.

In short, in the interim board's first four months, it accomplished four of the five miracles it set for itself in its first meeting. The only uncompleted task was the development of an adequate systemwide reform plan. Using a process similar to that used to reshape the board's budget, Joan Jeter Slay appointed a special task force of staff and volunteers to redraft the board's reform plan. Distracted by the need also to design a training program for parents and potential LSC candidates and frustrated by resistance from administrative staff, Slay made little progress in putting together a reform plan before the opening of school. A small group of reform activists--led by Don Moore, the executive director of Slay's own organization, Designs for Change—compiled a draft plan with 42 goals embodying the central elements of the reform act. Detail, however, was sparse. The plan did commit the system to working toward reaching national norms in student achievement, it focused attention on local school initiatives toward achieving that end, and it designated central and district office resources as the source of support for reform. Although lacking in detail required by the Chicago School Finance Authority (CSFA), which had been given oversight responsibility to monitor the implementation of reform, the plan was submitted to meet legally mandated reporting deadlines.

Successive iterations of this plan were developed under planning chief Bacchus. Later editions of the plan eliminated the more radical provisions of the "outsiders" plan, particularly those goals that focused on restructuring the central administration. As each plan submission was rejected, it became clear that the first year of reform implementation would be over before an acceptable plan would be submitted. It also became clear that the finance authority did not intend to evaluate the educational adequacy of the board's plan; it would only judge the plan on the basis of whether it met the individual regulations promulgated by the authority. Finally, in August 1990, following the recommendations of its consultant, Fenwick English, the CSFA approved 40% of the plan submitted for the 1990-1991 school year, even though English had called the plan "extremely conservative" (*Chicago Tribune,* August 15, 1990). The authority indicated that, if the implementing detail, summarizations of LSC plans, and accompanying cost projections were included in the board's next submission (due within 60 days), it was likely the entire plan would be adopted. Only authority member David Heller objected that such a conservative plan would be inadequate to create the change in Chicago schools that was desperately needed. Members of the authority never discussed the adequacy of the goals included in the plan, nor whether the plan's strategies would achieve either the plan's goals or the goals incorporated in the reform act.

OUTSIDE SUPPORT FOR REFORM

Had the school system been left to its own devices to implement school reform, the first year would have been a disaster. However, the groups active in designing the reform act and in pushing it through to enactment maintained their effort to improve Chicago's schools. In addition, once the reform act became law, groups that had not been involved in the effort and groups that had opposed dimensions of the reform proposals began to mobilize their own resources to provide assistance to individual schools and the system as a whole. One of the results of enacting reform legislation was a massive expansion of the number and kinds of people offering their assistance to the public schools.

The Chicago School Reform Act explicitly recognized the need for extensive training for Local School Council members. The act gives LSCs the right to direct the board "to contract with personnel or not-for-profit organizations not associated with the school district to train or assist council members" (P.A. 85-1418, Sec. 34-2.3.10). The board's obligation was limited to up to 30 hours of training per year. The law requires that council members shall receive training in at least the following areas:

1. School budgets.
2. Educational theory pertinent to the attendance center's particular needs, including the development of the school improvement plan and the principal's performance contract.
3. Personnel selection. (P.A. 85-1418, Sec. 34-2.3.10)

As has already been noted, during the spring of 1989, the Citywide Coalition for School Reform established a training task force that worked throughout the spring to design a common, comprehensive curriculum to be utilized by all members in providing training to potential LSC candidates before the election and to LSC members once the councils were established. Designs for Change, whose staff had provided leadership in the training task force, produced the most finished version of this curriculum in a bound volume titled *Kids First* (Designs for Change, 1989). Each organization developed its own set of workshop materials, built on the common curriculum design, and each developed its own pedagogical style and program emphasis. More than 35 groups established their own training efforts. Together, the major training groups, such as Designs for Change, the Chicago Panel, United Neighborhood Organization, Parents United for Responsible Education, and the Chicago Region PTA, provided training to more than 6,000 potential candidates before the elections. This represented about a third of the 17,000 persons who actually ran for election to a Local School Council. After the LSC elections in October, these organizations provided training opportunities attended by more than 10,000 participants. In most instances, LSC members who took training attended more than one session, and they frequently attended sessions conducted by different organizations, thereby exposing themselves to more than one perspective about the reform act. Best estimates are that the average LSC member attended two training sessions averaging two and one half hours in length. In addition, the board of education's Parent Training Center, with six full-time staff, claimed to have provided six or seven training sessions each week at the board's central offices or in schools across the system. Unfortunately, independent assessments regularly found the board's training confusing and self-contradictory while that provided by the reform groups was much more helpful (Bedard, Shauri, & Millender, 1990).

In addition to these more formal training sessions, a number of informational conferences and workshops were conducted by various groups. More than 1,000 parents, teachers, and principals jammed into the Hyatt Regency Hotel on Saturday, April 8, 1989, to participate in the Educational Partnership Conference. The partnership theme was designed to focus on the collaborative effort needed to improve local schools and reflected the diversity of the sponsoring groups: the Chicago Panel on Public School Policy and Finance, the Chicago Principals Association, the Chicago Region PTA, the Chicago Teachers Union, the Chicago Urban League, Citizens Schools Committee, and United Neighborhood Organization. Workshops explained the rights and responsibilities of Local School Councils, Professional Personnel Advisory Committees, and principals. Leaders outlined ways to promote effective communications within a school community. The plenary session speaker, Tom Corcoran of Rutgers University, spoke to the effect on school improvement efforts of staff working conditions in urban schools.

The conference was so well attended that the Citizens Schools Committee (CSC) scheduled a follow-up conference titled *21st Century Schools: How to Make Schools Work for Our Children.* Held two months later, it, too, attracted 1,000 participants. Similar conferences were scheduled by CSC and other sponsors, such as the Community Renewal Society and Roosevelt University, throughout the first year of implementation. Participation in these special conferences was in addition to the training programs already described.

Still, at the end of the first year of implementation, LSC members complained that they had not received adequate training for their task. In the ideal vision of the reformers, LSC members would have had several months to receive training before embarking upon their major tasks of principal evaluation/selection, school improvement planning, and budget setting. In reality, even before LSCs had organized, selected officers, and set meeting schedules, let alone written bylaws, they were informed that they must immediately decide how they would use their new discretionary State Chapter I funds, because the board was required to compile all of their decisions and report on the use of the funds to the Illinois State Board of Education by December 1, 1989! Thrust into making immediate decisions, which were frequently divisive, training was put aside, delayed, and fragmented. Frequently LSCs never did decide to secure common training, leaving individual members to attend training sessions on a "catch as catch can" basis. Meanwhile, the reform groups were training more people than they had ever previously served, and their resources were stretched to the limit.

In cooperation with the training efforts of nonprofit groups in the city, a number of large businesses actively encouraged their employees to become involved at their local schools. They arranged with the reform groups to offer preelection training to groups of interested employees during working hours and utilizing the company training facilities. Businesses such as Illinois Bell, AT&T, Harris Bank, First National Bank, Amoco, and Blue Cross provided such training, and in some cases provided continual training and support to those employees who won election to the councils. While in some quarters skepticism was expressed that this was a big business effort to capture control of the schools, our own experience with several of these companies revealed no overt or covert efforts of the business community to influence their employees to represent the company's interests or beliefs about schools and their communities. Our initial assessment has been that this was a genuine effort of the business community to encourage their employees to be good citizens even as the businesses were seeking to exercise their own civic responsibility in more direct action.

Business leaders had played an important role in the effort to enact reform legislation. Chicago United was active in bringing together civic groups and businessmen to act on their common concern. It was able to bring the secretary of education to Chicago to focus national attention on the problems of the city's schools.

With its counterpart, the Civic Committee of the Commercial Club, it mobilized business executives to lobby directly for passage of the reform act. After the legislation passed, these two groups combined to create Leadership for Quality Education (LQE) to be an enduring presence of the business community during the reform implementation stage. LQE's board was composed of equal representation from each of the founding organizations, augmented by several community-based educational activists. As has already been indicated, LQE's president was appointed a member of the interim board.

LQE quickly secured the financial commitment of nearly a million dollars from its sponsoring businesses and a few foundations. Some of those funds were used to sponsor training events for principals or special projects to support the board of education. LQE's leaders were able to convince philanthropic foundations to support other projects, such as the budget and reform planning transition task forces. Its most massive effort was suggested and engineered by the community-based members on its board.

During the summer of 1989, LQE distributed a request for proposals to community-based organizations across the city. The proposals were to show how potential grantees would use funds provided by the business community to organize an adequate supply of candidates to run for election to the Local School Councils and how they would mobilize a massive turnout on the election days. In July, LQE made the first awards of some $780,000, which they would grant to about 30 community organizations and civic groups across the city. The grants were carefully selected to assure the broadest possible coverage of the city's schools, with as little overlap as possible. An army of organizers, with roots in the local communities, hit the streets with a single purpose during the late summer and early fall. The organizers were required to attend citywide training sessions about the reform law and about effective voter organizing. A condition of the grants was that receiving organizations could not sponsor or endorse any particular candidates. The effort was mounted as a nonpartisan, get-out-the-vote campaign. An independent assessment by *Catalyst* was headlined, "Money made difference in voter turnout" (Joravsky, 1990). The article quoted Joe Reed, LQE's president, as saying, "I consider the turnout extraordinary, given the impediments we faced. Turnout was low in some black schools because these were the areas where skepticism about reform was strongest." The article asserted that "corporate money and aggressive community organizing generated big vote tallies in some unlikely places. . . . The powerful combination thrust some schools in impoverished black and Hispanic neighborhoods ahead of several largely white schools on the Northwest and Southwest sides, reversing traditional voting patterns."

Other observers noted that the organizing effort would have far broader political implications in the city. Joravsky noted that the United Neighborhood Organization (UNO), with branches then in five different communities across the city, primarily in Hispanic neighborhoods, was "the biggest winner" and was becoming a political force to be recognized. UNO's executive director, Dan Solis, coordinated the citywide organizing effort. He had been an early supporter of Richard Daley; his close colleague, Lourdes Monteagudo, was appointed deputy mayor; and Solis and Monteagudo were appointed by the mayor to the nominating commission, which would provide the mayor with slates of candidates to be appointed to the permanent board of education. One of the potentially important side effects of the Chicago school reform effort is the increased empowerment of inner-city citizens now involved in council election campaigns in their local neighborhoods, in winning a public office, and in serving on councils that are scrutinized by other community residents. The potential political impact of decentralized school-based management is enormous and will be closely watched.

Following the LSC elections, these community-based groups found themselves with organizers whose salaries had been provided for another nine months, but whose primary purpose had already been accomplished. The citywide coalition's organizing task force, which was virtually identical with the LQE organizers' meetings and which was led by UNO's Solis, sought to provide some common focus to efforts citywide. But, inevitably, these turf-oriented organizers began focusing on specific educational problems, and frequently ended up competing for school system resources. The Organization of the North East released a study of desegregation funding showing that minority students in schools in their area, many of whom were higher-achieving Asian students, received less funding than students in other parts of the city, and advocated far more funds for their students. Further to the north, GRADE, a joint effort of the Rogers Park Tenants Committee and the Nortown Civic League, focused on overcrowding and fostered the creation of a subdistrict overcrowding committee. They utilized the clout of the chair of the Illinois Senate Education Committee, who represented part of that area and claimed authorship of the reform bill because it came out of his legislative committee. The northside overcrowding committee was able to extort a promise to provide additional mobile classrooms to their northside community, while the more seriously overcrowded Hispanic neighborhoods on the southwestside got nothing.

Apparently bothered by the political implications of the organizing effort, LQE decided not to extend the grant program into a second year. In some parts of the city, with the loss of funds, organizers' efforts turned away from the schools as quickly as they had turned toward them the previous year. In other parts of the city, it appears that enduring relationships have been forged that are not as easily abandoned. In the absence of the organizing effort, LQE's major thrust entering the second year of reform implementation was unclear to outside observers. Its staff continued to provide organizational support for citywide reform efforts and to particular projects for the board of education. It provided support to the new superintendent's nationwide search for seven top administrative positions. It continued to play an active role in trying to shape the board's budget, particularly in ensuring a continued downsizing of the central administrative units. Beyond that, at the end of the first year of implementation, the thrust of the business community was uncertain.

In addition to the ongoing efforts of the nonprofit groups and the business community, a new level of volunteer assistance to the Chicago Public Schools emerged. Although the school system previously had worked hard to attract business interest through its Adopt-A-School effort, one example of which was examined in Chapter 2, and through its volunteer network, outsiders with significant expertise had few opportunities or little inclination to try to assist the public schools. With the launching of the school reform effort and the new responsibilities delegated to Local School Councils, a new need for expertise that could be made available to local schools became evident. Professionals in the city organized to fill that need.

During the spring of 1989, two public-interest legal groups joined forces to create the Lawyers Advisory Project on School Reform. The brainchild of Alex Polikoff of Business and Professional People in the Public Interest (BPI) and Ros Lieb of the Lawyers Committee for Civil Rights Under the Law, the project recruited lawyers to provide pro bono legal advice to LSCs as they were getting organized and as they entered into the principal selection process. More than a hundred lawyers volunteered their time, received training on the background of reform and the intent of the act, and on the types of assistance they should be ready to provide. In addition to creating and distributing a set of helpful materials on legal aspects of LSC operations (from open meetings act requirements to personnel selection guidelines) and answering hundreds of telephone inquiries, volunteer lawyers met with and assisted more than 85 councils with specific issues in the first year of implementation.

In a parallel effort, the CPAs in the Public Interest (CPAsPI) organized, trained, and assigned more than a hundred accountants to work with LSCs in developing budgets, analyzing staffs, and examining planning options. Meanwhile, starting from a small base at one West Side ghetto high school, the Executive Service Corps mobilized a team of 60 retired executives to work on a weekly basis with the staffs and councils of 30 West Side inner-city public schools. These former executives brought their management and planning skills to these schools at no cost. Many of the schools served by these various professional volunteer projects had never before received any outside expert assistance. The experience has been invaluable, both for the professionals, who have gained a new appreciation of the problems of inner-city schools, and for the schools, which have access to skilled assistance for the first time.

Universities, particularly those with schools of education, have had traditional ties into schools in America's urban centers. Chicago is no exception to this pattern. In most cases, those contacts were mutually beneficial. The universities gained access to training and research sites; schools benefited from additional staff and networks with educational experts; the system cultivated a supply of new graduates to fill the teaching ranks. On rare occasions, the system would call upon local academics to provide particular studies for which it wanted information. Rarely was the interaction anything other than helping to maintain the current status quo.

With the passage of the school reform act, a number of universities saw an opportunity to expand their efforts with the public schools, with outside support provided by both governments and foundations. With few exceptions, these universities had been notably absent from the reform effort, though many had been involved in efforts to improve individual schools. Like several other universities, De Paul created a network of inner-city schools to which it promised to provide technical assistance. Northeastern Illinois University, already active in creating a network of shared-decision-making schools through its project Co-Lead, dramatically expanded its contacts with city schools. Its counterpart on the southside, Chicago State, began offering training to a set of southside schools. Roosevelt University joined with the Community Renewal Society to sponsor a number of forums, around different subjects and problems, aimed at Local School Council members, school faculties, and principals. The University of Illinois at Chicago, Loyola, and National-Lewis similarly expanded their efforts, but were more represented by individual faculty members (notably Bill Ayres of UIC and Art Hyde of National) who were deeply involved in the reform movement.

The city's major philanthropies continued to provide support, both to local nonprofit agencies and to individual schools. As has already been indicated, several of the larger foundations, such as the Joyce Foundation, the John D. and Catherine T. MacArthur Foundation, and the Chicago Community Trust, provided direct support to the school system or other quasi-public entities (e.g., the school board nominating committee) for projects related to the reform effort. Several foundations and corporations provided funds directly to local schools, such as the Joyce Foundation's Educational Ventures Fund, the Whitman Corporation's Principals Awards, and Illinois Bell's Local School Council Awards Program. In some cases, foundation staff took direct roles in the creation of and deliberations by the Citywide Coalition on School Reform. General giving in support of school reform activity appears to have continued on an upward trend through the initial year of implementation.

Finally, as an outgrowth of the principals task force of the citywide coalition, a group of 50 Chicago Public Schools principals created "Project 'We Care.' " This coalition crystallized following a weekend retreat in Interlaken, Wisconsin, funded by several city foundations. The coalition was formed to give unified expression to support for the school reform effort and to rebut the negativity emanating from the Chicago Principals Association. The chairperson of the coalition was Sylvia Peters, principal of Dumas Elementary School in the inner-city Woodlawn community. Dumas had been a prereform site of parent organizing by Designs for Change, and Peters had been an active participant in the reform movement from the moment the legislation was enacted. The Project "We

Care" manifesto is indicative of the kinds of efforts and concerns these principals favored:

> We, the principals of public schools in the City of Chicago, County of Cook, and State of Illinois, do solemnly declare our commitment to the institutionalization of a restructured public school system. We support the efforts of parents, community, teachers, and school people to be involved in the evolutionary democratic process. We believe that these efforts will enable the children of Chicago who attend public schools to receive the most appropriate and most equitable education possible. . . .
>
> Let it be clearly understood that first and foremost in our minds is the need to develop an urban public school system that will deliver the finest educational services to children and their families in a manner that will enable them to become the empowered adults of the future, to develop responsible, civic-minded leaders, and to create young men and women who can truly enjoy and appreciate the "good life."
>
> Furthermore, this petition is a public declaration of our collective desire to be known as positive constructionists and not as obstructionists. As those who are in the forefront of this school reformation, we want you, the Chicago Board of Education to help us to move the schools we manage to a higher and more productive level. We need your strong concern and support.

The coalition listed three pages full of specific policy and resource requests covering finances, communication, buildings and grounds, transportation, and personnel. The manifesto and its requests was presented to the interim board, and the principals of the coalition have met with members of the administration to press their requests. It has been unfortunate that these principals had to organize outside their own union in order to express their commitment to school reform (the CPA is a member of the AFL/CIO, though it is not recognized by the board as a bargaining unit, since its members are considered part of management by the school system).

MAJOR IMPEDIMENTS TO REFORM

The first year of implementation did not go smoothly in all quarters. As had been intimated in the initial planning conducted by the 18 task forces established by the general superintendent early in 1989, most central office staff were resistant to efforts at reform. In April 1989, Dr. Byrd's demand that all principals create a three-year school improvement plan within four weeks looked to reformers like a transparent attempt to undermine one of the central responsibilities of the soon-to-be-elected Local School Councils. LSCs would be elected and embark upon their planning responsibilities only to be confronted with a hastily thrown together principal's improvement plan created with little parent, community, or faculty input. The reform act required LSCs to do a thorough needs assessment before undertaking school improvement planning and specifically directed the LSC to survey the concerns of the community and teachers (P.A. 85-1418, Sec. 34-2.4). Many principals simply ignored this mandate from the lame-duck superintendent. Others filed only cursory plans, which they considered "one more paperwork imposition."

Central office resistance was not unexpected, since one direct focus of the reform act was to decrease the size and power of the central bureaucracy. The interim board's clumsy handling of the dismissal of Dr. Byrd, its miscalculation in appointing Dr. Almo to replace him, and the prolonged delay in acquiring the services of a full-time superintendent, left the central office essentially leaderless for the initial eight months under the reform act. During the remainder of the first year, the new superintendent was struggling to gain control of the bureaucracy and to recruit new top leadership, which did not appear until the end of the summer of 1990.

In the Panel's January newsletter, we assessed the situation this way:

> As a result of the Board's undercutting of the superintendency, senior managers in the central offices have been free to go their own way. Some have done the best job they knew how to do. Sometimes their decisions have not won the support of the Interim Board, but that has been due to lack of [direction] rather than insubordination. However, other top administrators used their license to sow confusion, allow the reform effort to drift, or consciously attempt to subvert the intent of the Interim Board. (Chicago Panel, 1990a)

Unfortunately, the situation did not improve significantly during the initial months of the new superintendent's tenure. His own consultants from KPMG-Peat Marwick chronicled a long list of administrative foul-ups, miscommunications, and inaccuracies flowing from the central office to the schools. *Catalyst* (1990) reprinted one well-reported anecdote: "A school could not find the curriculum guides it ordered from the central warehouse. It turned out that the central office had packed the guides in boxes marked "apples." They were eventually discovered in the school's refrigerator."

Local School Councils found themselves deluged with forms to fill out, deadlines to meet, and reports to file. All seemed to arrive at the school with little rationale and arbitrarily set deadlines. Central office bureaucrats used every opportunity to shift the burden of reporting requirements off their own shoulders and onto the shoulders of Local School Council members. Deadlines were established with impossibly short timelines. For example, late in January, school councils that were to be engaged in the principal selection process were told they must inform their present principals by February 28 whether or not they would be retained. This date had been established by central office administrators, who had been lobbied by the Chicago Principals Association for an early decision date so that nonselected principals could become candidates at other schools prior to the legally mandated selection date of April 15. While there was an understandable rationale for the choice of the February 28 deadline, no one considered the crisis engendered at the school site when an LSC discovered it had less than a month to make a decision it had planned to make 75 days later. Only after PURE (Parents United for Responsible Education) filed suit did Superintendent Kimbrough reduce the February 28 deadline to a "suggestion."

Some council members felt they were being worn down in a war of attrition. Frequently, however, bureaucrats simply were backing up from state reporting deadlines and allowing themselves enough time to compile reports from 542 LSCs. Nobody monitored what the effect of these various demands would be upon the local schools. In the leadership vacuum, no clearinghouse was established as an advocate for the schools within the administration, and few administrators were willing to take the heat from the state or other jurisdictions to protect the school councils. To his credit, the general superintendent acknowledged this problem when it was reported by his consultants and indicated that a more carefully thought through year-long calendar of required reports and deadlines would be available for LSCs when school opened for the second year of implementation in the fall of 1990.

Still, it was the superintendent who violated an interim board indication that LSCs would not have to wait until the second year of reform to control their own budgets. By requiring the newly elected LSCs to decide about the use of discretionary State Chapter I funds immediately upon their election, the board encouraged LSCs to assume control of all discretionary spending at the school. Often principals concurred in this process, and together the local leaders planned their expenditures for the year. They were then shocked to discover, in the second week of May, that their unexpended funds had been summarily frozen by order of the superintendent. In an effort to stockpile funds to underwrite an expected 7% increase in employee salaries, Superintendent Kimbrough froze spending at the end of the year. Technically, the law did not give local schools control of their own resources until the second year of reform, so the superintendent was within his legal rights. However, the board had clearly indicated to LSCs that they should begin exercising that control in the first year, and the superintendent's action created great confusion in those schools who had planned summer projects or had restrained spending in order to be well prepared for the beginning of school in the fall of 1990 (the board's fiscal year ends August 31).

One of the stratagems used by central office administrators to hang on to their positions during the summer of 1989 was to accuse the interim board, and through it, Mayor Daley, of embarking upon a racially motivated plan to eliminate blacks from positions of power. This effort culminated in a highly publicized and well-reported press conference featuring Jesse Jackson, of Operation Push, confronting board Vice President Singer. Daley's own hiring practices since taking over the city had been reportedly unbalanced toward replacing blacks with whites, which gave support to Jackson's concerns. Indeed, it must be acknowledged that the board of education had been notorious for dealing primarily with white, male contractors prior to the financial collapse of 1979-1980. Only with the appointment of a minority-dominated board in 1980 did that picture begin to change, and real progress was not made until Operation Push's Francis Davis assumed a seat on the board. Davis was removed from the board, along with most of its other members, when the interim board was seated. Thus, although the interim board had continued the minority and women's preferences in contracting, concern about protecting high-paid minority jobs was not entirely unreasonable. However, even Jackson was embarrassed when he was asked if he was more interested in protecting black administrators' jobs than in improving the education of black children. Jackson quickly backed away from his more radical statements and soon thereafter returned to Washington, D.C. He was not significantly involved with the Chicago Public Schools during the remainder of the first year of reform implementation. However, the racial polarization that culminated with his mid-July press conference continued to smolder throughout the first year (cf. Poinsett, 1990; Starks, 1990).

A more direct impediment to implementation of reform was a suit filed in Cook County Circuit Court by the Chicago Principals Association. Primarily angered by the loss of tenure, leaders of the CPA filed suit to protect their interests. Their legal strategy was to challenge the constitutionality of the reform act on two grounds: First, that tenure was a property right granted to principals, which could not be taken away arbitrarily, once granted; and second, that the election procedure for the LSCs, with each constituency electing its own members (parents voting for parents, etc.), violated the one-man, one-vote provisions of the Constitution. The board of education had been given taxing authority under the reform act. The suit argued that, since LSCs selected district council representatives, who, in turn, selected representatives to the school board nominating commission, from whose recommendations the mayor must select members of the permanent board of education, an illegal basis for taxation was established. If the suit had been based simply upon the first argument, some compromise might have been possible under which existing principals would be guaranteed jobs in the system (which in effect was granted to teachers), while newly selected principals would operate under the new provisions and would never be granted tenure. However, the second rationale for the suit went to the heart of the reform act, and a judgment on this point in the principals' favor would effectively scuttle the entire effort.

The suit was quickly dismissed from county court, allowing the first year of reform implementation to proceed. The CPA then attempted to refile the case in federal court, but the federal judges refused to hear the case until every local appeal had been exhausted. The original suit was then appealed in the state courts and the State Supreme Court agreed to bypass other appeals levels and hear the case directly. In November 1990, the court declared the voting procedures unconstitutional, but invited the legislature to design a new voting pattern before its judgment was finalized.

In another dispute with a group of employees, LSCs were forced to find alternative sites to meet. Long-standing agreements between the board of education and the Operating Engineers Union had restricted the nonstandard use of school buildings to four nights a year, two of which were traditionally used for parents to pick up report cards and consult with their children's teachers. Under this agreement, without additional compensation, custodians would only open the school for two other evening meetings during the school year. The interim board had paid the overtime systemwide to accommodate the public hearings at each school to acquaint voters with the LSC candidates and the actual day of voting. When administrators balked at paying for any meetings the LSCs decided they needed, the custodians refused to open the buildings for meetings. For weeks, while they were themselves trying to get organized, LSCs found themselves scrambling to secure a public meeting site. Finally, the board negotiated a compensatory time-off agreement with the engineers union, which would permit two meetings per month at each school. However, the controversy added confusion to the initial efforts of LSCs and highlighted the constraints under which councils would have to work in creating more extensive utilization of their buildings. As reform headed into its second year, a satisfactory resolution of this problem had not yet been found.

THE STATUS OF REFORM AFTER ONE YEAR

At the end of the first full year of reform implementation, the success in installing the structural changes mandated under the Chicago School Reform Act has pleasantly surprised most observers. I certainly did not expect as many of the elements to have been put in place at the end of the first year of the reform effort. The resistance and impediments that have been encountered, while frustrating to council members and all others seeking to improve the city's public schools, were anticipated in the legislation. Certainly there will be a period during which LSCs and the central administration will be tussling over where the proper division of authority should be located. That also is to be expected. But it had not been clear at the outset that it would be possible to decrease the size of the central administration significantly or to reallocate significant resources to the school level. Yet, to an important degree, both of those systemwide goals had been accomplished.

More importantly, the critical elements of school-based management had also been put into place.

Local School Councils were elected at each of the city's 542 schools, and they are for the most part operating as described in the reform act. At some schools there have been nonperforming LSC members, and the law provides no simple mechanism to force their resignation or allow for their removal. Thus, at a few schools, LSCs have had difficulty achieving a quorum or accumulating enough votes to approve actions (the reform act requires six affirmative votes to pass most items of business, rather than a simple majority of a quorum). But in most schools, the LSCs were in place and were taking appropriate action. It is too early to tell how effective their actions will be.

All but about 81 schools had adopted and submitted to the central administration school improvement plans. One nonprofit agency that provided fee-based facilitation of improvement planning at about 30 schools issued a very encouraging report summarizing the planning at those schools (Institute of Cultural Affairs, 1990). In connection with an awards program, I was able to undertake a cursory review of about a dozen school improvement plans. As part of the Panel's reform monitoring project, our staff reviewed another dozen representative plans. On the basis of this fragmentary evidence, it did not appear to us that LSCs had yet designed educational efforts that would produce significant changes in the ways their students learn in the classroom. Two outside observers, Chester E. Finn, Jr., and Stephen K. Clements (1990), on the basis of experiences with four schools, came to a similar conclusion. They expressed their concerns in a *Catalyst* article entitled "Complacency could blow 'grand opportunity.' " After declaring that "school reform in Chicago is off to an encouraging start in terms of structure, process, and community energy," they offered the following caution, "What concerns us is whether this new system, once fully born, will be able to put into place a radically altered educational vision, a profoundly different set of ideas about teaching and learning, school organization and process, curriculum and pedagogy, student assessment and parent participation" (Finn & Clements, 1990). Thus, the challenge that is before the Chicago school reform movement now is to find ways to encourage LSCs to seize the opportunity they have to make substantial changes in the way in which the educative process is conducted. Without significant changes in the ways in which teachers and students interact in classrooms, it is unlikely that we will see major changes in the achievement levels and capabilities of the city's children. But it is no small achievement that more than 80% of the system's schools have embarked upon the process of analyzing the needs of their students and designing a plan to improve their potential achievement.

Similarly, the superintendent has reported that all but 40 LSCs had submitted budgets for the new school year. Once again, there has as yet been no detailed analysis of changes in these budgets, though staff from the Chicago Panel have begun such an effort. But LSC members have sat around tables, poring over the numbers that represent the resources they have to commit to the learning enterprise, and they have made the hard decisions about allocating precious funds. This is a significant step in capacity-building for council members.

Finally, principals have been selected at 276 of the system's 542 schools. As noted in Chapter 6, about 150 principals have assumed their current jobs since the original passage of the school reform act in July of 1988. More new principals will surely be selected during the second year of reform, all of which means there has been a significant change in school-level leadership during the past two years. But that does not necessarily imply that there will be radical change as a result of these changes. Tom Andreoli (1990), in assessing the principal selection process in an article titled "Councils Stick with Insiders in Picking New Principals," points out that 82% of schools selecting principals in the first round decided to keep their incumbents. In many cases, these incumbents were interim principals who had only been at their schools since the beginning of the first year of reform. In a sense, these newly assigned principals were being given a full term to see what they could do. In many cases, they had won the confidence of the new LSCs by their cooperation in launching their schools on the reform seas. Principals will be selected at the remaining 266 schools during the second year.

MONITORING FUTURE DEVELOPMENTS IN SCHOOL REFORM

This book has been based on the extensive research and monitoring base that has been built up by the Chicago Panel on Public

School Policy and Finance over the preceding eight years. The Panel has developed a detailed data base on the Chicago board's finances and staffing that spans a dozen fiscal years. It helped develop the board's cohort analysis capacity for tracking dropouts. It has compiled an extensive array of statistics about every school in the system, and has reproduced that data base in book form as the *Chicago Public Schools DataBook* (Chicago Panel, 1990b). In short, the panel has established itself as the primary independent monitor and analyst of the performance of the Chicago Public Schools.

The Chicago Panel has launched a major five-year effort to track the successes and failures of the movement to restructure Chicago's schools. This project, "Monitoring and Researching School Reform in Chicago," has been supported by six major foundations in the city. It is designed around 11 monitoring projects and 4 related research projects that combine massive citywide quantitative data for every school (test scores, attendance rates, dropout rates, retention and failure rates, budget items, staff changes) with qualitative investigations of governance and classroom instruction in a representative sample of schools. Initial reports from this project have provided some data for this book. However, many of the reports have primarily been compiled to provide a base line from which change can be measured during the five years described in the reform act. Interim reports tracking these changes will be issued at regular intervals and may be obtained from the Panel by any interested observer. We anticipate that, at the end of the five-year implementation period, a book-length assessment of the reform effort will be prepared and released.

Appendix A lists several sources of information for those who desire to track the reform effort as it is in progress.

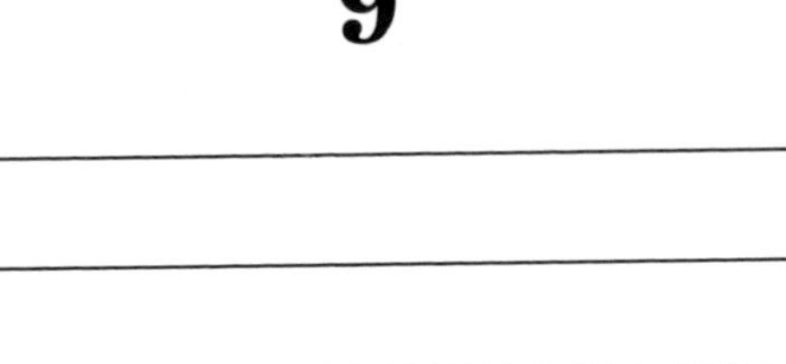

9

Too Much Democracy or Too Little?

Chicago's school reform has been critiqued as being both too radical and not radical enough. That situation may mean it is just about where it ought to be, radical enough to get the job done but not so radical as to be wish dreaming or raising hypothetical stalking horses that are disconnected from reality. The relevant question to ask about school reform is, "What is the problem you are trying to solve?"

The Chicago School Reform Act was carefully fashioned to meet very specific circumstances in the city of the broad shoulders, as Carl Sandburg (1916) once christened it. Its solutions are based in solid educational research and the most recent thinking about business organization. That does not mean that every provision in the act will work as expected, nor does it mean that the reformers did not overlook some critical areas. I have tried to point to some areas where the critics have already raised cautions that should be carefully heeded as reform is implemented. As we go down the path laid out in the reform act, further problem areas are likely to arise. No one in Chicago has suggested the act is perfect as it is.

But it is an effort to address the problems experienced in large urban and some countywide school districts. It is not addressed to improving the capacities of high-achieving suburban school districts to become more competitive with West Germany or Japan. It is not even clear to those focused on the urban scene that matching the Japanese is a problem that, given other significant values in the American educational system, it is important to redress. The Chicago reform effort, similarly, does not address the problem of low-achieving rural school districts, and it certainly gives no support to those concerned with forcing consolidation upon rural districts, though it may provide a model of how local control could be maintained while creating larger districts. But the centralization involved in consolidation, whether mandated by state legislatures or indirectly imposed by enacting choice legislation designed to drive smaller districts out of existence, would not be sympathetically applauded by Chicago reformers interested in local school autonomy and control. In sum, the Chicago School Reform Act is an attempt to address the problem of poorly performing urban schools, not to address the general level of excellence in our nation's schools (though if it is successful in raising the bottom schools, it will raise the overall level nationally).

The mainline education establishment has castigated the Chicago reform effort for being too radical. In major cities across the country, education leaders have been heard to say, "We'd better get going, or somebody will impose a Chicago-style solution on us." New shared decision-making agreements have been created in cities like Philadelphia in the wake of the Chicago legislation, and others may follow. Some in the mainstream have correctly critiqued the Chicago effort as not guaranteeing improvement in student achievement levels. The act was never intended to solve student achievement problems itself. In fact, the philosophy behind the act is that there is no one best solution or "one best system" (Tyack, 1974). The philosophy was to create the opportunity for local actors to solve the different problems encountered in different locales within the city. Thus, the act is not intended to solve the problems by itself but to create the opportunity for the problems to be solved. The long-term questions are, did the opportunity get adequately created and did people take advantage of the opportunity to make changes radical enough to improve the learning opportunities for students (cf. Finn & Clements, 1990).

The basic response to the critics who say the Chicago reform effort is too radical is to ask whether anything less radical would have been sufficient. In some situations, in some cities, something less radical may be sufficient. That is an empirical question that can be evaluated as the various reforms now underway mature. It is not a question that should be answered, as some recent authors are wont to do, argumentatively, hypothetically, and derisively. Let us look at the evidence as it accumulates, and judge from that perspective. In cities like Pittsburgh, Cambridge, and in District 4 in New York, there is some indication that less radical approaches have worked. It is not clear that their strategies would have been sufficient under the conditions in Chicago. In a moment, I shall analyze current reform efforts from the Chicago perspective and try to show where Chicago fits in the 1980s reform movement.

Market-oriented proponents, on the other hand, have suggested that the Chicago reform effort does not go far enough. In Chicago, the City Club issued a report as school opened for the first year of reform implementation that suggested that this reform effort will fail, that only vouchers can succeed (Marciniak, 1989). But the known interest of the primary author and his cohorts on the City Club's Education Committee in finding a way to underwrite the economically troubled parochial schools of the city undermined any significant local impact of the report.

Two of the more outspoken critics of all reforms undertaken during the 1980s, including the Chicago reforms, are John Chubb and Terry Moe (1990). For Chubb and Moe, the Chicago reforms are not radical enough, for they are still subject to the processes of democratic control, rather than market control. As such, they contend, the Chicago reform will never be able to deal with the fundamental bureaucratizing tendency of democratic institutions and therefore will never be able to give schools enough autonomy, over a prolonged enough time, to create the conditions necessary for effective schools. After examining the currently operative reform efforts, I shall analyze the more theoretical critique of the market-oriented advocates.

DO CURRENT REFORMS GO FAR ENOUGH?

In Chapter 4 I examined the background of the national reform movement, which created the context in which Chicago school restructuring developed. I gave some indications of how the Chicago reform act was related to those efforts. Now, I shall try to assess the significance of school reform efforts nationwide from the perspective of the Chicago effort.

Accountability and Testing

The first wave of school reform focused upon accountability, testing, higher standards for certification of teachers, incentives for better performance, and, in some places, higher salaries. Nearly every state made some effort to increase graduation standards. While everyone would like to have higher performance by students, setting higher graduation standards certainly did not produce that result. As the *Chicago Tribune* reported on its front page on August 28, 1990, "Verbal scores on SAT sink to a 10-year low." The story reported that "Average scores on the verbal section of the Scholastic Aptitude Test in the 1989-90 school year fell 3 points to 424—the lowest since 1980 and equal to the lowest levels since annual averages were first compiled in 1971." While it is not entirely appropriate to judge the success or failure of reform efforts on one measure, this story exemplifies other reports that indicate that wishing for higher achievement by setting higher standards did not make it happen. Of course, higher standards and testing could not be expected to improve achievement unless the only achievement problem was that students were not trying hard enough. While student effort may not be as high as it should be, simply blaming the students for not trying hard enough was not enough to improve the schools. Testing has helped to reveal the seriousness of the educational problem, at least in the urban school districts, and its importance for the Chicago reform movement was emphasized in Chapter 3.

But testing does not correct the problems it reveals. It does create some other problems, of which the Chicago effort may feel the effects. To the extent that Chicago's goals of reaching national norms on standardized tests drive the curriculum efforts at the city's schools, particularly through the use of the Iowa tests, which are reported to focus on basic skills, it may be that the reforms in Chicago will narrow the educational effort and may be counterproductive. This is certainly the concern of at least one testing expert who has been following the system's efforts (Lloyd Bond, a consultant to the Joyce Foundation).

Increasing teacher certification requirements may have some effect on Chicago, which, as Orfield (1984) has shown, relies upon the least selective teacher preparation university in the state. But this effect is likely to be in the long term, if at all. Some reformers have argued that any higher abilities of teachers entering the Chicago system would be worn down by the existing teacher culture, if that current culture is not changed by reform. Chicago could probably benefit from alternative certification procedures, particularly for persons skilled in science and math. However, the current practice of maintaining, as part of the Chicago classroom force of 23,000 teachers, a pool of some 4,000 FTBs (full-time basis substitutes) is worrisome. The administration has been accused of perpetuating the FTB pool simply to reduce costs. Without changing this work force management milieu, an alternative induction approach is likely to be completely subverted. And while efforts like the Princeton Project (*New York Times,* June 20, 1990) are flashy and exciting from the perspective of new college graduates who commit to teach for two years, the numbers involved are far short of the work force demands our schools will be facing as a large number of our veteran faculty members retire during the 1990s. This is a large-scale problem, which the Chicago reforms do not adequately address either.

Finally, the influx of new dollars, which happened in some states but minimally in Illinois (Nelson, Hess, & Yong, 1985), is unlikely to have much effect on schools except to the extent that those funds are earmarked for new programs. In Illinois, a small portion of the new funds in 1985 were thus earmarked for early childhood programs (at a level to serve one sixth of the qualifying disadvantaged three- and four-year-olds), reading assistance (grades 1-6), and dropout prevention. Chicago received about $25 million out of those three programs, a small part (a little over 1%) of its $1.8 billion budget. These new programs were helpful, but hardly sufficient to turn the system around. Other new funds were eaten up in teacher salaries, which paid the current teacher force more money for doing the same things they had previously done. Since teacher salaries had lost ground to inflation during the late 1970s and early 1980s, these raises were probably appropriate, but they had little effect on improving education in Chicago. I suspect the situation was similar in other urban districts.

Teacher Professionalization Models

The second wave of school reform nationally focused on teacher professionalization and restructuring. The teacher professionalization effort has had several different foci. Its shared decision-making facet, I believe, is critical to reforms working in any school system. If teachers do not get involved in, and assume ownership of, reform efforts at each school, there is little prospect for significant changes in that school. If reform stays in the corridors of the school and never gets into the classroom, there is little prospect of improving student achievement and capacity. If teachers do not get involved in reform, they can simply close the door of their classroom and continue as they have always done. Short of a massive expulsion of such noncooperating teachers, raising the very real question in this time of a growing teacher shortage of who would replace them, there is little that can be done to improve schools without securing the active involvement of the teaching faculty. The danger in the Chicago situation would be if lay control of the Local School Councils were used for confrontational purposes to the extent that teachers refuse to cooperate. Where LSCs emphasize a collaborative approach, the prospects of real change are much brighter.

From the Chicago perspective, the questions for those districts relying upon a shared decision-making approach is whether real power devolves from the central administration to the school level and what the level of accountability is. It must be acknowledged that, as Washington state's program, "Schools of the 21st Century," found out, schools may have had much more power to make changes all along than they realized they had (*Education Week,* April 11, 1990). Still, in large urban districts, and probably in some countywide districts, without a lifting of the informal network of sanctions, school leaders are reluctant to risk their careers to claim every power they may legally have.

In some school districts, like Hammond and Dade County and San Diego, who have confident and secure administrators, leadership from the top may see to it that schools are given a significant amount of autonomy and encouraged to use it. As long as those leaders stay in those districts, the shared decision-making model may prove to be sufficient. Once again, this is an empirical question to be evaluated as the plans in these districts mature. To date, the Hammond plan, which is the oldest in this set, has been well accepted systemwide, noncooperating principals have been replaced, and all reports are positive, but student achievement has not improved significantly. Reformers across the country will continue to keep a close watch on these districts.

But my major concern about this voluntarily shared autonomy approach is its dependence upon the effective leadership of a few key individuals. With the inevitable movement of those individuals into other positions or retirement, the concern is whether the effort will persist. The experience in Salt Lake City, after the departure of Superintendent Don Thomas, is not encouraging in this regard. To the extent that plans in these cities are incorporated into union agreements between boards of education and teachers' unions, there is some hope for institutionalization that will surmount the individuals involved. It must be remembered, however, that union agreements are renegotiated regularly, and what goes into an agreement can also come back out of it.

The teacher preparation dimensions of enhancing the professionalization of teachers, as has already been indicated in considering teacher certification, is a critical concern, but in itself not sufficient to occasion major changes in urban school districts. This is a major concern for schools of education, and in Chapter 6 I tried to indicate some of the implications for schools of education of greater reliance on shared decision-making and school-based management in urban school systems. Those of us active in such reform efforts should be willing to work with schools of education as they consider their own restructuring efforts. But changes in the colleges of education alone will not be sufficient to improve urban school systems.

More significant for school districts like Chicago are the teacher retraining efforts of a system like Pittsburgh. Combining retraining with a reorientation of the system's curriculum and several other improvement projects, Pittsburgh has significantly improved its student achievement levels systemwide (Wallace, 1986). I believe it is inevitable that other major urban school systems will emulate Pittsburgh, as Dade County has. The Mayor's Education Summit agreements, in Chicago, included a Schenley Teacher Training Center-type provision. Following advice from Judy Johnston, the director of the Schenley Center, we required that teachers be involved in planning what a Chicago retraining effort should look like. It is unlikely that the Schenley model would be copied exactly, but it seems critical that the Chicago Board of Education make some significant move in systemwide teacher retraining if school reform in Chicago is to be successful. In stultifying urban school systems, even the best of teachers get beaten down after a while. A chance to step back from the immediacy of teaching, to catch up on the latest developments in one's field, and to review one's own pedagogical practices is a tremendously important part of revitalizing what goes on in classrooms. To date, in Chicago, other than expressions of interest from the teachers union and a number of reformers, little has been done to incorporate the teacher retraining element of the education summit agreements.

The potential weakness of the shared decision-making approach is that there are no guarantees as to how teachers will use their new empowerment. Perhaps they will acquire this new opportunity and simply use it to do what they have always done. Obviously, little improvement is likely to occur if that happens. The Chicago reforms suffer from exactly the same threat. On the other hand, the shared-decision model might be used by teachers to focus entirely upon improving teacher working conditions, which, as Tom Corcoran and his colleagues point out (1988), are far from those most other professionals encounter. What other professionals would work without access to a telephone, without the ability to go to the bathroom whenever necessary, and without other adult interaction for the predominant part of each work day? But it is not clear that improving these working conditions will necessarily result in improved performance in the classroom and improved achievement for students, though it might. Once again, this is an issue to be tracked empirically. But it does raise the concern whether teachers will benefit from shared decision-making at the expense of students. Accountability of school staff to lay-dominated Local School Councils is the mechanism for trying to deal with this concern in Chicago. Its effectiveness also has to be assessed.

Restructuring

As I have described the restructuring aspect of the second wave of school reform, it has two components, both of which have to do with empowering lay participants in the school enterprise. Some have described this dimension as empowering users of the system or consumers, but from my perspective, that narrows the issue to the market-focused response, which I think is only one part of this effort. But that is the part I shall consider first.

It seems to me that there are two different kinds of choice plans currently in operation. Several predominantly rural states have enacted statewide choice plans (e.g., Minnesota, Iowa, Nebraska). It seems these plans are primarily aimed at small rural school districts, which are perceived to be inefficient and offering an insufficient curriculum. Choice is a vehicle to force these school districts to change their way of operating, primarily by releasing their captive students to attend more efficient districts where the curriculum is more rounded. Under such an approach, the mark of success will be whether these small districts are forced to consolidate or close, without great blame attaching to the legislators who designed and sponsored the choice legislation. Thus, the real goal is blameless consolidation. However, because the populations involved in such situations are quite small and marginal to the total state school enrollment, it is not clear to me that such an effort has much to do with improving student achievement statewide. It may have some valuable benefits to individual students involved, and it may solve some political problems for the state legislature, but it does not address the major issues of school improvement, certainly not the issue of improving the poorest-performing schools in our urban centers.

Of much more interest to urban reformers are the district-level choice programs that have been undertaken in Cambridge, Massachusetts, and in District 4 in East Harlem. In both of these situations, enrollment choice is combined with significant program diversity established at most schools, and a number of other improvement efforts, to create dynamic programs of districtwide improvement. Both districts report that student achievement has improved significantly (Peterkin & Jones, 1989; Fliegel, 1989). I believe both of these districts should be watched closely for their ability to sustain this success, but other districts should be evaluating the elements that have made them successful and the aspects of their efforts that are applicable in their own situations. The lesson from Cambridge, it seems to me, is that to prevent the creation of a two-tiered system, as magnet and specialty school choice has done in Chicago, a controlled choice program needs to be systemwide, making every school a school of choice.

The Chicago reform plan has some language encouraging greater within-district choice, but it certainly does not mandate it. The reform act explicitly delegates to the board of education the power to determine school enrollment patterns in order to prevent resegregation of schools in predominantly white neighborhoods. However, having empowered local leaders, it is probably not appropriate now to impose an open enrollment plan upon the fledgling LSCs. With enhanced local authority, once-simple decisions now entail building a consensus among 542 different schools. That is significantly more difficult, but consistent with the notion that schools will improve only as local leaders concur in the major actions that affect them.

A second lesson from East Harlem is that schools and buildings need not be thought of as identical. District 4 has some 49 schools in 19 buildings, which creates many smaller, more homogeneous (though racially diverse) schools in which individual students are well known and well served. Chicago, with some elementary schools exceeding 1,700 students, could benefit from emulating the diversity of schools in East Harlem. But once again, this is a decision that now should be made at the Local School Council level, not imposed by the central office or board. It is my hope that as some LSCs in these huge elementary schools struggle with how they may better serve their students, they will consider dividing into several different "schools" within the same building. In that way, program diversity may be increased, learning options for students increased, and, with a better match between student and teacher interest, learning increased. But the lesson from East Harlem is that such an effort cannot be imposed from the top down, though it can be encouraged and supported centrally.

A third lesson from East Harlem, it seems to me, is that program diversity must precede enrollment choice. Trying to drive diversity by giving students choice, in a system that does not have enough seats for students now, does not appear to be a very fruitful prospect. In Chicago, the schools from which students have been fleeing for some years do not now feel terribly underutilized; they have little incentive to seek more students. But it seems obvious that if an LSC sets up a school program that is focused in a particular way, or perhaps four programs focused in four different ways, then both students and teachers must be given some option about staying in that program or choosing between the multiple options. Students (and teachers) who are not comfortable with the particular program an LSC decides to establish to improve its school should not be forced to endure the results of that choice. Thus, enrollment choice logically follows from program diversity.

The less market-driven aspect of restructuring is the diversity of efforts at school-based management, which emphasize lay participation. As I noted in Chapter 4, most of these plans have been voluntary plans, introduced by an enterprising superintendent. As Malen and Ogawa (1988) noted, these voluntary approaches tend to deal with few really significant issues; when they do, the professionals tend to dominate the decision process. It also seems that the issues least likely to be addressed are the ones most determining student achievement: accountability of staff and significant changes in program, time, and pedagogical patterns. Furthermore, to the extent that entry into the school-based management program itself is voluntary (some school districts require a two-thirds majority vote by the faculty), it is likely that the schools that most need improvement are the very ones that are least likely to enlist. It may be that this does not prove to be the case and that significant improvement will occur in districts using voluntary approaches; the data should be evaluated. From the Chicago perspective, without a progressive administrator and with reluctant principals, a mandatory approach was required. Its success must also be tested, for coercion does not always lead to successful change either.

Chicago's Reform Utilizes Elements of All Approaches

It should be obvious that the Chicago School Reform Act, while primarily seen as a mandatory school-based management reform effort, in fact utilizes aspects of all of the reform efforts of the 1980s. Each has been carefully selected to meet some particular aspects of the problems of this particular urban school system. In other districts, a somewhat different set of strategies might be more appropriate. This, it seems to me, is the essence of careful reform planning. While some theorists (Chubb & Moe, 1990) derisively label this a "grab bag" approach, it seems to be the more appropriate response to the complexity of large urban school systems and much more appropriate than a simplistic *one-shot-solves-all-problems* approach.

At the same time, it must be noted that the Chicago reform effort takes very seriously Chubb and Moe's criticism that many of the national reforms of the 1980s do not adequately account for the institutional pressures toward bureaucratization and that those pressures can overwhelm the good intentions of high-minded professionals. To us in Chicago, it seemed obvious that the incentives inherent in professionalism alone would not be adequate to overcome the tendency toward bureaucratic growth and centralization of power. If school autonomy was to be significant in Chicago, institutional constraints upon the growth of the bureaucracy and the recentralization of power had to be put in place. The effectiveness of these constraints must also be evaluated as the Chicago experiment goes forward.

CAN PUBLIC EDUCATION SURVIVE UNDER DEMOCRATIC CONTROL?

Chubb and Moe (1990) have suggested that all of the foregoing reforms are doomed to fail because they do not escape from democratic control. They argue that democratic control leads to bureaucratization and the imposition of values that are not always locally acceptable and therefore, democratic control necessarily is antithetical to local autonomy. They argue that private schools—market-driven schools—escape from the forces of democratic control and imposed values and therefore more frequently have the autonomy associated with effective schools.

While their argument stumbles over the acknowledged effectiveness of suburban schools and virtually ignores the ineffective autonomy of many rural schools, its impact for large urban school districts must be addressed. The core of their critique is the demand that reformers must adopt an institutional approach if they hope to be successful. "Schools, we believe, are products of their institutional settings" (Chubb & Moe, 1990, p. 67). Chicago reformers would agree with this contention and equally question reforms that do not "call for truly fundamental reforms—new institutions of educational governance" (Chubb & Moe, 1990, p. 11). However, unlike Chubb and Moe, I believe the validity of this concern is an empirical, not dogmatic, question.

Chubb and Moe also criticize democratic control for imposing higher values on local communities. "The raison d'etre of democratic control is to impose higher-order values on schools, and thus to limit their autonomy. . . . All public authorities, in seeking to impose higher-order values on schools—values that many in society, including many in the schools, may not embrace—face serious control problems" (Chubb & Moe, 1990, pp. 38, 41). They suggest that these imposed higher-order values create opposition among parents and faculties, thereby creating internal dissension. Thus, the market advocates present two forceful criticisms of democratic control—that centralized bureaucracies are encouraged, thereby restricting local autonomy, and that external values are imposed creating consumer dissatisfaction.

Can Autonomy be Maintained Under Democratic Control?

The central impact of Chubb and Moe's argument for Chicago is whether or not the recentralizing tendencies of large urban bureaucracies can be constrained enough to allow school autonomy to flourish. This is not a question to be answered hypothetically; it is an empirical question that will be tested over time.

The Chicago reformers were firmly committed to keeping the public schools under democratic control. For the most part, with the exception of a few businessmen, they felt that market-driven solutions would not be adequate in the Second City. They were concerned that attention and resources must focus on what Sylvia Peters, the leader of the "We Care" principals, called "the lowest third," the students doing most poorly in the current system. They felt that our market economy, in general, had either abused or ignored the most disadvantaged and that market-driven educational models had provided little assurance that the disadvantaged would be the primary beneficiaries. In short, the Chicago reformers felt there were some higher-order values democracy should insist upon, including equality of educational opportunity. Thus, their concern was to find ways to make the system of democratic control work better, rather than to abandon it. They utilized an institutional approach, but came to different conclusions from those reached by Chubb and Moe.

Principally, what the Chicago reform approach contends is that what has been lost under large-scale urban bureaucracies is the people's voice. Chubb and Moe would agree that parents and local residents have little control but would contend that they never can have that control under democracy:

> A frequent complaint is that parents and students are not well enough organized to be very powerful. . . . What it implies is that parents and students would get the kind of schools they wanted if they could somehow gain "appropriate" clout—if democracy, in other words, were less imperfect and did a better job of reflecting their interests. This is simply not the case. . . . Parents and students have a right to participate too. But they have no right to win. (Chubb & Moe, 1990, pp. 31f.)

The Chicago reformers vehemently disagree with Chubb and Moe that parents do not have a right to win under democratic control. They have constructed a system under which parents have both the right to win and the votes to win. By establishing in law a set of constraints upon the centralizing tendencies of the urban democratic system and establishing a council membership that favors lay control, the Chicago school reform has sought to maintain the values of democratic public schools and to assure local school autonomy. Instead of doing away with democratic control, the Chicago reform effort seeks to put that control in the hands of the *demos,* the people. Chicagoans have rejected the notion that there is too much democratic control; they think there has not been enough democracy. The Chicago solution is not to abandon democracy but to extend it.

Chubb and Moe themselves, in a footnote hidden in small print in the back of their book (1990, p. 305, note 20), acknowledge that the process of democratic control they have described could work to the advantage of those who would constrain the normal tendencies. If reformers can use the system to gain control and can maintain their control long enough for a new constituency to grow that is interested in maintaining local school autonomy, the system can be long lived. This appears to have happened in New York City, though Chubb and Moe worry about recent actions affecting the District 4 experiment. The perpetuation of local autonomy seems to be well under way through union contract codifications in places like Hammond and Dade County. Local autonomy seems well established in Cambridge. In Salt Lake City, however, it appears a favorable constituency did not emerge, and the school-based management experiment waned after the superintendent's departure. It remains to be seen whether the system in Chicago is adequate to constrain recentralization and whether a constituency in favor of local autonomy will develop. At the end of the first year of implementation, it appears that the reform forces remain unified and have the continuing political support necessary to keep the system in place throughout the stated five-year reform period. It is an empirical question whether the Local School Councils will continue to exist and whether they exercise real authority. It is also an empirical question whether enough of a constituency will have developed to maintain the achieved autonomy beyond the five-year experimental period embodied in the reform act.

MARKS OF SUCCESS FOR CHICAGO

As discussed in Chapter 5, the Chicago School Reform Act establishes a set of goals that will be the primary criteria for judging the success of the experiment. They are lofty goals, seeking to move the system to national norms in achievement and student behavior in five short years. While achieving national norms is an appropriate target, five years may be impossibly optimistic as a time frame for reaching them. Are there other marks of success that might give observers reason to believe the Chicago experiment has been worthwhile?

Are Resources Reallocated to the School Level?

There are at least four dimensions in which the potential success of the Chicago school restructuring effort can be assessed. The first is whether the centralized governance structures are focused on supporting and encouraging school-based management. There are many subcategories of this area of concern that can be examined over the next five years, such as how central office units redefine their missions, whether attitudes among the central staff shift to embody a service mentality, how hiring procedures are shifted to facilitate local school staffing decisions, etc. The most important of these measures involves the reallocation of the system's resources. Do the resources of the system continue to be refocused toward the local school level, and do they provide greater flexibility for Local School Councils? The allocation of resources and the programs and staff that they can purchase can be carefully measured. For the first year of reform implementation, about $40 million was redirected to school-level use. One measure of success will be if there is a continuation of resource reallocation toward the school level.

Do Teachers Receive Significant Retraining, Systemwide?

Many teachers in Chicago, as in other major urban centers, have grown tired and frustrated as they have tried to help students learn under intolerable conditions. Some teachers have inadequate skills to meet the needs of their students. Many teachers have lost contact with the latest developments in their own primary fields. While much can be done at the local school level to meet the immediate staff development needs of school faculties, a more systematic effort is required to meet the basic inadequacies of the current teacher force. This was the genius of the Schenley Teacher Training Center and its primary and intermediate school counterparts in Pittsburgh. While a Chicago effort would probably not exactly match the Schenley model, if some such systematic teacher retraining effort is not launched, it is questionable whether the Chicago teacher force will be adequate to the task of dramatically improving the educational opportunities available to Chicago young people.

Do Local School Councils Significantly Alter the Educational Efforts of Schools?

The greatest frustration for school reform in Chicago would be if restructuring the governance of the system resulted in no significant change in the way students experience their classrooms. If the educational process does not change in response to a change in governance, school reform in Chicago will have failed. I have already noted several critical areas to be monitored in this regard.

Do teachers become involved in the process of changing the educational program at their schools? If teachers do not become involved in the change process at the local school, it is unlikely that any significant differences will be experienced by students. Teacher retraining is focused on improving the skills of teachers as they meet their students, but it should also focus upon schoolwide improvement strategies that a faculty might seek to introduce. It is critical that teachers become knowledgeably involved in the school improvement planning process. A key to their improvement is the tone set by the parent and community representatives on the LSCs. If they adopt a confrontational stance toward the educational professionals, we may expect to see the professionals shutting down and backing away from active engagement. In some schools a confrontation may be necessary to effect a change in leadership, replacing a principal. If that should occur, the lay members would do well to keep the confrontation focused away from the teachers, for they are the key coworkers, along with the council, in turning around poorly performing schools.

Closely related to teacher involvement is the development of the school improvement plan. If LSCs do not adopt school improvement plans that require radical change at local schools, it is unlikely that the school system will be radically changed. This is the concern that Finn and Clements (1990) articulated in *Catalyst.* One group that provided paid facilitation to LSCs creating improvement plans has released a far more encouraging report on the 30 schools with which they worked (Institute of Cultural Affairs, 1990). However, our review of about two dozen random improvement plans at the Chicago Panel supports Finn and Clements and their concerns. Still, LSCs had little time to put together their first improvement plans. Many will have to alter their plans significantly in the second year of reform implementation if significant changes are to begin happening in school instructional programs.

Finally, assuming some significant plans begin to be developed, do they produce school programs that differ from one another in important ways? Does the opportunity for diversity produce real diversity? If most schools continue to do the same things they have always done, just trying to do them a little better, it is unlikely that the diverse needs of students across the city will be met. If real diversity does emerge, then students and teachers will demand the freedom to escape from programs that do not meet their needs and to seek out other programs that do. Movement that is based in differentiation of program emphasis rather than differences in quality should enhance the overall performance of the system.

Does the Two-tiered System Begin to Break Down?

If teachers become involved in changing the instructional approaches of schools, if school improvement plans are created that require significant changes in schools, if programs begin to diverge so that students are attracted to schools because of differences in programs rather than differences in perceived quality, then the achievement differences between the top tier of schools and the bottom tier should begin to diminish. Students in previously poorly performing schools should be improving their achievement, and these schools should be attractive to students who are now transferring away from them. Schools that in the past have been highly selective of their entering students should find themselves accepting a more diverse student body. The school system should become more unitary in its diversity. It is, of course, quite conceivable that some better-performing students could be transferred to schools where students have been performing more poorly, the gap diminished, but median scores across the system not improve. Under the current structure, such a scenario is possible, but highly unlikely. But if the system became more unitary *and* scores rose systemwide, then it could be said that reform was moving the system in the right direction.

CONCLUSION

The Chicago School Reform Act is a bold venture in public policy seeking to revitalize an urban school system in desperate need of improvement. It is based upon the conviction that local people, if given the opportunity, are in the best place to solve differing local educational problems. It reorients the resources of the system so that schools facing the most difficult educational situations will have the most resources to deal with those problems. It seeks to change the nature of the central administration of the school system from a controller and director into a servant, and seeks to constrain its ability to exercise direct control over local schools. It does not address the larger educational system problems relating to teacher supply and initial teacher training. It is based upon a fundamental faith in local school leaders, both professional and lay.

There are many points of both faith and practice that can be criticized in the Chicago School Reform Act. But it is a carefully constructed effort, built upon some fundamental educational and organizational research, and designed to utilize the unique history and experiences of the Chicago system. It is designed to attack problems in the educational system particularly endemic to large urban school systems and to some countywide school systems.

Many critics have decried the expanded democratic control of the schools. Some say that lay control over educational professionals is sure to fail, though they do not make that same assessment relative to suburban school districts. Others, as we have just seen, say that democratic control itself is the problem, though they also exempt the suburbs. School reformers in Chicago would do well to listen to the criticisms from both camps, and to seek to assure themselves that they have taken every possible action to meet potential negative consequences identified in those criticisms. But the ultimate test is not the dogmatic assertions of the critics. The ultimate test is in the outcomes of the reform implementation effort.

Is the problem with the Chicago Public Schools that they have been too much under democratic control? The reform movement in Chicago answers with a resounding “No!” From our perspective, the problem is that there has been too little democracy. The Chicago School Reform Act is an effort to revitalize the people’s voice, not to eliminate the arena in which they may fight for control.

Appendix A

Sources of Continuing Information on the Implementation of School Restructuring in Chicago

Monitoring and Researching the Effects of School Reform in Chicago, John Q. Easton, director; a project of the Chicago Panel on Public School Policy and Finance; 220 South State Street, Suite 1212, Chicago, IL 60604. Phone: (312) 939-2202; Fax: (312) 939-2564.

Catalyst: Voices of Chicago School Reform, Linda Lenz, editor; a publication of the Community Renewal Society; 332 South Michigan Avenue, Chicago, IL 60604. Phone: (312) 427-4830.

Designs for Change, Donald R. Moore, executive director; 220 South State Street, Suite 1910, Chicago, IL 60604. Phone: (312) 922-0317.

Chicago Board of Education, Ted Kimbrough, general superintendent; Office of Reform Implementation; 1819 West Pershing Road, Chicago, IL 60609. Phone: (312) 890-8000.

Appendix B

Member Organizations of the *Chicago Panel on Public School Policy and Finance*

American Jewish Committee

Aspira of Illinois

Center for Neighborhood Technology

Chicago Region PTA

Chicago United

Chicago Urban League

Chicago Westside Branch N.A.A.C.P.

Citizens Schools Committee

Community Renewal Society

Erie Neighborhood House

Jewish Council on Urban Affairs

Junior League of Chicago, Inc.

Latino Institute

Lawyers Committee for Civil Rights Under Law

League of Women Voters of Chicago

Metropolitan Mission Strategy Organization of United Methodist Church

Mexican-American Legal Defense and Education Fund

The Woodlawn Organization

United Neighborhood Organization of Chicago

Youth Guidance

References

Alinsky, S. D. (1946). *Reveille for radicals.* Chicago: University of Chicago Press.

Andreoli, T. (1990). Councils stick with insiders in picking new principals. *Catalyst, 1,*(4), 12-14, 16.

Armor, D., Comy-Oseguera, P., Cox, M., King, N., McDonnell, L., Pascal, V., Pauly, K., & Zellman, G. (1976). *Analysis of the school preferred reading program in selected Los Angeles minority schools.* Santa Monica, CA: Rand.

Bakalis, M. (1983). *Community schools study commission,* Springfield: Illinois General Assembly.

Banas, C. (December 3, 1986). Eight schools found cutting class time. *Chicago Tribune,* pp. 1, 10.

Barr, R., & Dreeben, R. (1981). *School policy, production, and productivity.* Unpublished manuscript. University of Chicago.

Bastian, A., Fruchter, N., Gittell, M., Greer, C., & Haskins, K. (1985). *Choosing equality: The case for democratic schooling.* New York: New World Foundation.

Bedard, A., Shauri, H. K., & Millender, N. (1990). Two "thumbs up," one "thumbs down" on training. *Catalyst, 1*(3), 4-5.

Bloom, B. S. (1981, May). *The new directions in educational research and measurement: Alterable variables.* Paper presented at the meeting of the American Educational Research Association, Los Angeles.

Bloom, B. S., Davis, A., Hess, R. (1965). *Compensatory education for cultural deprivation.* New York: Holt, Rinehart & Winston.

Braddock, J. H., II, & McPartland, J. M. (1990). Alternatives to tracking. *Educational Leadership, 47*(7), 76-79.

Brookover, W. B., & Lezotte, L. W. (1979). *Changes in school characteristics coincident with changes in student achievement.* East Lansing: Michigan State University.

Brookover, W. B., & Schneider, J. M. (1975). Academic environments and elementary school achievement. *Journal of Research and Development in Education, 9,* 82-91.

Camayd-Freixas, Y. (1986). *A working document on the dropout problem in Boston public schools.* Boston: Boston Public Schools.

Carnegie Forum (1986). *A nation prepared: Teachers for the 21st century.* New York: Carnegie Forum on Education and the Economy.

Catalyst (1990). Bulletins: Reform updates. *2*(1), 16.

Chance, W. (1986). *"The best of educations": Reforming America's public schools in the 1980s.* Washington, DC: John D. and Catherine T. MacArthur Foundation.

Chicago Board of Education (1984). *Racial/ethnic survey—students.* Chicago.

Chicago Board of Education (1985). *Racial/ethnic survey—students.* Chicago.

Chicago Panel (1988a). *Testimony before the Chicago Board of Education.* Chicago: Unpublished testimony distributed by the Chicago Panel on Public School Policy and Finance.

Chicago Panel (1988b). *Illegal use of State Chapter I funds.* Paper distributed by Chicago Panel on Public School Policy and Finance.

Chicago Panel (1989a). *Panel Update: Newsletter of the Chicago Panel on Public School Policy and Finance. 6*(2), 1, 8.

Chicago Panel (1989b). *Panel Update: Newsletter of the Chicago Panel on Public School Policy and Finance, 6*(3), 5-6.

Chicago Panel (1990a). *Panel Update: Newsletter of the Chicago Panel on Public School Policy and Finance, 6*(4), 5-8.

Chicago Panel (1990b). *Chicago public schools databook, school year 1988-89.* Chicago: Chicago Panel on Public School Policy and Finance.

Chicago Sun Times (April 24, 1985). School dropout rate nearly 50%! p. 1.

Chicago Sun Times (December 27, 1986). Fake study halls: Tip of an outrage, p. 12.

Chicago Sun Times (October 11, 1987). School critics battle cry: Decentralize! pp. 4-5.

Chicago Sun Times (November 7, 1987). City's schools called worst, p. 1.

Chicago Teachers Union (1986). *Perspectives from the classroom—II.*

Chicago Tribune (December 17, 1986). How high schools cheat students, sec. 1, p. 22.

Chicago Tribune (January 18, 1987). Byrd defends school anti-dropout role, sec. 4, p. 2.

Chicago Tribune (March 5, 1987). Giving students a full school day, sec. 1, p. 26.

Chicago Tribune (December 11, 1987). Elected school boards urged, sec. 1, p. 1.

Chicago Tribune (August 15, 1990). "Fuzzy" school plan rejected, sec. 2, pp. 1, 8.

Chicago Tribune (August 28, 1990). Verbal scores on SAT sink to a 10-year low, sec. 1, pp. 1, 11.

Chicago Tribune (1988). *Chicago's schools: Worst in America?*

Chicago United (1981). *Report of the special task force on education: Chicago school system.* Chicago: Chicago United.

Chubb, J. E., & Moe, T. M. (1990). *Politics, markets, and America's schools.* Washington, DC: Brookings Institution.

Cibulka, J. G. (1975). School decentralization in Chicago. *Education and Urban Society, 7*(4), 412-438.

Cippolone, A. (1986). *Boston Compact in the schools: Does it make a difference?* Unpublished paper presented at American Educational Research Association Annual Meeting in San Francisco.

Citizens Schools Committee (1984). *Consumer's guide to Chicago public high schools.* Chicago.

Coleman, J. S., Campbell, E. Q., Hobson, C. J., et al. (1966). *Equality of educational opportunity.* Washington, DC: Government Printing Office.

Coleman, J. S., Hoffer, T., & Kilgore, S. (1982). *High school achievement: Public, Catholic, and private schools compared.* New York: Basic Books.

Coons, J. E., & Sugarman, S. D. (1978). *Education by choice: The case for family control.* Berkeley: University of California Press.

Corcoran, T., Walker, L. J., & White, J. L. (1988). *Working in urban schools.* Washington, DC: Institute for Educational Leadership.

Council of Great City Schools (1987). *Challenges to urban education: Results in the making.* Washington, DC: Council of Great City Schools.

Deming, W. E. (1982). *Quality, productivity, and competitive position.* Cambridge: MIT Press.

Denton, S. E., & LeMahieu, P. G. (1985). Evaluation research as an integral part of an inservice staff development center. *Evaluation Bulletin, 6*(3), 45-50.

Designs for Change (1985). *The bottom line: Chicago's failing schools and how to save them.* Chicago: Designs for Change.

Designs for Change (1989). *Kids first.* Chicago: Designs for Change.

Doyle, D. P., & Hartle, T. W. (1985). *Excellence in education: The states take charge.* Washington, DC: American Enterprise Institute for Public Policy Research.

Drucker, P. F. (1986). *The frontiers of management.* New York: E. P. Dutton.

Edmonds, R. (1979, October). Effective schools for the urban poor. *Educational Leadership, 37,* 15-18.

Edmonds, R. R., & Frederiksen, J. R. (1979). *Search for effective schools: The identification and analysis of city schools that are instructionally effective for poor children.* ERIC Document Reproduction Service No. ED 470 396.

Education Week (1990, April 11). Unexpectedly little interest found in state offers to waive key rules, pp. 1, 19.

Elmore, R. F. (1978). Organizational models of social program implementation. In D. Mann (Ed.), *Making Change Happen* (pp. 185-224). New York: Teachers College Press.

Elmore, R. F. (1979). Backward mapping: Implementation research and policy decisions. *Political Science Quarterly, 94,* 601-616.

Elmore, R. F. (1988). *Models of restructuring schools.* Unpublished paper presented at the American Educational Research Association, New Orleans.

Faulkner, L. (1990, September). A first year report card. *Chicago,* p. 126.

Finn, C. E., & Clements, S. K. (1990). Complacency could blow "grand opportunity." *Catalyst, 1*(4), 2-6.

Fliegel, S. (1989). Parental choice in East Harlem schools. In J. Nathan (Ed.), *Public schools by choice* (pp. 95-112). Minneapolis: Institute for Learning and Teaching.

Friedman, M., & Friedman, R. (1981). *Free to choose: A personal statement.* Avon.

Gelder, S., & Rawles, N. (1980). School system abandons dropouts as rate hits 55 percent. *Chicago Reporter, 9*(5).

Glass, T. E., & Sanders, W. D. (1978). *Community control in education: A study in power transition.* Midland, MI: Pendell.

Hallett, A. C., & Hess, G. A., Jr. (1982). *Budget cuts at the board of education.* Chicago: Chicago Panel on Public School Finances.

Hammack, F. M. (1986). Large school systems' dropout report: An analysis of definitions, procedures, and findings. *Teachers College Record, 87*(3), 324-341.

Henderson, A., Marburger, C. L., & Ooms, T. (1986). *Beyond the bake sale.* Columbia, MD: National Committee for Citizens in Education.

Herrick, M. J. (1984). *The Chicago schools: A social and political history.* Beverly Hills, CA: Sage.

Hess, G. A., Jr. (1984). Renegotiating a multicultural society: Participation in desegregation planning in Chicago. *Journal of Negro Education, 53* (Spring), 132-146.

Hess, G. A., Jr. (1986). Educational triage in an urban school setting. *Metropolitan EDUCATION, 2* (Fall), 39-52.

Hess, G. A., Jr. (1987a). *Donors forum 1985 education survey, ages 0-18,* Chicago: Donor's Forum.

Hess, G. A., Jr. (1987b). *Testimony before the Chicago board of education.* Chicago: Unpublished testimony distributed by the Chicago Panel on Public School Policy and Finance, October 14.

Hess, G. A., Jr., Green, D. O., Stapleton, A. E., & Reyes, O. (1988). *Invisibly pregnant: Teenage mothers and the Chicago public schools.* Chicago: Chicago Panel on Public School Policy and Finance.

Hess, G. A., Jr., & Greer, J. L. (1987). *Bending the twig: The elementary years and dropout rates in the Chicago public schools.* Chicago: Chicago Panel on Public School Policy and Finance.

Hess, G. A., Jr., & Lauber, D. (1985). *Dropouts from the Chicago public schools.* Chicago: Chicago Panel on Public School Policy and Finance.

Hess, G. A., Jr., Lyons, A., & Corsino, L. (1989). *Against the odds: The early identification of dropouts.* Chicago: Chicago Panel on Public School Policy and Finance.

Hess, G. A., Jr., & Meara, H. (1984). *Teacher transfers and classroom disruption.* Chicago: Chicago Panel on Public School Finances.

Hess, G. A., Jr., & Sandro, P. (1986). *Education and unemployment in Chicago.* Chicago: Unpublished white paper for Mayor's Education Summit distributed by the mayor's office.

Hess, G. A., Jr., & Warden, C. A. (1987). *Who benefits from desegregation?* Chicago: Chicago Panel on Public School Policy and Finance.

Hess, G. A., Jr., & Warden, C. A. (1988). Who benefits from desegregation now? *Journal of Negro Education, 57* (Fall), 536-551.

Hess, G. A., Jr., Wells, E., Prindle, C., Kaplan, B., & Liffman, P. (1986). *"Where's Room 185?" How schools can reduce their dropout problem.* Chicago: Chicago Panel on Public School Policy and Finance.

Hess, G. A., Jr., Wells, E., Prindle, C., Kaplan, B., & Liffman, P. (1987). "Where's room 185?" How schools can reduce their dropout problem. *Education and Urban Society, 19*(3), 330-355.

Hoffer, E. (1951). *True believer: Thoughts on the nature of mass movements.* New York: Harper.

Holli, M. G., & Green, P. M. (1989). *Bashing Chicago tradition: Harold Washington's last campaign, Chicago, 1987.* Grand Rapids, MI: William B. Eerdmans.

Holmes Group (1986). *Tomorrow's teachers.* East Lansing, MI: Holmes Group.

Institute of Cultural Affairs (1990). *A summary of participative planning with elementary local school councils (LSC) and professional personnel advisory committees.* Chicago: Institute of Cultural Affairs.

Jencks, C., Smith, M., Acland, H., Bane, M. J., Cohen, D., Gintis, H., Heyns, B., Michelson, S. (1972). *Inequality: A reassessment of the effect of family and schooling in America.* New York: Basic Books.

Jennings, L. (1988a). New Jersey moves to take control of school district. *Education Week, 7*(36), 2, 12.

Jennings, L. (1988b). Partial takeover of district backed. *Education Week, 7*(39), 23.

Johnston, J. A., Bickel, W. E., & Wallace, R. C., Jr. (1990, May). Building and sustaining change in the culture of secondary schools. *Educational Leadership,* pp. 46-48.

Joravsky, B. (1990). Money made difference in voter turnout. *Catalyst, 1*(1), 12-15.

King, T. C. (1987). *Reassessment of the report of the 1981 special task force on education.* Chicago: Chicago United.

Kyle, C. (1984). *Aspira Chicago Hispanic dropout study.* Chicago: Aspira, Inc., of Illinois.

Kyle, C., Lane, J., Sween, J., & Triana, A. (1986). *We have a choice: Students at risk of leaving Chicago public schools.* Chicago: Chicago Area Studies Center.

Lauber, D., & Hess, G. A., Jr. (1987). *1986-1987 Assessment of school site budgeting practice of the Chicago public schools.* Chicago: Chicago Panel on Public School Policy and Finance.

LeCompte, M. D., & Dworkin, A. G. (1988). Educational programs—indirect linkages and unfulfilled expectations. In H. D. Rodgers, (Ed.), *Beyond Welfare.* New York: M. E. Sharpe.

Lenz, L. (December 3, 1986). Panel charges three schools fake "study halls." *Chicago Sun Times*, p. 3.

Lezotte, L. W., Edmonds, R., & Ratner, G. (1974). *A final report: Remedy for school failure to equitably deliver basic school skills.* East Lansing: Michigan State University.

Lieberman, M. (1989). *Privatization and educational choice.* New York: St. Martin's Press.

Malen, B., & Ogawa, R. T. (1988). Professional-patron influence on site based governance councils: A confounding case study. *Educational Evaluation and Policy Analysis, 10*(4), 251-270.

Marburger, C. L. (1983). *School based management.* Columbia, MD: National Committee for Citizens in Education.

Marburger, C. L. (1985). *One school at a time.* Columbia, MD: National Committee for Citizens in Education.

March, J. G., & Olsen, J. P. (1976). *Integrity and choice in organization.* Bergen, Norway: Universitetsforlaget.

Marciniak, E. (1989). *Report of the task force on education.* Chicago: City Club.

Massachusetts Advocacy Center (1986). *The way out: Student exclusion practices in middle schools.* Boston: Massachusetts Advocacy Center.

McLaughlin, M. W. (1978). Implementation as mutual adaptation: change in classroom organization. In D. Mann (Ed.), *Making Change Happen,* (pp. 19-32). New York: Teachers College Press.

Menacker, J., Herzog, L., Hurwitz, E., & Weldon, W. (1990). Most principals, councils get thumbs up. *Catalyst, 1*(1), 2-5.

METROSTAT (1987). *METROSTAT databook: Educational statistics on schools and school districts in the Chicago metropolitan area, base year: 1987-1988.* Chicago: Chicago Panel on Public School Policy and Finance.

Mirel, J. E. (1990). What history can teach us about school decentralization. *Network News & Views, 9*(8), 40-47.

Moore, D. R., & Hyde, A. (1981). *Making sense of staff development: An analysis of staff development programs and their costs in three urban school districts.* Chicago: Designs for Change.

Moore, D. R., & Radford-Hill, S. (1982). *Caught in the web: Misplaced children in Chicago's classes for the mentally retarded.* Chicago: Designs for Change.

Morris, V. C., Crowson, R., Porter-Gehrie, C., & Hurwitz, E. (1984). *Principals in action: The reality of managing schools.* Columbus, OH: Charles E. Merrill.

Mortimore, P., & Sammons, P. (1987). New evidence on effective elementary schools. *Educational Leadership, 45* (September), 4-8.

Moynihan, D. P. (1969). *Maximum feasible misunderstanding: Community action in the war on poverty.* New York: Free Press.

National Commission on Excellence in Education (1983). *A nation at risk: The imperative for educational reform.* Washington, DC: Government Printing Office.

National Governors' Association (1986). *Time for results: The governors' 1991 report on education.* Washington, DC: National Governors' Association.

The Nation Responds (1984). Washington, DC: Department of Education.

National Coalition of Advocates for Children (1985). *Barriers to excellence: Our children at risk.* Boston: National Coalition of Advocates for Children.

Nelson, F. H., Yong, R., & Hess, G. A., Jr. (1985). *Implementing educational reform in Illinois.* Chicago: Chicago Panel on Public School Finances.

New York Times (August 24, 1988). Chancellor seeks dropout program in New York's elementary schools, sec. N, p. 14, sec. L, p. 83.

New York Times (June 20, 1990). Princeton student's brainstorm: A peace corps to train teachers, sec. A, p. 1, sec. B, p. 7.

Oakes, J. (1985). *Keeping track: How schools structure inequality.* New Haven: Yale University Press.

Office of Civil Rights (1982). *Survey of elementary and secondary school districts, and schools in selected school districts: School year 1980-1981.* Washington, DC: Department of Education.

Orfield, G. (1984). *The Chicago study of access and choice.* Chicago: University of Chicago Public Policy Committee.

O'Rourke, P. (1987). Shared decision making at the school site: Moving toward a professional model. *American Educator* (Spring), 10-17, 46.

Perpich, Rudy (1989). Foreword. In J. Nathan (Ed.), *Public schools by choice,* (pp. 1-3). Minneapolis: Institute for Learning and Teaching.

Peterkin, R. S., & Jones, D. S. (1989). Schools of choice in Cambridge, Massachusetts. In J. Nathan (Ed.), *Public schools by choice* (pp. 125-148). Minneapolis: The Institute for Learning and Teaching.

Peters, T. J., & Waterman, R. H., Jr. (1982). *In search of excellence: Lessons from America's best-run companies.* New York: Harper & Row.

Peterson, P. E. (1976). *School politics: Chicago style.* Chicago: University of Chicago Press.

Poinsett, A. (1990). School reform, black leaders: Their impact on each other. *Catalyst, 1*(4), 7-11, 43.

Purkey, S. C., & Smith, M. S. (1983). Effective schools: A review. *The Elementary School Journal, 81*(1), 426-452.

Rogers, D. (1968). *110 Livingston Street: Politics and bureaucracy in the New York City schools.* New York: Random House.

Rogers, D., & Chung, N. H. (1983). *110 Livingston Street revisited: Decentralization in action.* New York: New York University Press.

Rutter, M., Maughan, B., Mortimore, P., Ouston, J., & Smith, A. (1979). *Fifteen thousand hours: Secondary schools and their effects on children.* Cambridge, MA: Harvard University Press.

Ryan, W. (1976). *Blaming the victim.* New York: Random House.

Sandburg, C. (1916). Chicago. In F. O. Matthiessen (Ed.), *Oxford book of American verse,* Oxford, UK: Oxford University Press (1950).

Schwartz, R. S., & Hargroves, J. (1986). The Boston compact. *Metropolitan EDUCATION, 3,* 14-24.

Starks, R. T. (1990). School reform shaped to preserve white power. *Catalyst, 2*(2), 10-11.

Stephenson, R. S. (1985). *A study of the longitudinal dropout rate: 1980 eighth-grade cohort followed from June 1980 through February, 1985.* Miami: Dade County Public Schools.

Toles, R., Scholz, E. M., & Rice, W. K., Jr. (1986). A study of variation in dropout rates attributable to effects of high schools. *Metropolitan EDUCATION, 2,* 30-38.

Trisman, D. A., Waller, M. I., & Wilder, C. (1976). *A descriptive and analytic study of compensatory reading programs: Final report* (Vol. 2) (PR 75 26). Princeton, NJ: Educational Testing Service.

Tyack, D. B. (1974). *The one best system: A history of American urban education.* Cambridge, MA: Harvard University Press.

Walberg, H. J. (1984). Improving the productivity of America's schools. *Educational Leadership, 41*(8), 19-30.

Walberg, H. J., Bakalis, M., Bast, J., & Baer, S. (1988). *We can rescue our children: The cure for Chicago's public school crisis—with lessons for the rest of America.* Chicago: Heartland Institute.

Wallace, R. C., Jr. (1986). Data-driven educational leadership. *Evaluation Practice, 7*(3), 5-15.

Warden, C. A., Lauber, D., & Hess, G. A., Jr. (1988). *1987-1988 assessment of school site budgeting practices of the Chicago public schools.* Chicago: Chicago Panel on Public School Policy and Finance.

Weick, K. P. (1976). Educational organizations as loosely coupled systems. *Administrative Science Quarterly, 24*(1), 1-19.

Author Index

Subject Index